ORCAS OF
THE GULF

SIERRA CLUB BOOKS   SAN FRANCISCO

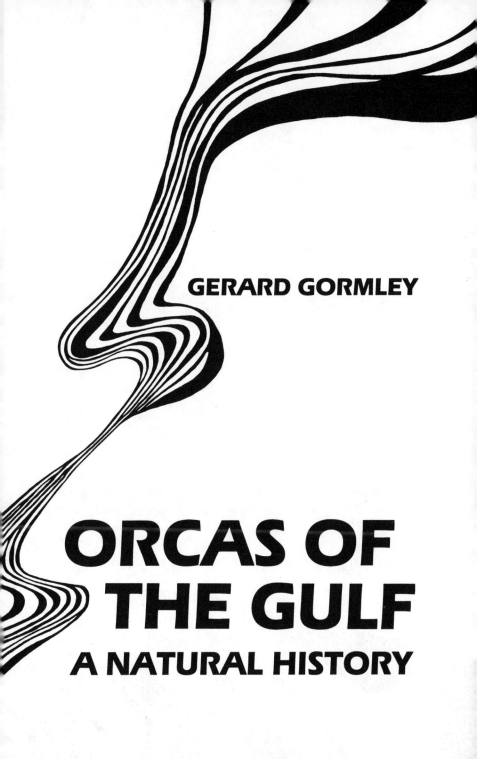

GERARD GORMLEY

ORCAS OF
THE GULF
A NATURAL HISTORY

Library of Congress Cataloging-in-Publication Data
Gormley, Gerard.
Orcas of the Gulf : a natural history / Gerard Gormley.
p.   cm.
ISBN 0-87156-601-X
0-87156-624-9 (pbk.)
1. Killer whale—Behavior. I. Title.
QL737.C432G685   1990
599.5'3—dc20   89-27662
CIP

Cover / Jacket design by Bonnie Smetts
Book design by Abigail Johnston

Printed in the United States of America
10 9 8 7 6 5 4 3 2 1

For my late brother Jim,
whose love of the sea helped inspire my own

CONTENTS

FOREWORD • *ix*

ACKNOWLEDGMENTS • *xiii*

1 • 1

2 • 20

3 • 33

4 • 43

5 • 60

6 • 69

7 • 92

8 • 106

9 • 117

10 • 130

APPENDIX • 139

NOTES • 169

BIBLIOGRAPHY • 183

INDEX • 201

FOREWORD

This is a natural history of *Orcinus orca* in the western North Atlantic. Orcas here seem always on the move, covering vast ranges and spending most of their time well offshore, so the species has been little studied in this habitat. No one knows where orcas come from to visit the Gulf of Maine, or where they go when they leave. They are probably not numerous in this area, though as many as fifty have been seen at one time. Most sightings involve about ten orcas, so it is possible that several pods range over our continental shelf, joining forces now and then to hunt and socialize. The pods appear to spend much of their time well offshore, probably in continental slope waters where they can calve and rear their young near the warming influence of the Gulf Stream without having to migrate far from major food stocks. They seem to move close inshore only to visit various oceanic bights where experience tells them they will find favored prey at certain times. In the Gulf of Maine, most orca sightings occur in late summer and early autumn. Accordingly, this book's narrative covers a period of about ten weeks, from mid-August through October.

When I set out to write this book, one of my first research steps was to compile all available sighting reports for the western

North Atlantic. These are presented in the appendix. Some sighting reports are dramatized in my narrative, but not necessarily in actual sequence or time frame. Consequently, my orca pod is a composite, but its actions are based on behavior reported by sighting networks and scientific literature, or related to me by firsthand observers. Most behavioral anecdotes come from the western North Atlantic. A few originate from other oceans. None are based on captives. Thus, although this book uses a narrative framework, it is based on fact. Where lack of data forces me to speculate, I say so.

Many people are confused, and rightly so, by the various names applied to orcas. Fishermen often refer to them as grampus or blackfish. Whalers used to call them fat-choppers because of the way they fed on harpooned whales. Even the taxonomic classification, *Orcinus orca,* is variously interpreted. Some think *Orcinus* may be derived from the Latin *orcynus,* meaning "a kind of tunny," referring to the orca's resemblance to tuna or (more likely) to its habit of preying on tuna. Some sources suggest that *orca* might translate loosely as "devil whale," since Orcus was the Roman god of the underworld. Others note that the Latin word *Orcinus* means "of or belonging to the realms of the dead," and that *orca* denotes "a kind of whale." Hence, "killer whale," some scholars conclude, though others claim that the name "killer whale" arose from a mistranslation of an early Spanish term meaning "whale killers." Still others interpret *Orcinus orca* as "bringer of death."

The *American Heritage Dictionary* suggests other roots: "orc (ork) *n.* The killer whale (see). (Old French *orque,* from Latin *orca,* whale, probably from Greek *oruga,* accusative of *orux,* a pickax, hence (from its horn), narwhal, from orussein, to dig.)"

Indeed, puzzling references to horns and narwhals do appear among various regional names for *Orcinus orca.* It is known as "swordfish" or "sword-whale" in Eastern Canada, Quebec, Germany, the Netherlands, Denmark, and Iceland. The Norwegian names for orca translate to "farmer's pole, swinging back and forth," "pole-shaped horn," and "pole-whale." At least ten local and national names refer to orcas as swordfish, sword-whales, or pole-whales. The dorsal fins of adult male orcas are often described as swordlike, so this may explain the "sword-whale" references. It may also explain why *Orcinus orca* was earlier called *Orca gladiator.* "Farmer's pole" may refer to a wagon tongue, the long tapering wooden shaft extending from a vehicle's front axle to the collars of the draft animals. "Pole-shaped horn" and "pole-whale" suggest that early Norwegian observers may have confused orcas with narwhals while the two species were interacting.

Taxonomists classify *Orcinus orca* as the only species in the genus *Orcinus* in the family Delphinidae (dolphins) in the suborder Odontoceti (toothed whales) in the order Cetacea (whales). Three other species, all of which look more like pilot whales than orcas, prey on marine mammals as well as on fish, and so are commonly referred to as various types of killer whales: namely, the false killer whale (*Pseudorca crassidens*), the pygmy killer whale (*Feresa attenuata*), and the little killer whale or melon-headed whale (*Peponocephala electra*). These, together with *Orcinus orca,* are the only cetacean species known to prey on fellow cetaceans, but other species may do so, especially now that food stocks are dwindling worldwide.

The taxonomic inclusion of orcas with dolphins brings to mind another source of confusion, the interchangeable use of the terms dolphin and porpoise. Dolphins (Delphinidae) generally have pronounced beaks, conical teeth, and prominent sickle-shaped dorsal fins. Porpoises (Phocoenidae) generally lack beaks and have spatulate teeth; their dorsal fins, if any, are low and triangular. Although orcas lack beaks, they are classified as dolpins rather than porpoises, presumably because they have conical teeth and prominent sickle-shaped dorsal fins.

To sum up this confusing situation in the simplest possible terms, all cetaceans are whales, dolphins are relatively small-toothed whales, and orcas are large dolphins that include other marine mammals in their diet.

Owing to their size (twenty to thirty feet), speed (up to thirty knots), intelligence, and cooperative hunting techniques, orcas are the sea's supreme natural predators. Even great white sharks and sperm whales are not immune to orca attack. Orcas have no natural predators, and throughout most of recorded history they had little to fear from man. Now, though, hard times brought about by overfishing are forcing orcas to compete boldly with us for dwindling food supplies, and this does not bode well for orcas or ourselves.

Orcas fascinate us for many reasons. For centuries they were feared as the sea's most bloodthirsty predators. Only recently have we learned that these largest of dolphins can be gently tolerant toward people. Now millions of us each year visit oceanaria and come away viewing orcas as playful pets. Which are they: savage killers or gentle dolphins? The answer is both, and this makes them even more fascinating.

Join me now in imagining what it might be like to live amongst a pod of orcas summering in the Gulf of Maine.

Gerard Gormley
Manchester-by-the-Sea, Massachusetts
Summer 1989

ACKNOWLEDGMENTS

As always, Scott Mercer of New England Whale Watch in Newburyport, Massachusetts, has been an ongoing source of helpful information. Thanks also to shipmasters Bill and Mike Neelon of New England Whale Watch. Mrs. Clive Tucceri, administrative director of the Stout Aquatic Library (an extension of the Marine Advisory Service, University of Rhode Island, Narragansett, Rhode Island) was a great help in locating pertinent books and periodicals. Dr. John Heiser of the Shoals Marine Laboratory, Isles of Shoals, New Hampshire, gave me valuable time on Appledore Island. Captain Charles Mayo, Jr., spent many hours with me in Provincetown, Massachusetts, sharing his memories of orcas and bluefins. Thanks also to his son, Dr. Charles Mayo III, for giving me time from his busy schedule at Provincetown's Center for Coastal Studies, and to the center's Phil Clapham for his views on population studies. On that same subject, I owe a debt of thanks to Drs. Marilyn Dahlheim of the NMFS National Marine Mammal Laboratory in Seattle and Gerald Joyce, chief scientist on the IWC/IDCR survey project, for their long conversations with me.

Dr. James Mead and Matthew Hare kindly shared orca data from the Marine Mammal Events Program at the Division of

Mammals, Smithsonian Institution, Washington, D.C. Dave
Crestin and Doug Beach at the National Marine Fisheries Service (NMFS) in Gloucester, Massachusetts, were very cooperative on numerous occasions, as were Dr. Steve Turner and Larry
Hansen at NMFS/Miami. Drs. Steven Katona and Judith Beard
at the College of the Atlantic in Bar Harbor, Maine, generously
shared their sighting data and reference books with me.

My thanks to Dr. Howard E. Winn, Robert Kenney, and
Marilyn Nigrelli at the Graduate School of Oceanography,
University of Rhode Island, for the Cetacean and Turtle Assessment program (CETAP) data, sound recordings, and other information supplied to me over the years. I am grateful to
Thomas Fritts and Randy Jennings at the University of New
Mexico for the Gulf of Mexico data, and to Dr. Ray Gambell
and Mrs. V. J. Hunter at the International Whaling Commission Secretariat in Cambridge, England, for the helpful statistics
and reports. My thanks also to Dr. Frank Mather, scientist
emeritus at Woods Hole Oceanographic Institution, Falmouth,
Massachusetts, for his kind translations of foreign papers and
his helpful comments.

Special thanks to the Canadian scientists who helped me in
collecting orca research data: Drs. David Sergeant, Edward
Mitchell, and Randall Reeves at the Arctic Biological Station,
Ste. Anne de Bellevue, Province of Quebec; Dr. Michael A.
Bigg at the Pacific Biological Station in Nanaimo, British Co-
lumbia; and Dr. John Ford of the West Coast Whale Research
Foundation in Vancouver, British Columbia, who so generously
shared his knowledge of orca acoustics.

Mid-August. Over cobalt-blue water eighty miles south of Nantucket, Massachusetts, an albatross soared in the early morning light. Since sunrise the wind had been freshening out of the southwest, opposing the prevailing current and raising steep waves, but the weather was fair. Apart from a diagonal brushstroke of cirrus cloud far to the north, the sky was a flawless blue vault, the air so clear that the albatross could see waves crimping the horizon six miles away.

Pointing upwind when it wished to slow and examine the surface, swinging off the wind to speed up, the great bird followed a habitat interface marked by a change of sea color from cobalt to green. Now and again the bird swooped down to snatch food from a wave, then swung back into the wind and rose some fifty feet before resuming its zigzag course. Rarely did it need to beat its slender, ten-foot wings.

Twelve orcas came into view, swimming eastward over the continental shelf break. Like the albatross, they were following the habitat interface, but in the opposite direction. The pod's youngsters leapt from wave to wave. The adults maintained a more leisurely pace, boring through the eight-foot seas with fluid ease, their bodies straddling the troughs as they left one wave and penetrated the next.

The albatross turned and followed the orcas, but seeing no signs of feeding from which it might be able to scavenge, it soon swung back into the wind and moved out of sight.

The orca pod included two bulls, marked by their high dorsal fins and heavyset builds. Though not much longer than the cows, they were much stockier. One bull, a twenty-two-footer with scarcely a mark on his body, looked recently matured. The other was nearly thirty feet long and weighed eight tons. His back was laced with crisscross scars and pockmarks. Three bullet holes had perforated his dorsal fin, which was as tall as a man and came to a curly point. His sides bore puckered dents from tissue lost in accidents or fights. His teeth, the size and shape of half bananas, were darkened and worn. The gum tissue on the right side of his jaw was swollen as big as a seal's head. The two bulls seemed clearly related. Their dorsal fins were tipped with similar wavy hooks, and both bulls bore unusual gray chevrons on their left flippers.

Leading the pod was a twenty-four-foot cow at least as old as the ailing bull. She and he had identical gray patches behind their dorsal fins and similar white patterns on the undersides of their flukes. Her left flipper had a chevron similar to his, and her saddle patch and fluke patterns suggested kinship at least to the old bull, if not to both males. Her dorsal fin, a third as large as theirs, had no genetic tale to tell, but an old fisheries tag embedded in the base of her fin bore a 1919 date.

In addition to the old cow and two mature bulls, the pod included three other cows, two immature males, and four immature females, one of them a nine-foot suckling still showing the pointed snout and pink patches characteristic of first-year orcas. Soon her snout would round out and the pink would fade to ivory. By the time she was a year old, she would sport the same jet black and snowy white coloration as the adults.

Staying to one side of the pod, the old bull swam with his mouth partly open to cool his infected jaw. At one point he gnashed his teeth as if in pain, and the growth spewed bloody pus. A cow drew alongside him and uttered a lengthy pulsed phrase that sounded like a creaking door hinge. As she sonared the bull's swollen jaw and tried to investigate it with her tongue, he patted her with his flipper, then gently pushed her away.

White bellies flashing, two young males corkscrewed underneath the bull, then together shot out of the water ahead of the pod and bellywhopped. They wriggled and rolled against each other, dove, and popped up on opposite sides of the pod. As they bobbed in the wave crests, whistling to each other, the younger bull slipped a six-foot flipper under one of them and upended him. Buzzing like a chain saw, the juvenile chased the bull and hurdled him. With amazing agility the bull did a snap roll and snatched the youngster out of the air with his great paddlelike flippers, then hugging him against his chest, completed the roll and pulled him under. Apparently in need of air, the young male struggled desperately to get free. The bull held him underwater a while longer, then released him, rolled, and spanked him hard with his five-foot dorsal fin. The youngster rejoined his playmate, and they resumed their antics.

As the pod entered an area where great currents were colliding, the waves became steeper and lost all semblance of rhythm. Rather than waste energy fighting the craggy seas, the orcas began swimming in a series of shallow dives, each lasting about seven minutes. As they swam, they simultaneously called to each other and probed the sea with sharp pulses of sound. Their sonar clicks picked up a school of hake far below, but they did not give chase. Orcas typically prefer not to dive much deeper than 15 fathoms, though if necessary they can plunge many times that depth.[1]

From all directions came a commotion of natural and mechanical sounds, but the orcas' sharp sonar clicks and strident communication calls stood out sharply from the background noise, so they had no interference problems. Still, they often remained silent for extended periods, the better to take prey by surprise, or simply to assess various sounds for their survival value. Just now, for example, they heard slow cataracts of mud and sand hiss down along the shelf break 90 fathoms below and knew that the tide was ebbing from the Gulf of Maine. From 170 fathoms below and to their right came a *boing,* followed by heavy snapping sounds that told them sperm whales were down there, hunting squid. Deeper still and farther out, a submarine purred through the blackness. Listening through acoustic windows located in various parts of their bodies, orcas are able to monitor sounds from all directions without having to change course.

Overhead drifted a stray from the sapphire blue Gulf Stream, a Portugese man-of-war, its body an iridescent bubble in the sunlight, its deadly purple tentacles trailing so deep that several orcas had to avoid them. As the pod surfaced for air, seventy saddleback dolphins came skipping along from the south, then sensed the orcas and swung back out to sea. Shortly afterward, fifty pilot whales rose out of the darkness, spotted the orcas, and went deep again without even taking air. When orcas are not hunting in earnest, many animals tolerate them to come close, even swim among them, but those included in the orcas' diet know when to stay well clear. And this was one of those times.

The orcas had just returned to swimming depth when the old cow applied full drag with flippers and flukes, coasted to a stop, and hovered head down, listening. The others followed her example. The keenly alert old cow had detected a faint sizzle of turbulence as two large bodies sped through the darkness far below the pod. Judging by the bottom sounds that framed the racing whispers, the unseen animals were inside the shelf break. That meant they could be no more than 90 fathoms deep. A quick estimate of angular velocity, based on past experience, told the orcas that the creatures below them were reaching speeds of forty knots. Such speed suggested bluefin tuna or some other warm-blooded sprinter equally good to eat. Still silent, the orcas listened and waited.

The faint hiss of cavitation faded, suggesting that the animals had plunged over the shelf break, but soon the sound returned, growing louder and louder. Moments later a ten-foot swordfish flashed out of the depths ahead of the pod, with a large mako in pursuit some five fathoms below. The broadbill rocketed through the waves and soared twenty feet into the air, its purple-blue back and silver-gray undersides glistening in the sunlight. A second later the mako, twelve feet of driving muscle sheathed in iridescent blue and snowy white, burst through the surface and bared its long curved teeth. It seemed certain to intercept the broadbill in midair and rip out its belly, but just as the shark broke water, the swordfish executed a marvelous maneuver. Throwing off a great arch of sparkling spray, the fish jackknifed, pointed its sword downward, and plunged like a living harpoon. The three-foot sword rammed into the mako's open mouth and burst through the back of its skull. With a heavy slap the two fish struck the water, then rolled over and over, the mako snapping off teeth as it tried to bite through the sword. The combined strength of the combatants severed the sword two feet from the tip, leaving the mako permanently impaled and unable to use its jaws effectively. Massive volumes of blood billowed darkly from its head. It tried to escape, but brain damaged, could only swim in circles.

The orcas approached. Seemingly oblivious to them, the broadbill rammed the mako with its splintered remnant of sword. As the broadbill circled to make another charge, the young bull orca darted in and severed its tail, then the mako's. Neatly biting off thick steaks of firm flesh, the orcas consumed the broadbill and the mako, leaving only their heads to spiral into the depths, joined in death as they sank to the bottom. For all their great size, the mako and broadbill had yielded only a few hundred pounds of meat. Divided among eleven orcas (the suckling took little solid food as yet), that amounted to a mere snack for each.

A while later, again moving silently near the surface, the orcas surprised two eighty-foot blue whales that nearly swam right over them. Defecating in alarm, the whales took deep breaths, popped their nostrils shut, and sounded. By the time their flukes arched gracefully beneath the waves, the whales were making fifteen knots and were quickly working their way toward twenty. With scarcely a glance at the blue whales, the orcas continued on their way. Perhaps they were not quite hungry enough to take on such swift, powerful prey, for a well-fed blue whale that size weighs over a hundred tons.

The calf of that year, swimming safe and snug between her mother and the old bull, squealed and nuzzled her mother. The cow twisted her flippers, more winglike than the bull's broad paddles, and rolled onto her side. Still on the move, the calf pressed against her mother's belly and nursed. While the pod slowed to accommodate cow and calf, two juvenile females rubbed against the younger mature bull and excited him, then coquettishly avoided his advances. A juvenile male tried to nurse along with the calf and was rebuffed.

When the calf had drunk her fill, the pod resumed its original pace, about the speed of a brisk walk. The calf napped on the move, once again safely tucked between her mother and one of the bulls. For the better part of an hour the pod ambled along, staying generally over the shelf break.

From somewhere west of the pod came a cupped clap of sound. Still silent, the orcas spyhopped and scanned the area. they saw a minke clear the water and come down on its belly with a loud splash. The orcas headed that way.

Minutes later they came within sight of the minke, which was so busy feeding on mackerel stunned by its breaching that it did not sense the danger until too late. While most of the orcas spread out behind the whale, the younger bull circled wide ahead of it and doubled back. Frightened by the approaching pod, the minke sped up and tried to go deep, but the bull was waiting. With a broadside body block that could be heard for a mile, he slammed into the minke and slowed it down, then seized its sharply pointed snout in his jaws and held the whale in place. Although the minke was twenty-five feet long, several feet longer than its attacker, it could not break the orca's grip. The minke went limp, then began to shudder and moan.

The rest of the orcas arrived, trailed by the senior bull, who merely looked on while one cow seized the minke's flukes and another sank her teeth into its genital slit and ripped open the skin. Then, while she gripped the flap of loose skin, the other cow and the young bull began to roll. They spun the minke like a piece of work being turned on a lathe, skinning it so neatly that it began to look like a freshly peeled fruit. As each long sheet of skin and subcutaneous fat was peeled away from the blubber, the orcas divided it among themselves, the senior bull getting first share. It took some twenty minutes to flay the minke, which through it all continued to shudder and moan. Suprisingly little blood was shed, but the surface all around became covered with a film of oil that formed rainbows and made water bead up on the orcas' backs. The youngest orcas watched the first part of the skinning process, then lost interest and began playing nearby.

The two adults who had been holding the minke shared the last sheet of skin between them, nibbled away the minke's lips, then forced open the whale's mouth and ripped out its tongue. Hemorrhaging massively, the minke went limp and appeared to lose consciousness. The orcas shared the tongue among themselves, leaving the rest of the minke, its blubber intact, to scavengers. Still bleeding heavily from the mouth, its flayed body glowing grotesquely orange against the dark depths, the minke sank slowly out of sight.

During the hour or so that the orcas fed on the minke, hundreds of sharks had been attracted to the scene. As some took exploratory bites on the sunken whale, the minke came to and made a feeble attempt to swim away, but then the sharks struck in force and brought its suffering to a bloody climax. Frothy pink bubbles rose and burst. Scraps of blubber floated to the surface. Scavenging jaegers mobbed the area, darting and swooping over the surface, fiercely contesting every morsel.

Slowly the sounds of ripping flesh became fainter and then inaudible as the orcas drifted back toward the shelf break. While the elders napped at the surface, the youngsters darted among them, chasing each other and anything else that came within range. The younger bull rolled belly-up and let the suckling calf ride on his belly. When he needed air, he rolled and gently dumped her to one side. She tried to swim atop his back and failing that, returned to her mother's flank. The bull moved close, affording the calf a snug space between himself and her mother.

When the shelf break was once again audible below them, the orcas resumed their eastward course, sonaring as they went. They soon began receiving strong echoes from a score of halibut that had ventured near the surface to feed. The orcas took air, went deep, and spread out. Without subjecting themselves to uncomfortable depths, they were able to dive below the halibut and herd them up against the surface, where the orcas easily outmaneuvered the frantic fish. The pod's two big bulls, despite their heavy builds and tall wobbly dorsal fins, staged an impressive show of speed and agility, turning tighter and tighter circles until their chosen halibut were caught.

Although the big bull had the look of a fading old scrapper who kept himself going on sheer grit, he was the first to catch a halibut. The catching proved easier than the eating, though. The hundred-pound flatfish was five feet long and half as wide, far too big to swallow whole, and the bull's infected jaw made it difficult for him for him to tear the flapping fish into pieces. The powerful halibut's struggles must have caused the bull great pain, for suddenly he flipped it over his back and struck it a mighty blow with his flukes. The halibut soared thirty feet into the air, hit the surface with a heavy slap, and lay there stunned. Four juvenile orcas shared it among themselves, then hurried to catch up with the others.

Moving sometimes in a cluster, other times in twos or threes, the orcas seemed to dislike doing anything the same way for very long. Now and then an adult surfaced and left a fish for a juvenile. All in all, though, pickings were lean for the next hour or so. As if swimming randomly until a meal presented itself, the orcas cast this way and that along the shelf break.

• • •

Outside the northeast shelf break lies a thirty-mile-wide belt of blue-green "slope" water, so called because it flows over the continental slope, where the bottom drops one mile in ten. Here cold currents from the Gulf of Maine and Nova Scotia are tempered by the Gulf Stream, keeping slope water temperatures near 50 degrees Fahrenheit year round and making the region a favorite wintering place for many species of fish and mammals.

North of the pod's present position lie Nantucket Shoals. Ahead, in sunlit shallows above vast submarine mesas, are some of the world's richest fisheries. Over Georges Bank, Browns Bank, and several smaller inshore banks, giant bluefin tuna and other prime prey begin feeding in spring. By August of each year they have fattened themselves into prime condition. It is then, between July and September, that orcas are most frequently seen inside the Gulf of Maine. They are not seen in the Gulf every year, though they may be there and simply go unreported. (For more information on the habits and movements of orcas in the western North Atlantic, see Appendix I.)

The orcas are about to enter an area of great mixing. Cold tidal outflow from the Gulf of Maine, discharged through Great South Channel between Cape Cod and Georges Bank, spills southward over the edge of the continental shelf and collides with prevailing deep-ocean currents and warm eddies from the Gulf Stream. This meeting stirs the sea to great depths, mixing cold and warm water with bottom nutrients and exposing the mixture to the energizing effects of sunlight. The resulting vitalization supports a tremendous abundance of life, while the diversity of habitats along the shelf break fosters a great diversity of life. This general rule—that habitat diversity seems to foster species diversity — is particularly true of habitat interfaces such as the shelf break. Where forest meets meadow, for example, you usually find a greater diversity of species than in forest or meadow alone.

•   •   •

The air remained clear and bright, the sea spangled with light. For miles around the sky was still cloudless, but far away a thunderhead grew treelike on a dark trunk of rain.

As the orcas continued northeastward over the shelf break, they felt the prevailing westward current joined by a colder flow from the north. The upper waters began to swarm with sand lances, short-finned squid, and many species of fish that had gathered to prey on sand lances and each other. Picking off what squid and fish they could without exerting themselves, for energy would be wasted in pursuit of small prey, the orcas turned northward into Great South Channel. Within minutes the water temperature dropped from 65 to 55 degrees Fahrenheit.

The old bull opened his mouth wide and curled his tongue to channel the cooler water against his abscessed jaw. He passed the old cow, who had stopped and was facing northeast, listening to something. The others doubled back and gathered around her. The old bull circled the pod and continued to cool his swollen jaw. The two immature males began butting each other and splashing noisily. With an outcry that sounded like the clang of a heavy iron gate, the old cow silenced them.

Several kittiwakes appeared out of the southwest and passed overhead, their wingbeats rapid, their flight path straight and purposeful. The old cow reared back with her head above the surface and watched the kittiwakes fly out of sight. Now a dozen greater shearwaters appeared over the southeast horizon, flying in the same general direction as the kittiwakes. From the south and not far behind the shearwaters came a flock of skuas. Three different species of birds seemed to be converging on a spot miles to the northeast. The old cow made a guttural sound akin to a gargle. The young bull repeated the sound, and together they led the pod northeastward. The ailing bull followed.

A five-mile swim brought them within sight of some thirty humpback whales, which were diving under schools of sand lances, then blowing great clouds of bubbles that drove the small fish to the surface and concealed the whales as they rose to swallow their prey. The roaring sound made as the whales released air underwater was similar to the old orca cow's guttural signal.

Kittiwakes, shearwaters, and skuas were feeding on fish spilled from whales' mouths at the surface. Just below the surface, a dozen giant bluefin tuna swam alongside the humpbacks to catch sand lances dribbling from the whales' mouths. Some of the humpbacks slapped the tuna away with their flippers.

One humpback detected the orcas and trumpeted a warning. The bluefin tuna fled the area at speeds approaching fifty knots. The humpbacks broke off their feeding and gathered in small groups at the surface. Nursing cows and their escorts protectively flanked calves that, though thirty feet long, were still nursing and quite dependent. The adult humpbacks' breathing became rapid and took on a wheezing sound.

The orcas dove and swam below the herd while the humpbacks remained at the surface, flippers and flukes curled inward to protect their underbellies. Shafts of sunlight, redirected by surface chop, probed the orcas' formation like flickering spotlights. Spiraling strings of bubbles formed by the sweep of humpback flippers and flukes sparkled in the light.

All at once the young orca bull sounded a chilling scream and flashed through the humpback herd, rushing one whale after another, passing so close to some that the tip of his dorsal fin grazed their bellies. As though swept up in the spirit of the hunt, most of the orcas followed the young bull's example. The water became clouded with the feces of frightened humpbacks.

Humpbacks are the slowest of the rorquals, toothless and

seemingly defenseless, yet what promised to be a massive slaughter instead became a clash of titans. Bellowing and trumpeting like enraged elephants, the humpbacks lashed the sea white as they defended themselves against the streaking orcas. Flukes clapped like thunder. Flippers flashed like mammoth swords. And through this scene of awesome power the orcas — half the size of their prey — darted and weaved, screaming as they went, seeming to revel in the shrieking excitement as they whipped the humpbacks into a frenzy.

Meanwhile the old orca cow and bull, guarding the suckling calf, cruised well below the herd and gauged the humpbacks' reactions. It appeared that the orcas had hoped to stampede the humpbacks and pick off a straggler. If so, the strategy was failing, for the humpbacks were holding their positions.

Leaving the old bull to guard the calf, the senior cow recalled the attackers and signaled a change in tactics. Led by the old cow, the orcas began seizing humpbacks by the flukes, then darting clear as the various rorquals proved able to defend themselves. Moving in pairs throughout the herd, the orcas thus attacked one after another of the humpbacks. The rorquals suffered little more than deep scratches, for the orcas were merely testing their strength and mettle.

Then the orcas came upon six adult humpbacks gathered at the surface with heads together and bodies extended like the arms of a gigantic starfish. The circle enclosed by their heads sheltered three calves. In this formation the adults could breathe at will and avoid attack from above or ahead, while using flippers and flukes to protect their flanks and bellies. The orcas circled the formation and made feinting rushes, but the humpbacks lashed out with their flukes and repelled them.

Having completed one full circuit of the humpback herd, the old cow led her pod back about half a mile. There, at a signal from her, the orcas rushed a humpback calf flanked by its fifty-foot mother and her smaller male escort. The adult humpbacks began trumpeting and lashing the water white. It was remarkable how well the big whales maneuvered: they could swim forward or backward, wheel and turn within half their lengths, and whip their bodies into snap rolls that spun their fifteen-foot flippers like gigantic blades. Lashing out with their powerful flippers and flukes at any orcas that came within striking range, the two adult humpbacks kept the calf between them and defied their attackers.

Although the orcas outnumbered this humpback maternal group by ten to three (the ailing bull and suckling calf merely observed), five of the orcas were young and inexperienced. They tried to mob the calf, but with body blocks that sounded like big boats colliding, the adult humpbacks bumped them away and struck out at them. Colossal sheets of bubbles trailed from the humpbacks' one-ton flippers as they cut through the water in lethal edgewise chops. Even more dangerous were their flukes, which could strike above and below with crushing force or slash sideways with even greater speed and strength than the flippers. Although the orcas pressed the attack from all directions, they could not penetrate the humpbacks' defenses.

At a signal from the old cow, the orcas broke off the attack and left the area, but no sooner were they out of sight than they went deep and quietly circled back. When the humpbacks were once again visibly overhead, silhouetted against the surface glow, the orcas attacked silently out of the darkness.

The humpbacks sensed their approach, but too late. The young bull orca slammed into a calf and sank his teeth into its flank. An extraordinary clap of sound as the orca split open the young humpback's skin was followed by a gargantuan ripping noise as the bull spun and peeled away a foot-thick slab of blubber weighing at least a hundred pounds. The calf's blubber had separated from its underlying muscle tissue as cleanly as the peel from a thick-skinned orange.

Feces clouded the water, obscuring the orcas' vision as the humpback mother swung under her calf and lashed out at the attacking bull with flukes and flippers. The old orca cow sounded a loud danger call. Narrowly escaping injury, the young bull surfaced at a safe distance and settled down to eat. He was joined by the old bull and cow, with whom he readily shared his prize. The calf had been nursing for eight months and was in prime condition. Its blubber, which resembled stringy bacon, was apparently a great delicacy, for rather than wolfing it down, the orcas bit off ham-size chunks and seemed to savor each bite. While they ate, the rest of the pod attacked another trio of humpbacks.

Leaving the last portion of blubber for the ailing bull, the old cow and young bull went back for more.

Although not yet fully grown, the young bull was a formidable animal. He could streak through the sea at thirty knots, maneuver like a dolphin, and bite like a great white shark. As he matured, he would add another six feet and two or three tons and be a match for anything in the sea except perhaps a bull sperm whale. With maturity he would also acquire a bit more caution. Meanwhile, his cockiness sometimes got him into trouble, as was about to happen now.

Sounding a strident call, he darted ahead of the old cow and attacked an adult humpback that had become separated from the rest. The old cow and several others hurried over to help. While two cows seized the humpback's flippers and a third gripped its flukes, the young bull sank his teeth into the whale's genital slit and tried to rip open its belly. With a might born of desperation, the fifty-foot humpback freed its left flipper, which it swept downward in a vicious edgewise chop toward the young bull's back.

The old bull had finished the last of the blubber and was approaching the attack scene at the moment the humpback tore its flipper free. Seeing what was about to happen, the old bull accelerated from five to thirty knots within seconds and seized the humpback's flipper just before it struck the young bull. The old bull's momentum twisted the one-ton flipper safely clear, but the impact burst his abscess and dislodged two teeth already loosened by infection and bone damage. As he rolled clear and released his grip, sharp barnacles on the humpback's flipper lacerated his lips and tongue.

The big bull's charge threw the other orcas off balance, enabling the terrified humpback to break free and fight off its attackers long enough to reach a nearby group of other humpbacks. The orcas did not follow.

Bleeding heavily from his mouth, the old orca bull rested at the surface and gingerly flexed his jaw to make sure it was not broken. Then he used the tip of his tongue to probe his teeth. One was gone altogether. Another had been ripped halfway out of its socket and was sticking sideways into his mouth. Rolling and puffing in the swells, he prodded the loose tooth with his tongue and managed to push it out of his mouth. Blood now poured freely from both tooth sockets. Having no doubt put the worst of his pain behind him, after what may have been many months of suffering, he closed his eyes and rested.[2] The young bull swam over and floated next to him.

The rest of the orcas made no further attempts to launch lethal attacks on the humpbacks. It may be more energy efficient to eat a fifty-ton whale than to chase down thousands of smaller animals, but even the most formidable predators must weigh efficiency against risk. Serious injury can mean death for any predator, and it appeared that the humpbacks in this herd were too strong and feisty for the orcas to make a kill.

Nonetheless, for an hour or more the orcas followed the herd, now and then separating some hapless humpback from a hundred or more pounds of its blubber. None of the rorquals was mortally injured, but many were left with wounds a foot deep and several feet across. The orcas fed primarily from the flanks, which the humpbacks had difficulty protecting. Little of the muscle tissue underlying the blubber was damaged. Some tried to force open the humpbacks' mouths to get at their tongues—which can weigh several tons apiece and are prized by orcas—but were unsuccessful.

At last the orcas left the humpbacks in peace and swam back to rejoin the bulls, who were now ten miles away, napping at the surface and calling occasionally to mark their position. The others gathered around them and went to sleep. Dozing in the current, they drifted back toward the shelf break.

Apparently too winded to dive, the humpbacks continued to wheeze and puff their way along the surface. Many left wakes greasy with oil and pink with blood. Some had lost hundreds of pounds of blubber. One would think that their suffering must be great, yet evidence indicates that a whale's blubber is fairly insensitive to pain.[3] If so, the loss of a hundred-pound slab of blubber may be no worse an ordeal for a whale than is a badly skinned knee for a person.

After fifteen minutes or so, the humpbacks dove and headed northeastward.

• • •

A number of reliable observers have described orca attacks on minkes.[4] In some cases, the orcas ate only the skin and subcutaneous fat layer. (This part of a seal, called *muk-tuk,* is relished by Inuit and polar bears.) Usually the orcas ate the tongue, as well. Sometimes all or most of the minke was eaten.

The minke attacked in this chapter suffered greatly, but this is not to suggest that orcas are particularly cruel. Lions often take hours to kill large prey, such as buffalo, and predation in general is a cruel business. As for orcas' habit of flaying whales, is it any more cruel than wild dogs eating the internal organs of a wildebeest while the hapless animal watches its own ordeal? And is either of these more cruel than a songbird dismembering a caterpillar and eating it alive? If we wince less at a caterpillar's demise, it is probably a matter of scale and whatever personal values we bring to these events.

The more sensitive among us may find comfort in the belief that prey animals go into shock and are spared the worst of their agony. We have no way of measuring another creature's pain, but the annals of surgery prior to the introduction of general anesthesia indicate that patients often screamed and struggled throughout lengthy operations. Many prey animals must suffer just as badly. For reasons unclear, nature has imposed cruel standards of suffering on its creatures. Imagine the pain wild animals like the old bull orca must endure when they develop severe infections or tumors.

Attacks like the preceding orca-humpback scene have been witnessed on three different occasions by Canadian biologist Hal Whitehead over Grand Banks, Newfoundland.[5] The "starfish" defensive formation used by humpbacks was described to me by Douglas Beach, a biologist at the National Marine Fisheries Service in Gloucester, Massachusetts. About a third of the humpbacks seen in the Gulf of Maine bear parallel scars thought to be caused by the teeth of orcas.[6]

By taking only a modicum of blubber from each whale, orcas are certainly conserving a resource, but it is unlikely that they do so purposely. More likely, they take what they can get with minimal risk. Orcas are not unique in their preference for tongue meat. Many terrestrial predators also regard the tongues of their prey as delicacies. Tongues and livers are often the first body parts eaten.

While resting on the move, orcas usually swim very slowly, covering only a few hundred yards on each long dive. Resting pods have been seen to enter tidal rips and be pushed backward for up to thirty minutes. Wild orcas appear to need only a few hours of sleep a day, most naps probably lasting ten to twenty minutes. Having no natural enemies, they may spend much of their waking time in a state of relaxed meditation, and thus need little in the way of sound sleep.

Assuming the narrative's events to be current, the 1919 fisheries tag (an artistic liberty) suggests that the old cow has lived for at least seventy years. Most reference books estimate life expectancy for *Orcinus orca* at thirty to thirty-five years, based on the counting of tooth layers and ovarian scars, but the validity and accuracy of these aging techniques have long been questioned.[7]

Recent findings suggest that the life expectancy of *Orcinus orca* is equivalent to our own. In 1981 the International Whal-

ing Commission's Scientific Committee concluded that the age
of orca females at first pregnancy is at least seven to eight years,
and that male orcas do not mature sexually until about sixteen years of age. It seems unlikely that males destined to live
only thirty to thirty-five years would take half their lives to
mature.

Michael A. Bigg, a research scientist with the Canadian Department of Fisheries and Oceans, who has closely studied the
orcas of British Colombia since 1971, states that "the life span
and ages of sexual maturity of the species are probably close
to our own."[8] Moclips (now known as the Whale Museum),
a nonprofit research organization in Friday Harbor, Washington, has been studying the orcas of Puget Sound since 1976.
From Moclips's studies and Dr. Biggs's research, it is estimated
that female orcas in the wild can live up to one hundred years
and that males can live from forty to sixty years.

All evidence considered, it appears that orca maturation and
longevity correspond to our own. This, together with clannishness, may explain the species' low reproduction rate of four
to five percent per year. In many parts of the world, men have
been killing orcas faster than given communities can reproduce,
and the animals may tend not to breed across community lines.
In habitats where orcas have been heavily exploited, the species
may be endangered. (For more on this, see Appendix II.)

Assuming that orcas of the western North Atlantic maintain extended families of the type found in British Columbia,
the old cow in our story is probably the mother of both bulls,
and most likely matriarch to the entire pod. In British Columbia, sixteen pods of orcas that live near shore year round
have been studied by scientists since 1971. These "resident" pods
number about ten to fifteen animals each and appear to be
genetically isolated extended families with lifelong membership for all, including adolescent and mature males. While going
their separate ways for the most part, various pods stay in touch
acoustically over considerable distances, and occasionally get
together to socialize or hunt.[9,10]

Similar temporary amalgamations of pods may take place in the Gulf of Maine. Pods seen there typically number ten animals or less, but as many as one hundred orcas were seen in one group near Cape Ann, Massachusetts, within the past decade. The second-largest group reliably reported in the Gulf of Maine was forty to fifty strong. It is possible that the habitat hosts an unusually large pod of some one hundred orcas, which may periodically break up into smaller hunting groups. Still, groups larger than ten to fifteen are rarely sighted, so it seems more likely that smaller pods occasionally join forces to form larger ones. (For more on these matters, see Appendix.)

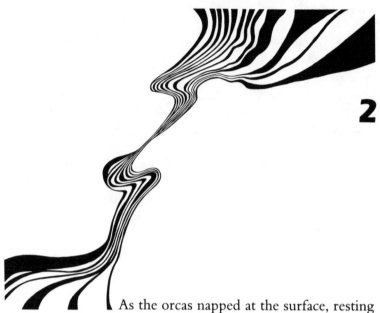

2

As the orcas napped at the surface, resting from their attack on the humpbacks, the sun approached its zenith and beat hot on their backs. To avoid sunburn and over-heating, they began resting in a series of dives, swimming slowly and rising for air every few minutes in groups of two or three. They maintained a northwesterly heading in the general direction of Nantucket, sleeping lightly with ears attuned to the raspy sound of big propellers, for they were now near busy shipping lanes.

First to stir from its nap was the calf of that spring. She popped to the surface and took air. A few miles east of her, a big tanker was passing, the *shoosh-shoosh* of its propellers like the sound of a big seal scratching itself underwater. Then she heard the whine of a large pump and recognized it as the sound ships made when they defecated.

After watching a towering flock of phalaropes drift smoke-like along the horizon, she caught up with the pod and swung beneath her mother to nurse. Having drunk her fill of thick fishy milk, she meandered through the pod, bumping others and making a general nuisance of herself. Perhaps at the request of sleepy adults, two juvenile females led the calf some distance away and kept her amused while the others continued to nap.

The calf teased the juveniles and got them to chase her, then in her excitement swam directly over the old bull as he was rising for air. Breaking water like a big black rock, he lifted the nine-foot baby high and dry on his broad back, then rolled and dumped her to one side. She squealed and swam atop the bull's head, blocking his blowhole. He exhaled a blast of air against her belly, tickling her so much that she rolled off his head and got water into her blowhole. Sneezing and chuffing to clear her nostril, she again swam atop his head and again he tickled her belly with a blast of air. They played this game several times, then the bull rolled and pushed her away with his left flipper. She squealed at him. With his abscess draining, the old bull no doubt felt better than he had for a long time, but it was uncomfortably warm there at the surface. He puffed a few clouds of sparkling vapor into the hot sunlight, then slipped beneath the waves to continue his nap.

The juveniles led the calf off to one side of the resting group. Too restless to remain quiet for long, she began slapping her tail against the surface. The juvenile females tried to silence her, then apparently gave up and decided to make the best of the situation by showing her proper lobtailing technique. The three of them floated side by side, smacking their tails against the surface. The juveniles knew how to cup their flukes and strike the surface at just the right angle to create loud claps of sound. The calf's flukes were only about two feet across, but she still managed to make plenty of noise. This was good practice, for lobtailing is one way of herding fish during hunts, and even the youngest can help.

Soon all the others were stirring from their naps and starting to play. The calf and her playmates stood on their heads and thrust their tails high in the air. The younger bull copied them, but finished his headstand by striking his tail hard against the surface. His great flukes, seven feet across, produced a thunderclap of sound. Some adults reared back with their heads above water and churned the sea into foam with their flippers. The younger adult bull performed a series of soaring breaches that culminated in booming bellywhops. Then he began doing barrel rolls and landing on his side, clapping thunder with his big dorsal fin. Even the old bull joined in the play, swimming belly-up and using his flippers like big paddles as he planed across the surface. His version of the backstroke created a mighty disturbance of sound and white water.

Some of the orcas played with seaweed, dragging it along in their mouths or draping it over their dorsal fins and flukes. The younger bull hooked a long strand of kelp on one flipper and towed it around until an adolescent male stole it from him. The bull snorted and gave chase. Snout to tail all the way, the two males flashed through the water and soared through the air. The swift passage of their big bodies raised six-foot waves. At last the bull intercepted the younger male from the side and delivered a thumping body block that could be heard for half a mile. But no sooner did he recapture his kelp than he lost interest and let it drift away.

A juvenile male left the group, zigzagging as if in pursuit of something, then returned and floated motionless in front of the little calf. He whistled some sort of repetitive signal. She clicked at him. He opened his mouth and out swam a twenty-inch silver hake. When the fish was about a foot from him, almost within the calf's reach, the male sucked it back into his mouth.[1] The calf squealed and clicked at him again. He opened his mouth and out swam the hake, only to be sucked back in just as the calf tried to seize it. They played this game five times, then the male held the hake by the tail and let the calf take it. She tried to play the game, but the fish was too big to fit inside her mouth. Besides, it was half dead. The calf swam through the pod with the hake's tail sticking out one side of her mouth until a juvenile male stole the fish from her, turned it with his tongue, and swallowed it headfirst. She slapped him with her flukes, then darted back to the safety of her mother's flank.

Perhaps attracted by the pod's commotion, a greater shearwater began circling the area, banking so sharply that the tip of one long wing nearly brushed the water. Then a dozen gannets appeared, circling high overhead. It seemed at first that the birds thought the orcas were feeding and hoped to share in the catch, but the gannets had spotted fish nearby. One after another, they folded their wings and plunged from a height of a hundred feet. A split second before impact, they swept their wings straight back behind them and speared the water to a depth of ten feet.

Moments later the gannets popped to the surface and took wing. All but one bird. About to take flight, it was pulled back underwater by a young female orca. Two juvenile females took turns dragging the big bird to a depth of some three fathoms and releasing it. Each time the terrified bird struggled back to the surface and tried to fly away, the orcas recaptured it.

The calf darted over and tried to join the game, but the gannet was bigger and stronger than she had realized. It was the size of a goose, and its heavy bill came to a sharp point. When she tried to grab the bird, it pecked her and nearly put out her eye. Bleeding from a deep gash in her face, she backed away and watched as the game continued for another ten minutes until the gannet drowned.

The females nudged the bird as though hoping to revive it. Failing that, one of them held it by the neck above the surface, then with a sideways snap of her head, separated skin and feathers from the body, which flew through the air and was retrieved by the other female. Neatly plucked, the bird was then shared by the two females.[2]

Meanwhile, play between the younger adult bull and the two adolescent males had grown increasingly rough. They were now slamming into each other with jarring force and raking each other with their teeth. After a few minutes of this, the adolescents abandoned the game and moved off stiffly, gasping for breath and nursing many bruises.

Panting from exertion, the younger bull joined the old one.

The two males floated side by side, puffing rainbows into the sunlight, then arched their backs and went deep to escape the heat. At a depth of some three fathoms, they joined up with the old cow. As she and the two bulls exchanged fond rubs, they were joined by two younger females, one of them the calf's mother. Now the calf arrived, escorted by the other three juvenile females. Soon all members of the pod had come together. Swimming slowly a few feet apart, they rested from their play.

The calf heard the old bull echo-scanning the bottom. She tried to do the same but could make little sense of her echoes. This much she knew; there was a lot of water under her.

• • •

What the orcas heard would be a spectacular sight, were it visible. Ninety fathoms below the pod lies the edge of the continental shelf, which plunges sheerly for a thousand fathoms, then gradually falls away to a depth of several miles.[3] Just a few miles north, in the cool green waters of Georges Bank, are places so shallow that the old bull could rest his tail on the bottom and slap his flippers against the surface.

Ahead of the pod lie 36,000 square miles of oceanic bight known as the Gulf of Maine, which in many respects is like a huge tidal pool cupped on the continental shelf. On its seaward side the Gulf extends from Cape Cod to Cape Sable, Nova Scotia. Between these headlands it is bounded by Nantucket Shoals, Georges Bank, and Browns Bank. Its landward boundaries include the coasts of northern Massachusetts, New Hampshire, Maine, and parts of New Brunswick and Nova Scotia.

Beneath this cold backwater of the north Atlantic, the wide plateaus of Georges Bank and Browns Bank fall away into a broad valley punctuated by twenty-one deep basins (Georges Basin plummets two hundred fathoms) and nearly as many buttes. The many and varied seamounts form rich inshore fishing grounds, such as Stellwagen Bank and Jeffreys Ledge. To the north the Gulf narrows into the Bay of Fundy, a natural bottleneck whose upper reaches boast the world's highest tides, ranging as much as fifty-three feet between low and high water.

Because Georges Bank, Browns Bank, and Nantucket Shoals are so shallow, the Gulf of Maine is largely isolated from the warm, sapphire blue Gulf Stream and the rest of the Atlantic. That isolation is rendered nearly complete by temperature/salinity mixtures that set up fluid density barriers. As a result, the Gulf differs from the Atlantic in temperature, color, salinity, physical processes, flora, and fauna. All these characteristics change abruptly at the shelf break, where the orcas are now. The Gulf is a boreal environment that bounds on a subtropical one by way of the Gulf Stream. The southern and western limits of the Gulf are the northern limits for many southern species of marine life.

The geological history of the Gulf also differs sharply from that of the Atlantic. Scientists interpreting the geological record have concluded that fifteen to twenty million years ago, the Gulf was a smooth, shallow seaward-sloping shelf much like our present mid-Atlantic continental shelf. Back then none of the complex banks, gulleys, ridges, and basins existed that define the Gulf today. About fifteen million years ago, sea level fell, or the sea bottom rose, leaving the area high and dry. Streams eroded the exposed lowland, carving out the vast troughs of Northeast Channel and Great South Channel and eroding the inner border of Georges Bank into what is now a steep northward-facing slope. Erosion also carved out a number of river valleys that were later broadened into major basins by glaciers during the most recent ice age, one to two million years ago. About thirteen thousand years ago, glacial ice retreated from the Gulf, which remained high and dry for a thousand years. During that time, erosion completed the sculpture of the Gulf as we know it today; then the sea rose to its present level and reclaimed the Gulf.[4] To this day, the nets of fishing vessels bring up the occasional ancient tree trunk from one of the Gulf's banks.

The Gulf's isolation from the warm Gulf Stream is one reason it has some of the world's richest fisheries, for cold water absorbs more oxygen and so can support more marine life than warmer waters. Another reason these fisheries are so rich is that the banks are shallow, so marine plants get enough sunlight to support photosynthesis. Marine plants thrive, marine animals that eat the plants thrive, and so on up the pyramid of life.

From April through November the Gulf of Maine teems with life, then food stocks run low and water temperatures start to fall. For want of food or warmer water, many species abandon the Gulf for the winter, and the ecosystem has a few months in which to replenish itself. During the winter, storms churn nutrients from the great depths beyond the continental shelf and mix them, together with oxygen, into the waters of the Gulf. Once again rich with nutrients, the submarine banks are revitalized by the increased sunlight of spring, which triggers the explosive growth of planktonic life that supports the entire food cycle. By April, migratory species are returning in force, and the Gulf teems with life for another eight months.

This year, though, major changes have been occurring within the Gulf, as the orcas will learn over the next few weeks. Above-normal winter water temperatures encouraged many migratory species to stay in the Gulf all winter. No one knows how this may have affected the balance of life, but by spring there were signs that collapses and geographical shifts in major bait fish populations were causing predatory species to change their habits. For example, the humpback whales failed to show up on Stellwagen Bank, cetacean species normally never seen in the Gulf were being sighted, and the once-ubiquitous dogfish (only recently being exploited for England's fish-and-chips market) were nowhere to be found nearshore.

All in all, the experience gained by the orcas during past visits to the Gulf may prove irrelevant this summer.

•   •   •

It was midafternoon of that same day. Obscured behind a high bank of clouds, the sun's disk was a vague luminosity, but its light fanned downward in discrete rays that silvered the western horizon. The orcas had progressed some thirty miles northwest of the shelf break and were passing the Nantucket lightship. Once clear of the lightship, they headed due north between the southernmost banks of Nantucket Shoals and Great South Channel. The orcas were swimming on a steady course now, staying deep for four to five minutes, surfacing long enough to take several breaths, and coasting back into the depths without showing their flukes. Their speed was about five knots.

They were starting to see many signs of people now. Large oceanic vessels loomed on the eastern horizon, plying the shipping channels to and from Boston. Now and then the orcas encountered iridescent wavy bands of petrochemicals drifting on the surface. The elders swam around or under such waste. As a rule, all the youngers followed their example, but at one point the suckling tried to play with a floating plastic jug and inadvertently swallowed some chemical. Minutes later, she vomited. Whatever she had swallowed made her stomach burn and left with her a throbbing headache.

When the little one stopped retching, the orcas resumed their journey. West of the pod, two treelike shapes blossomed in black smoke, then a pair of draggers hove into view, running broad abeam of each other on a pair-trawl. A dark gray longliner passed on the pod's right, sinking behind one swell and soaring on the next like a porpoising whale. It passed a southbound sloop, which sank behind a swell so big that the top third of its sail cut the sea like a dorsal fin. Then the sloop soared into full view, and the orcas could see men in the cockpit watching them through binoculars.

As the orcas moved along the eastern periphery of Phelps Bank, they saw white birds with long black-tipped wings circling far ahead. Even before they got close enough to see the birds' yellow heads and thick pointed bills, they knew they were gannets. One bird swept back its wings and made a quick drop, then changed its mind and circled again. The birds gathered into a tight circling flock. The old cow signaled for silence. She knew the gannets had something in sight. They were not just searching.

As the orcas quietly approached, the birds circled higher, then folded back their wings and plunged like arrows, and the orcas saw fish spurt out of the water. Listening through the water and looking through the air, the orcas watched the long-winged black-and-white birds, which had by now regained the air and were again working high over the water. The big birds dipped again, slanting their wings for a dive, then swinging this way and that as they followed fish. Now the orcas saw a bulge move along the water, the sort of bulge big predators raise as they swim near the surface. Maybe it was a school of giant bluefin tuna. Still silent, the orcas hurried to the scene, but by the time they reached the area below the gannets, they found no sign of anything larger than tinker mackerel. With bursts of sound and bubbles, they herded a few hundred tinkers into a tight ball and took turns feeding on them.

The suckling calf followed her mother as she went in to feed, then lost interest and wandered outside the circling pod. Hearing a splash, she swam over to investigate. A tinker mackerel, apparently injured by the feeding gannets, was swimming in circles on its side. The calf flipped it into the air and caught it, then spat it out and whacked it high in the air with her flukes.

She was still splashing around and amusing herself when something bumped her so hard in the belly that it nearly knocked the wind out of her. Instinctively she leapt straight up out of the water, only to find herself falling back on top of a thirteen-foot white shark, which had bumped her with its snout to gauge her edibility. The shark was apparently trying to figure out where she had disappeared to, for when she fell broadside onto its back, it streaked out of sight as if it thought the tables had been turned. While the shark shot off in one direction, the frightened calf skipped across the water in the opposite direction and was met by her mother and the young bull. When the shark recovered its composure and circled back to make another try for the calf, it found itself confronted by twenty-two feet of very feisty bull orca. There was a brief standoff, then the shark turned tail and went deep. While the calf composed herself at the teat, her mother patted her with her flipper.

A small yellow aircraft came into view several miles north of the pod. The old cow reared back at the surface and watched as the plane flew a series of gridlike sweeps, moving generally northwestward as it went. She sounded a strident call. The others fell silent. The old cow submerged her head and listened. Even the little calf listened, wondering which of the many sounds she was hearing had caught the elder's attention. So many ships, so many propeller sounds. And fish, croaking and squeaking by the millions. And bubbling, farting whales and clicking, whistling dolphins. What was it that had the old mother so absorbed?

The eldest cow exchanged clicks and whistles with the old bull, then the family headed northwestward. For the rest of that day and night they swam, pausing to feed as opportunities presented themselves.

• • •

It is not common knowledge, but great white sharks are regular summer visitors to the Gulf of Maine.

While waiting for the island ferry to Portsmouth, New Hampshire one summer day in 1986, I struck up a conversation with a sport fisherman. I was hoping to get some orca anecdotes, for when killer whales are in the area, tuna fisherman usually see them. This man had seen orcas five or six years earlier, but his recollections were vague. "I hope I never see killers again," he said, "because when they show up, you might as well forget about catching tuna." Then, in the course of bemoaning the sorry state of bluefin tuna stocks, he happened to mention that great white sharks (*Carcharadon carcharias*) are often reported over Nantucket Shoals.

At that point the ferry arrived, and I embarked on a research trip to the Isles of Shoals, ten miles off the coast. On Appledore Island, I met with John B. Heiser and other scientists at the Shoals Marine Laboratory, a teaching facility jointly operated by Cornell University and the University of New Hampshire. Although I had gone there primarily to talk about orcas, I mentioned the fisherman's comment about great white sharks over Nantucket Shoals. To my surprise, Dr. Heiser said that great whites are thought to be fairly common as far north as the Isles of Shoals.

Upon returning home, I checked my references on great whites. Burton and Burton[5] confirmed my general impression that the "man-eater" is a pelagic warm-water shark that occasionally strays into temperate seas. But the water near the Isles of Shoals could hardly be called temperate. Subarctic, perhaps.

Checking further, I was surprised to find in Bigelow and Schroeder[6] that "man-eaters" (white sharks) were reliably reported more often from southwestern parts of the Gulf of Maine than from any area of comparable size along the entire Atlantic coast of North America. The "southwestern parts" of the Gulf include not only Nantucket Shoals but the crowded beaches of Cape Cod and the islands as well. A chilling thought.

As for this apparent anomaly — warm-water sharks being found in the frigid waters near the Isles of Shoals — it appears that great whites are not warm-water sharks at all. Ellis[7] reports that they are most commonly found in cold-water areas of California, South Australia, South Africa, New England, and the Canadian Maritimes. They apparently visit these areas to hunt the large populations of seals and sea lions. (The Isles of Shoals are the whelping grounds for a colony of harbor seals.)

The ability of the great white sharks to tolerate cold water may be due in part to their size. (Big bodies retain heat better than small ones.) Still, were that the only reason, very young white sharks could not survive in the Gulf of Maine, yet they do. One white shark harpooned near the Boston lightship in

July 1948 was only three feet long and is apparently the smallest white shark on record. (The formidable teeth and healthy condition of even the smallest white sharks captured to date show them to be self-sufficient predators within a few months of birth.) Based on umbilical scars found on four-foot white sharks, the three-foot specimen could not have been more than a few months old.[8]

Until fairly recently it was thought that all sharks and bony fishes were cold-blooded creatures unable to regulate their body temperatures because they lost body heat through their gills. Over the past decade, in vivo muscle temperature experiments have revealed quite a few warm-blooded species. Among these are bluefin tuna (*Thunnus thynnus*), which grow to be one of the largest (up to fifteen hundred pounds) and fastest (up to forty-eight knots) bony fishes in the world.

Large, fast animals need elevated body temperatures not only to survive in cold water but also to speed up nerve impulses and muscle contractions. Thus it would seem reasonable to assume that the fastest of the sharks are warm-blooded.

This is known to be true of the makos and porbeagles, two genera in the mackerel shark family. Experiments have shown that these sharks are able to minimize heat loss through their gills. Great whites are in the same family as makos and porbeagles, so they are likely warm-blooded as well.

Ellis cites warm-bloodedness with respect to mackerel sharks only,[9] but it is likely that other species can regulate their body temperatures. For example, the Greenland shark (*Somniosus microcephalus*) and the basking shark (*Cetorhinus maximus*) regularly inhabit the temperate-boreal zone of the North Atlantic. Both have the heat-retention advantage of great size (twenty feet or more) but they may also be able to minimize heat loss through their gills, like mackerel sharks.

Great whites have been recorded at least as far north as St. Pierre Bank south of Newfoundland, where according to an 1874 record cited by Bigelow and Schroeder, one attacked a fisherman's dory and left some of its teeth in the gunwale.[10]

Ellis reports that another dory was allegedly sunk by a twelve-foot white shark off Cape Breton Island, Nova Scotia.[11] No year is given. Burton and Burton cite a man-eater attack on a fishing dory in Nova Scotia as having occurred in 1953.[12] In such attacks, the sharks may be mistaking boats for prey.

All things considered, it appears that great whites are more common in New England waters than most of us would like to think, but attacks on people are certainly rare in this region. Of 1,652 cases in the Shark Attack File (maintained by the Shark Research Panel of the American Institute of Biological Sciences under the sponsorship of the Office of Naval Research from 1958 to 1969, then discontinued for lack of funding), only one involved a great white attacking a person in New England. That was a fatal attack in Buzzards Bay, Cape Cod, during the summer of 1936. Worldwide, the Shark Attack File attributed thirty-three attacks to great whites, but in a third of those cases, species identification was questionable, as it is in most shark attacks.[13]

Great whites can never be taken lightly, but it appears that they are no more dangerous to people than many other shark species. And regardless of species, in two out of three shark attacks on people, the victims escape with their lives. The sharks appear to mouth people, then release them, as if they dislike the taste of human flesh. (Perhaps our heavy bone structure puts them off.) Unfortunately, their exploratory bites usually inflict serious injury.

Considering the enormous number of sharks in the world's oceans and the number of people they undoubtedly encounter, attacks are remarkably few and far between. Far more people are struck by lightning than by sharks. Each year in the United States alone, lightning kills at least five hundred people and injures another fifteen hundred. Worldwide fatalities must reach many thousands, for lightning strikes the earth some half-million times each day.

3

By dawn of the following day, they had traveled some eighty miles to the northerly reaches of Cape Cod.[1] There, at first light, they again saw the yellow aircraft circling; then it flew out of sight to the west.

The weather was clear. Sea and sky, the same deep blue, flowed one into the other. In deep water several miles off Cape Cod's northeast shore, on a flat calm sea, two men were fishing from an outboard skiff. One man glanced seaward, then sat bolt upright, tapped his companion, and pointed. Wide-eyed, the men watched a series of strange swellings move along the surface toward their boat. Patches of white were visible inside the watery mounds. Now a bubbling fin broke the silky smoothness, then a plume of mist erupted with a loud *kawoosh,* followed by other blows and other fins, two of them towering over the seated men. "Killer whales!" exclaimed one man in a harsh whisper. His companion paled and gripped the gunwales.

The strange mounds are caused by surface tension. As the orcas rise for air, the water bulges eighteen inches before the animals' dorsal fins break the surface tension. Seen through this mound of water, each orca looks like a fetus in its sac.

Agog, the men clutched the gunwales of their rocking skiff as a dozen phantasmal shapes flowed swiftly around them and glided away toward shore.

Pausing about two miles offshore, the old cow and bull spun on their tails and scanned the sky. Only one aircraft was visible, flying high and straight toward the north. The orcas submerged and moved inshore.

Over sandbars off Cape Cod National Seashore, they found the water roiled by tidal currents. Swimming slowly near the bottom, they cruised a vast expanse of white sand. Dappled with sunlight, rippled by waves, the sandbars were so shallow in spots that even the youngest calf could strand herself. Carefully the elders felt their way with sonar clicks, keeping to the deeper channels as they searched for prey.

Near the light at North Truro, people on the shore photographed the orcas investigating fish traps. Generations of orcas had exploited these traps every summer, stealing many bluefin tuna, but now the traps were empty.

Once again the elders scanned sea and sky, then led the pod toward the tip of the Cape. On their left, towering sand dunes rolled like golden waves almost to the water's edge, streaming sandy spindrift from their peaks. The wind was freshening now as the sun ascended.

From a commotion of tidal rips off Race Point, the orcas' sonar clicks returned some solid moving echoes. The noise of rushing water made identification of the prey impossible, but the elders whistled for the pod to start a sweep.

They formed a single line abreast, thirty to sixty feet apart, the smallest of them close to shore and the rest ranked by size on out to the big bulls. To people watching from the point, they presented a formidable line extending a quarter mile from shore, their fin heights ranging from the porpoiselike dorsals of the juveniles to the man-high sails of the bulls. The one exception to the ranking was that year's calf, who stayed beside her mother. Sweeping the shoreline at the pace of a brisk walk, the pod swam with a rocking motion, surfacing with heads high and smashing their chins against the water, then smacking their flukes as they submerged. All the while they sounded harsh cries.

Soon a large patch of flat water came to a boil, then silvery shad began to jump, checking the surface to see what they were up against. Now the shad moved ahead of the pod, parallel to the shoreline, trying to swing around the orcas' formation and make a dash for open water.

On signal, all the orcas swam at top speed. The larger of them being faster swimmers, their formation automatically curved toward shore, encircling the fish like a living net. Trapped in the shallows, a hundred two-pound shad were taken, enough to take the edge off the orcas' hunger.

• • •

Orcas often sweep shorelines this way, ranked by size. When they all swim at top speed, their line automatically curves shoreward because, within a given species, larger animals can swim faster than smaller ones. This is a matter of scale. To illustrate, let us say that an orca moves one body length for each thrust of its flukes. This same propulsion ratio would apply to all orcas because they all have the same body design, so a twenty-foot orca would move twenty feet with each thrust of its flukes, while a ten-footer would move only ten feet.

This is why we find only fish of the same age and size schooling together. For a given fin thrust, they all move the same distance at equal speed and so can maintain their tight formations.

• • •

Again ranked according to size, the orcas made a long sweep of the Cape's northeast coast. Along Peaked Hill Bar, they surprised some five-foot sand sharks trying to trap young striped bass against the shore. The orcas chopped up a few of the sand sharks but ate little of their flesh. When the stripers ventured out of the shallows and made a dash for open water, the orcas caught quite a few of them. They were ten-pounders and even tastier than the shad, but there were not enough of them to feed the pod. The average orca needs some four hundred pounds of food a day, and the pod's intake so far this morning was but a fraction of its daily requirement.

While the gulls fought over floating scraps, the orcas rested and the little calf nursed. The big bulls gathered a short distance from the others.

After a twenty-minute rest, they continued on around the tip of Cape Cod, led now by the old bull. Past Race Point they swam, well within view of people standing on the shore, then they rounded Wood End and swung northeast toward Long Point. As they approached Long Point light, they stopped and milled about, then the old bull continued on alone.

Turning the hook of Long Point, he reared back at the surface and looked into Provincetown Harbor. He could see the high square monument on the hill above town and the weathered old houses crowding the hillside all the way down to the water's edge. He scanned the vessels in the harbor, then looked them over again, as if searching for a particular one. There were draggers off-loading or preparing for trips, a few sport fishing boats that had not yet put out to sea, and many pleasure boats. He studied the harbor and listened to its many sounds for a few minutes more, then slipped beneath the surface and headed back to rejoin the pod.

As soon as he moved away from the high noise levels at the harbor's mouth, the old bull heard the distant thrum of diesel engines. Swinging his head from side to side, he zeroed in on the sound. It was coming from somewhere near the center of Cape Cod Bay. He reared back with his head well out of water and saw a small yellow aircraft circling very far away. It looked like the same one they had seen earlier that morning and yesterday, and it was circling steadily over one particular area.

As soon as the bull slipped back into the water, he heard himself being called by the old cow, who had apparently heard the vessel and seen the plane and reached the same conclusion. He listened to her message, then set off on an angle to intercept the pod, which was already racing toward the sound. They rendezvoused and swam toward the center of Cape Cod Bay, a distance of some eight miles, which they would cover in twenty minutes or less.

Halfway into their trip, as they had the aircraft in sight less than a mile ahead, it broke off its circling and made a pass directly above them. It circled them briefly, then climbed to a thousand feet, and the old bull heard the seiner's diesels speed up. He and the younger bull pulled ahead of the pod and, pushing themselves to their limit, covered the last few miles in six minutes. Just as the vessel came into view, the growl of diesels was joined by the whine of high-speed outboard motors and the hollow *kathunk* of aluminum hulls spanking the waves. Then the orcas heard underwater explosions.

• • •

In this scene, the orcas have not only recognized a particular type of vessel by its sound, but even know which one it is, for they have memorized the "voices" of many vessels they exploit. The vessel they are approaching is one of three purse seiners authorized by the National Marine Fisheries Service (NMFS) to fish for bluefin tuna in northeastern waters. The small yellow aircraft is a spotter plane used by the seiner to find schools of bluefin.

Successful seining calls for making a fast set on a moving school. A seiner captain must take into account wind, tidal currents, and vessel drift, as well as the speed and direction in which fish are traveling. When making a set, a purse seiner circles at twenty knots, paying out a perfect arc of float-supported net six hundred feet in radius. Within twenty minutes the ends of the net are joined and its open bottom is pursed, entrap-

ping the fish. Then a big winch hauls the catch aboard. Fishing
with a seine is like sifting a hemisphere of ocean a quarter mile
in diameter.

The explosions heard by the orcas are being caused by men
in motorboats throwing cherry bombs into the water to prevent the tuna from escaping. The orcas know by these sounds
that the seiner is already deploying its net.

• • •

The old bull leaped high above the water and assessed the situation, then he and the young bull took up positions that would
trap the tuna between them and the partially deployed seine.
Soon the rest of the pod arrived and spread out on either side
of the bulls, keeping the tuna between them and the open half
of the seine. Their usual practice was to pick off their fill before
the net was much more than half closed, but they were a bit
late this time. The seiner had already completed about half its
circle.

Still, they would have time to get their share, and their formation would actually help the fishermen by keeping the tuna
contained until the net was closed.

Encircled by noisy boats and confronted by orcas, the tuna
went deep. The orca bulls followed. Because they were in
relatively shallow water, the fishermen were using a seine only
fifteen fathoms deep. Even at that, there was a gap of only about
three fathoms between net and bottom. The bulls managed to
get under the tuna, a hundred or more giants, then drove them
back toward the surface and the waiting pod. The tuna seemed
to sense greater danger at the surface, and milled about in a
tight mass about halfway from the bottom.

By this time the seiner had paid out two-thirds of its four-
thousand-foot net. Soon it would join up with its net skiff,
then take in the purse line to close the bottom of the seine.
If the orcas took too long to make their kills, they could be
trapped along with their prey. Using acoustic windows located

in his head and near his flippers to monitor the sounds of the seiner and its net skiff, the old bull estimated the angle between them, their closing speed, and their distance from him. It would be too close. He signaled the old cow to lead the pod outside the net's circle.

Then, sounding terrifying screams, the bulls struck the north side of the milling tuna. The school exploded like a bomb burst, quickly regrouped, and with the orca bulls in close pursuit, circled the net at blurring speed. Glimpsing their one shot at freedom, the tuna turned toward the narrow gap remaining between seiner and skiff. Cherry bombs exploded ahead of them. Half the tuna reversed direction and darted back inside the net. The rest flashed through the gap, directly toward the other orcas, who were waiting a hundred yards beyond the boats. In the bloody melee that ensued, two six-foot bluefins were crippled, their caudal fins severed by the orcas. Another leaped out of the water at thirty-five knots and was intercepted in midair by the old cow, who bit a chunk the size of a bushel basket out of its belly. The two bulls accounted for another two giants. All told, the orcas managed to catch about a ton and a half of prime bluefin. The rest escaped. The fishermen had netted about half the original school.

As if oblivious to the fishermen, the orcas ate their kills on the spot. There was enough to satisfy the hunger of the entire pod. Their meal finished, they drifted and dozed.

•   •   •

Orcas the world over exploit all manner of fishing vessels. When taking advantage of purse seiners, they usually anticipate a set and work the prey between themselves and the open side of the seine. This maneuver often helps keep fish inside the fisherman's nets, though in terms of fish lost to orcas, the men pay a toll for the service. Still, this can work both ways, for artful fishermen often exploit orcas by making sets ahead of pods when they see them driving fish.

Atlantic purse seiners used to begin a season's bluefin fishing off the Virginia coast and work their way north, but now, due to National Marine Fisheries Service restrictions, they cannot fish for bluefins any farther south than New Jersey and cannot go after bluefin under 270 pounds (eight to nine years old). Accordingly, they do not concentrate on bluefin until about mid-August, and then they usually fish south of Nomans Land, in Cape Cod Bay, or around Cape Ann.

Bluefin tuna are now comparatively rare. As of 1982, their estimated numbers were down to about fifteen percent of the 1960 stock. Nonetheless, they are still seen in enormous schools from time to time, some so large (thousands of tons) that purse seiners dare not make a set for fear of exceeding their quotas. Thanks to protective measures enforced by the National Marine Fisheries Service over recent years, bluefin stocks could soon be up to about twenty percent of the 1960 level.

The giant bluefins (adults weighing 270 pounds or more), much in demand for Japanese *sashimi* markets, have been so heavily exploited that most bluefins now seen in the Gulf of Maine are young—in their ninth year or less and weighing no more than a few hundred pounds. The size of bluefin tuna seen feeding inshore increases south to north, from "footballs" off the Virginia coast to 900 pounds *average* around Nova Scotia. This distribution is a function of cold-water tolerance. The larger a bluefin is, the better it can withstand cold water. This relationship between size and tolerance to cold applies generally to all species, including marine mammals, and explains why many polar subspecies are larger than their counterparts in temperate zones.

Several of the fishermen I interviewed have said that bluefin are running neither in former numbers nor as close inshore as before because the bait is not there. Some think bluefish have been running so heavily since the mid-1970s that they are decimating the bait fish. (Bluefin tuna, by the way, have been observed eating bluefish as well as smaller bait fish.)

Generally speaking, the action does seem farther offshore than before. Off Cape Ann during 1986, one had to cruise thirty miles to Jeffreys Ledge, in particular the Fingers, to be sure of sighting humpbacks and bluefin tuna. Stellwagen Bank (Middle Bank to fishermen), where for years whales had been sighted consistently only ten miles offshore, was visited by far fewer whales and tuna in 1986. Still, 1987 brought signs that the offshore trend may be starting to reverse itself.

Bluefin tuna are often seen swimming under whales. Perhaps they, like their yellowfin cousins in the Pacific, are drawn to the shadows of floating objects or schools of dolphins. The reasons for this behavior are poorly understood, but Pacific tuna fishermen use it to great advantage by "fishing on porpoise." That is, they deploy their purse seines around herds of dolphins known to attract tuna. In the process, many thousands of dolphins die each year.

Bluefins in the Gulf of Maine often feed with whales. One fisherman told me that on a third of his 1985 trips, he had seen tuna mingling with whales. He saw one big finback followed by a large group of tuna, each about four feet long (about 400 pounds). When the finback took a turn, the tuna followed.

Another interesting thing about bluefin tuna is that they appear simultaneously north to south in all parts of the Gulf of Maine. They show up about the same time (mid- to late June) around Nova Scotia and Cape Ann as they do around Cape Cod, and when they leave the Gulf (late September to early October), they seem to drop out of sight. Recent findings show that they ride the Gulf Stream north from their spawning grounds in the Gulf of Mexico, then according to size (larger ones farther north), head inshore at various points along the coast to spend the summer feeding.

A closing thought about this fascinating species: the current decline in bluefin tuna stocks may be due in part to natural cycles. One Provincetown fisherman, now in his eighties, recalls that when he was a lad, some old fishermen (old then —

long-since dead) could remember a time when there were no "horse mackerel" (bluefin tuna) caught in the Truro traps. This decline may have occurred around 1860–1865. I hazard that guess because bluefins were scarce in Massachusetts Bay from 1902 to 1904, then again in 1943, after which the stock slowly built back up to a peak in 1948.[2] The data stop at 1951, but they hint at a forty-year cycle in bluefin stocks. We now appear to be at another natural low point, which makes the species all the more vulnerable to human exploitation.

4

The orcas spent the better part of a week in Cape Cod Bay. At night they foraged along the shoreline, trapping prey in the shallows. During the day they stayed farther offshore to avoid small motorboats, whose shrill propeller noise hurt their ears and sometimes interfered with whistled communications.

When not playing or actively pursuing prey, the orcas exerted themselves as little as possible. Although this conservation of energy made them seem lackadaisical, they were not as easygoing as they appeared. Even in the relatively small confines of Cape Cod Bay, the elders carefully planned the pod's every move, for the bay encompassed more than five hundred square miles of water and well over a hundred miles of shoreline. The elders were forever thinking ahead to the next meal. Where could they find enough food for all without working too hard to get it? And enough food for *all* was the key, because group strength was vital to each of them.

As long as food intake exceeded energy outlay, they passed up few feeding opportunities, however small. And they gorged themselves whenever possible, for there was no telling when they might get their next meal. If necessary, they would venture deep to feed on groundfish, such as cod and haddock, but deepwater foraging was not their style. Besides, they preferred oilier fish like the various species of mackerel, which could usually be found near the surface. One mackerel species in particular, bluefin tuna, was a major reason for visiting the Gulf of Maine each summer. Bluefins are rich sources of carbohydrates, proteins, and fats, and the big ones make very energy-efficient prey. It generally took a lot less effort for the orcas to bring down a thousand-pound bluefin than it did to catch ten hundred-pounders.

Historically the orcas had always been able to count on finding bluefin tuna throughout the Gulf of Maine. The giant adults had been especially plentiful near Nova Scotia, Cape Ann, and the tip of Cape Cod, but over the past ten years or so, tuna stocks had declined drastically. Bluefins still migrated into the Gulf of Maine every summer, but compared to their former numbers, they were difficult to find. The same was true of many bait fish preyed upon by the bluefins, *and* species preyed upon by the bait fish, so the orcas could no longer count on finding bluefins in certain areas. Food concentrations might vary daily, even hourly.

The orcas could echolocate big tuna from as far away as half a mile, but at the first burst of clicks, any cagey bluefins within earshot would sprint away at speeds no orca could hope to match. Sometimes the orcas were lucky enough to hear bluefins jumping and could slip up on them without having to make a sound. As a rule, though, successful bluefin hunts depended on strategy.

The most energy-efficient strategy was to exploit the purse seiners, but the orcas knew of only three vessels working the area, and those ventured out of port only when their spotter planes found tuna. Whenever the elders heard light aircraft during the day, they paused to scan the sky and look for telltale search patters. They could not hope to follow spotter planes over great distances — even the seiners were too fast to follow — but the orcas exploited tuna fishermen as opportunities arose. Their long swim from the shelf break to Cape Cod had been triggered in part by the sight of a spotter plane, but they would have been heading for Cape Cod within a day or two, anyway.

The second most energy-efficient strategy was to figure out where the tuna *would* be, get there before they did, with minimal effort, and lay a trap. One way to do this was to lie in wait at historically likely locations. Another was to guess where tuna would feed in the immediate future, based on certain sets of conditions favorable to bluefins. Likely locations were less reliable now than years ago, and the orcas could waste a lot of energy visiting likely spots, so they relied more on detecting ideal sets of conditions.

Such considerations kept the elders preoccupied much of the time. Even now, the old cow was investigating the approach to Wellfleet Harbor, an area so rife with shifting sandbars that the bottom changed with each turn of the tide. Swimming ahead of the pod at a leisurely pace, she let the sea flow across her tongue, checking the water's temperature and salinity and tasting it for signs of prey or bait. She listened to the myriad fish sounds pouring through the harbor approach. How many of these sounds were being made by mackerel, favored prey of bluefins? Did they sound stressed, as if they were being hunted? Diving to the bottom, she listened again, checking for temperature gradients that might mask sounds from the harbor or give false echoes when she and her kin used their sonar. Then sonaring softly, she mentally mapped the bottom topography, seeking out likely escape routes and hiding places. Juggling the many variables, her big brain compared all her sensory inputs to complex sets of conditions remembered from productive tuna hunts of the past. If her brain found a matching profile, she would experience a sense of environmental déjà vu.

Right now, at the mouth of this particular harbor, there was no match. Something was missing. One final time she swept the area's spectrum of sounds, tastes, temperatures, and sights, then led the pod southwestward to Barnstable Harbor. There too, conditions seemed poor for bluefins, but she could hear muted slaps and the bait fish sounded stressed. The orcas quietly entered the harbor mouth and surprised a school of young stripers working the cove inside Beach Point. The bass were feeding on smelt, stunning them with sharp slaps of their tails, then doubling back to swallow them. The stripers were chunky ten pounders, and the orcas took a hundred or more.

•   •   •

In terms of complexity, at least, my paradigm of orca information processing may be close to the truth. It certainly seems unlikely that orcas simply roam their range, eating what they want when they want it. They may have done this when marine life was still abundant, but predators must adapt to environmental change, and the Gulf of Maine has undergone sweeping changes.

Just fifteen to twenty years ago, you could have cruised Stellwagen Bank and thrilled to the sight of big bluefin tuna jumping from horizon to horizon. Schools covering several acres each were common sights. The same was true of mackerel. Tinker mackerel were so plentiful that when my sons and I set out for a day's fishing, we never bothered to bring bait from shore. We merely lowered a jig over the side, almost anywhere, and caught all the tinkers we needed. Groundfish were still plentiful, too. Almost at will, we could catch haddock and flounder for the dinner table.

Now haddock and flounder are so scarce that retail prices sometimes reach ten dollars a pound. Mackerel are scarce too, and each giant bluefin sighted is all but front-page news. We cannot catch even cod or herring very readily now. Compared to its former abundance, the Gulf of Maine seems a watery desert.

This is the situation in which the orcas find themselves. Most species of prey fish are on the decline. Some populations have crashed. Each bellyful of food is several times more difficult to obtain than it was twenty years ago. This grim picture affects all life forms, but I mention it here primarily to dramatize the gravity of the orcas' every hunt. Survival is a business in which one either turns a profit or dies. Turning a profit means earning more in the way of food than is spent in terms of energy required to catch that food.

Despite environmental declines, we still see orcas in the Gulf of Maine. How are they surviving? They may be preying on fellow cetaceans more than before. They are certainly preying on fish species they never used to eat and, in the process, are competing with fishermen as never before. In many parts of the world, the situation is approaching open warfare as orcas raid fishermen's lines and nets. Fishermen see this behavior as laziness, but considering the lethal reprisals that orcas brave to exploit the men, the animals seem more desperate than lazy. They are probably just competing for their share of declining food stocks.

The situation in Alaska is a good example. In 1985, longliners fishing Alaskan waters began losing up to twenty-five percent of their blackcod catch to orcas, who bite them off the big hooks at considerable risk to themselves. According to area biologists, blackcod (a deepwater species) is not historically part of the orca diet, so some ecological change must be forcing the orcas to risk the fishermen's hooks and guns. They are probably resorting to blackcod because traditional prey, such as salmon, are so scarce. And they may risk stripping longlines because the blackcod's habitat is too deep for them to reach.

Some fishermen are shooting orcas that raid their nets and lines. Still, the reasonable men among them appreciate the orcas' viewpoint, for in many habitats we are virtually taking badly needed food from the animals' mouths.

One thing is fairly certain. The orcas that have made it through this difficult period must be cagier than ever, for survival now demands a stringent energy budget. They cannot afford to burn up too much energy seeking preferred prey that is scarce. Neither can they afford to settle for alternatives that fail to give them what they need. Orcas prefer certain prey because experience has shown that it supplies an optimum balance of proteins, fats, and carbohydrates. It may be difficult for the animals to make major changes in their diets and still stay healthy.

For an orca, the bottom line in the business of survival is blubber thickness. When the animal is well fed and healthy, its blubber stays thick enough to keep it warm in cold seas and to provide a reserve in case food becomes scarce. Should an orca's blubber start to thin, the animal cannot stay in cold water or its body core temperature will fall, damaging the brain and heart. The animal can migrate to warmer water, as orcas do for part of each year anyway, but if it is forced to spend too much time in warmer, less productive water, its blubber will become even thinner. Thus, even a moderate thinning of the blubber could escalate into a potentially fatal situation.

It falls on the elders to direct a pod's movements, and it must be more crucial now than ever that they make the right decisions. Should they come up empty on too many hunts, the pod will become progressively weaker and less effective on each succeeding hunt. Beyond a certain point, they could be doomed.

Effective pod leadership must demand careful planning, especially in habitats such as the western North Atlantic, where orca ranges appear to be vast. From their infrequent but seasonally regular appearances in this habitat, it seems that the oldest, most experienced adults keep the pods on long-range timetables. They must have a staggering fund of knowledge about their environment. They appear to know precisely when and where gray seals and harbor seals whelp, for orcas usually reach the whelping grounds when the newly weaned pups are on their own but still naive. When bluefin tuna venture inshore to feed, orcas seem not to follow them right away, but instead wait for them to fatten into prime condition. Similarly, the ideal time to prey on any species is when its females are ripe with roe, and the oral record suggests that when the various races of Atlantic salmon and shad returned to spawn, they found orcas waiting for them at the mouths of their home rivers. Long gone are the hordes of anadromous fish available to orca generations past. Dams, pollution, and overfishing have taken a heavy toll. Still, improvements have been made on many rivers, enabling anadromous fish to spawn once again in respectable numbers. It is conceivable that orcas still time their movements to arrive at various river mouths when spawning runs are due to start.

From the data presented in the Appendix, it appears that orcas of the western North Atlantic range over much of the northeast shelf, probably synchronizing their movements with the migrations and birthings of their prey. How they keep track of all this is anyone's guess, but orcas are known to have excellent memories and sharp wits. It is possible that experienced orcas maintain a sort of calendar by keying on the seasonal habits of fishermen, by observing the changes in coastal foliage, and even by gauging the lengths of days and nights. Clearly their long-range planning involves more lore than instinct, for in many habitats they have shown that they can quickly adapt to changes in their environment.

In short, orcas are *smart,* perhaps even smarter than I give them credit for in my narrative.

·   ·   ·

Twice each day during their sojourn in Cape Cod Bay, the orcas visited the Cape Cod Canal. Tidal currents through the canal are swift, approaching five knots at the Buzzards Bay end, and nearly three knots at the end near Cape Cod Bay. On each turn of the tide, hordes of small bait fish are swept through the canal. In pursuit of them come predators, such as mackerel, hake, bluefish, striped bass, and bluefin tuna, compressed into a waterway only 250 yards wide and five fathoms deep. Despite the heavy traffic, it was a good place to hunt, so the elders planned the pod's foraging around two trips each day to the eastern mouth of the canal. Arriving at the approach waters just before the flood turn of the tide, they would wait for prey to come their way.

One morning about an hour before flood tide, the orcas gathered near number 1 bell buoy. While waiting for the tide to turn, they napped in a series of dives, staying well clear of the many vessels entering and leaving the canal. This was a noisy place, but most of the vessels were large, their sounds pitched so low that they did not interfere with the orcas' communications.

While the tide was still slack, the orcas heard heavy splashing to the east and went to investigate. A three-mile swim brought them to a point just northwest of the Barnstable bell buoy. While the rest of the pod waited quietly nearby, the old cow swam to the bell buoy. She waited until she heard another splash, then concealed herself behind the buoy, poked her head six feet out of the water, and peered through the buoy's superstructure. She knew roughly where the sounds had come from and could see herring gulls circling, but nothing broke the surface. Then, half a mile away, a big tuna rose into the air, glinting silvery blue in the sunlight. As it dropped back into the water, another rose and then another, and soon they were leaping all around a quarter-mile circle, soaring in long jumps and landing heavily on their sides. She knew what they were doing. Her kind used much the same tactics. While some of the tuna created a commotion at the surface, others were circling deep, driving the bait fish up into one big cluster for easier feeding. Now she saw signs of small fish finning, then the surface began to boil with bait. Gulls wheeled and dipped, scooping up silvery young herring as they broke the surface.

The tuna were feeding now, circling the bait fish to keep them contained, darting in every now and then to scoop up a mouthful. The old orca had seen at least thirty bluefins jumping, each a good seven hundred pounds, and probably as many more were working the bait from below.

She gave the tuna time to gorge themselves. There would

be all the more food for her and her kin if the tuna had full stomachs. Then she swam back to the pod and quietly gave instructions.

The main body of the pod waited near the bell buoy, due west of the tuna school. The two bulls circled wide to the north and came in on the eastern side of the school. They approached to within a hundred yards, then began smacking their broad flukes against the surface. *Kawap! Kawap!* The sounds rolled across the water like peals of thunder, bounced off the bottom thirteen fathoms below, and reverberated along the shore.

The tuna bunched up and started westward, making about ten knots and heading directly toward the waiting pod. There was no need for the bulls to use their sonar; the pounding of the bluefins' big hearts was like a beacon marking the school's position. Now and then the tuna tried to go deep, but the bulls kept them up by diving to the bottom, sweeping from side to side, and blowing noisy bursts of bubbles. At no time did they vocalize or get close enough for the bluefins to identify them, for had the timid fish known they were being stalked by orcas, they might have stampeded in all directions. Making enough noise to keep the big fish up and moving without throwing them into a panic, the bulls skillfully herded the tuna toward the other orcas, who silently waited to spring the trap.

Just as the bulls had the tuna almost within striking range of the pod, they heard boats approaching. While the young bull kept the tuna moving, the old bull spyhopped and checked out the surface. Six boats were approaching from various directions. Judging by their long bowsprits and pulpits, they were all harpoon boats.

Quickly the bulls drove their quarry the rest of the way into the ambush, but even as the pod was closing its trap, a boat moved in amongst the tuna and harpooned one. Streaming blood, the big bluefin dove straight down and tried to break the harpoon line against some rocks. Failing that, it headed east, towing the thirty-foot boat at walking speed.

To avoid the harpoons, the orcas went under the tuna school.

This kept the bluefins at the surface, making it easy for the other fishermen to move in and launch their harpoons. Six fish were harpooned as the orcas continued to keep them up and drive them westward, trying to get the school away from the boats.[1]

Soon all the boats had wandered off, towed in various directions by harpooned bluefins, and the orcas were able to close in for the kill. But it was difficult for twelve orcas to contain sixty fish that large, and the tuna were so skittish that as soon as the orcas showed signs of making their strike, the school exploded. In their desperate bid for freedom, some fish slammed blindly into the orcas as they tried to break through their formation. In the confusion, the little calf was nearly struck by a speeding tuna almost as large as herself. The orcas managed to take three fish, but the bulk of them shot off in all directions, then regrouped and sped northward, followed by a spotter aircraft that had arrived on the scene as the orcas were closing in to make their strike.

The tuna were in prime condition, and their stomachs bulged with herring, but the kill yielded barely a ton of meat. After all that work, the orcas had less than two hundred pounds of food for each of them. They ate, then took a nap.

The rest of the day was uneventful. The orcas kept pretty much to the center of Cape Cod Bay, just east of the main shipping lanes. The bay is a bowl-shaped depression only about twenty miles in diameter, so when the orcas were near the deep center, sounds from all around the basin were focused on them as though by an amphitheater. At their leisure, they could listen and sort out the various sounds, then investigate anything that interested them.

At dusk they heard what sounded like heavy feeding activity near the bay's eastern shoals. Following the sounds, they surprised a large band of bluefish that had struck an enormous school of alewives returning to the sea from Herring Brook in Wellfleet. The alewives were spent fish, gaunt from the strain of spawning, but the orcas were not interested in them. They jumped the bluefish, ripe ten-pounders so caught up in their feeding frenzy that the orcas put away a hundred or more before the blues smartened up to the fact that they the predators were now the prey.

Bearing a few wounds inflicted by bluefish — pound for pound one of the most vicious creatures in the sea — the orcas napped on the drift as they digested their meal. The tide was low, so Cape Cod Bay was fairly quiet for the first half of the night. But no sooner had the orcas begun to enjoy the lull than a humpback some ten miles to the north, near Provincetown, unwound a bright ribbon of song that rippled the length of the bay and back again. Apparently the whale found the acoustics to its liking, because it moved farther into the basin and sang for some time, running the gamut from pleasant pipings and buglings to great basso profundos that sounded like an entire herd of whales breaking wind.[2] Fed up with this sonic bombardment, the old bull orca faced north and cranked up his loudest scream. The humpback stopped dead in its musical tracks and was never heard from again.

Toward dawn the old cow and bull became excited over something they heard and led the pod northward. Shortly after daybreak, they came within sight of Long Point lighthouse at the tip of the Provincetown hook. Here and there for miles across the approaches to Provincetown Harbor, they could hear the heavy broadside slaps of leaping tuna. The orcas spread out and hurried toward the harbor, sounding piercing calls as they went. Many small schools of tuna were scattered across the harbor approaches, so the orcas spread their forces thin along a one-mile front, each of them zigzagging fifty yards left and right to prevent fish from slipping through the line. They made no attempts to kill but just kept driving the various schools in toward the harbor.

Not far from the Long Point bell buoy, a forty-foot charter fishing boat out of Provincetown was trolling live baits. The boat's captain had been working small, widely scattered patches of tuna, but now he spotted a school of several hundred five-

footers he knew would weigh in at two hundred pounds apiece.
They looked ripe to be caught, and conditions were ideal for
trolling, the only way this captain fished for bluefins. He found
chumming and still-fishing dull because tuna caught that way
usually stay deep when hooked. By trolling, he gave his customers the thrill of seeing the big bluefins jump while they
fought the line.

He trolled his baits carefully, trying to target on the lead
fish. The tuna began "cartwheeling" at the surface in a circle
so perfect that they appeared to be swimming inside a huge
submerged barrel. The captain trolled close around the circle,
expecting to get a strike right away, but nothing happened.
Even when his baits passed directly over the tunas' backs, the
big fish ignored them. Something was wrong. The captain
scanned the area and saw two killer whales a half mile south
of his position. He backed his boat off about fifty yards and
settled down to watch the action.

Swiftly the two orcas, the young bull and one of the cows,
closed to within a hundred yards, then slowed, and breathing
very quietly, approached the tuna like stalking cats. When they
had the tuna between themselves and the shore, they bombarded the fish with raspy sound, trying to drive them toward
the harbor, but the tuna maintained their tight circle, swimming with their dorsal fins breaking water. Within twenty
yards of the school now, the orcas went deep and swam under
the tuna. Several minutes passed, and still the tuna continued
to circle. The fishermen were speculating that the killer whales
had left the area when all at once they heard the thud of heavy
bodies colliding and the sea erupted like a geyser.

The killer whales had shot to the surface and struck the center
of the circle. The tuna leapt in all directions, arcing outward
like a great silvery blue fountain. So desperate were they to
escape that their tails were half out of the water and they could
not get enough thrust to reach full speed. The bull seized one
fish and dragged it deep, then bit it in half and shared it with

the cow. The rest of the tuna regrouped, swam over to the boat, and crowded against its side, as the captain had seen mackerel do when pursued by tuna.[3]

• • •

Relating the incident years later, the captain concludes that the tuna knew killer whales were somewhere nearby but were not sure how many or from which directions they might strike. He thinks they bunched in a circle because they were panic-stricken and could not decide which way to go. Although he heard nothing as the killer whales approached, he believes they were using sonar, because they seemed to know exactly where the tuna were. Judging by the way the tuna sought the safety of his boat, he feels they had been hunted by killer whales before.

Despite all he has seen during an adventurous lifetime at sea, the captain's attitude toward orcas still borders on awe. "You wouldn't believe a whale could move that fast. I've seen killer whales move like black-and-white streaks underwater. It's like having a car whiz past my house at thirty miles an hour."[4]

• • •

The two orcas had fallen far behind their pod. When they finished sharing the one tuna, they spread out, caught up with the others, and resumed their positions in the sweep, which continued to move toward the harbor.

As the twelve orcas entered the mouth of Provincetown Harbor, a deep approach two miles across, the sounds of feeding tuna doubled in volume. Was it luck or had the elders fully assessed the situation from ten miles away? The pod had arrived on the scene while many big tuna were inside the harbor, feeding on mackerel. These, added to the "schoolies" the orcas were driving ahead of them, brought to thousands the total number of tuna inside the harbor.

It was an ideal opportunity, but could twelve orcas blockade a harbor mouth two miles wide and five to twelve fathoms deep? With some prey species it would have been impossible, but despite their formidable size and speed, bluefin tuna are timid creatures. The mere presence of orcas outside the harbor sufficed to keep most tuna inside. And the orcas, well aware the tuna had no idea how many were waiting to pounce on them if they tried to escape, made enough noise to sound like twice their number. They continually bombarded the broad harbor mouth with clicks and screams, the former meant to detect escape attempts, the latter to discourage them.

The old bull and cow were first to go in and feed. While the rest of the pod maintained a noisy blockade, the elders entered the harbor at a leisurely pace, swimming at the surface. Just inside the hook of Long Point, they encountered several boats idling along with harpooners poised in their pulpits. Apparently the fishermen had figured out what the orcas were up to and intended to capitalize on their blockade.

With a nonchalance bordering on disdain, the orcas swam boldly between two boats that were running barely sixty feet apart. Each beat of the orcas' tails left big round "flukeprints" on the flat-calm surface, and the pressure fields from their massive bodies made the boats veer off course a bit. One harpooner turned and called to his mate on the flying bridge.

"Talk about *cocky*. You'd think they owned the damn harbor."

"Where does an eight-hundred pound gorilla sit?" said his mate.

Exhaling in loud unison, the whales continued on, the bull's tall dorsal fin like a black windsurfer gliding across the water.

Just outside a large fish trap, the orcas paused and listened. It sounded like the younger bluefins were bottling themselves up in the inner harbor, while older and wiser fish were keeping more to the east, where they had a better chance of reaching open water

The orcas turned east and heard many large bluefins near the shallows toward Pilgrim Lake. Sonaring now, the whales

spread out, sped up, and streaked along just below the surface. Medium-sized tuna squirted out of the water ahead of
them, but the whales had apparently selected their victims, for
they seemed oblivious to everything else. Either side of their
approach, great shoals of mackerel and other bait fish brought
large patches of surface to a rolling boil. Thousands of gulls
wheeled over the bait, but few dared touch down, for tuna
were now racing about and jumping all over the area.

A half mile off the eastern shore, a small boat was anchored
near the edge of the shoals. Two scientists, husband and wife,
were recording underwater sounds through a hydrophone. As
the man monitored the main recording through headphones,
he dictated comments into a smaller tape recorder. "The harbor is throbbing with the calls of orcas as they echolocate and
communicate. They make a wide variety of sounds, including
clicks, creaks, squeaks, squawks, trills, screams, whistles, roars,
and some sounds that I can't begin to describe. Some of their
strident screams are as loud as trumpet blasts, and can be heard
clearly through the air-water interface." The man listened for
a time, then made another observation. "The orcas' echolocation
clicks sound like a running boy snapping a stick along a picket
fence."

The orcas heard the depth ahead shoal rapidly, then with
a series of heavy thuds, six big tuna ripped through a fish trap,
struck the eastern shoals, and began wildly flopping about,
stranded in shallow water. The rest swerved to the right toward
deeper water, but the bull had anticipated their move and was
already darting in to cut them off. The tuna were racing along
the bottom in five fathoms of water, hugging the outer periphery of a fish trap. Accordingly, the bull's sonar beam was
aimed downward and sent back only a whispery echo from
the scientists' boat looming ahead.

Aboard the boat, the woman, who was not wearing headphones, turned and looked astern as pulses suddenly peppered
the boat's fiberglass hull. "Through the hull, they sound like

distant machine-gun fire," she commented into her own recorder. She continued to look astern, watching a big swell racing toward the boat. It looked too large for bluefin tuna.

Both scientists heard the next sound. *WEEEEEEEEE-oooo-
eeee!* The piercing call drove the recording volume meter into
the red. The man ripped off his headphones and rubbed his
ears. "Ouch! That one nearly blew my eardrums. They seem
to use that type of call a lot. It's the same three-note whistle
we use to call the dog."

The woman was still watching the swell when it suddenly
disappeared. She frowned. "I could have sworn one of them
was heading right toward us." Her husband shaded his eyes
and looked down through the water. "What's that?" They leaned
over the side and saw several nine-foot tuna flash along the
white sandy bottom. Moments later, their field of view was
completely filled by the massive form of a thirty-foot orca
streaking directly under the boat, so close that the tip of its
dorsal fin grazed the keel. "My God!" The boat spun violently
on its anchor, forcing the scientists to grab the gunwales and
brace themselves.

The whistle was heard again, receding rapidly, followed by
a rising arpeggio and a long warbling call. Then a burst of clicks
quickly soared to a whine, and off in the distance the surface
exploded.

A few hundred yards from the scientist's boat, the old bull
surfaced with an eight-hundred-pound tuna flapping and snapping in his jaws. Apparently the bull's mouth was still too sore
for him to effect a killing bite, for he simply held the great
fish high out of the water so that it could not gain leverage
with its caudal fins. The old cow caught up with him and bit
off the tuna's tail. The bull settled back into the water, released
the disabled bluefin, and flexed his ailing jaw. Then he and the
cow shared the kill. Gulls mobbed the area, sometimes paddling
within a few feet of the feeding whales, who ignored them.

The orcas finished feeding and resumed the hunt. This time

the cow caught a five-hundred pound tuna. Again, she and
the bull shared the fish. Sated, they left the harbor and were
replaced by another pair of hunters. And so it went until all
members of the pod had eaten their fill.

For two days the orcas kept thousands of bluefin tuna
trapped inside the harbor. The blood from their kills reddened
large sections of beach and attracted many sharks. Hundreds
of fishermen tried to capitalize on the situation, but the tuna
were too frightened to strike at baits. By the end of the second day, most of the giant tuna had made good their escapes.
The orcas abandoned the blockade.

• • •

This two-day bloodbath will never be forgotten by any who
witnessed it. The orcas drove so many tuna inside the hook
of Long Point that bluefins were dashing in blind panic all over
the harbor. They leaped over sandbars, darted among people
wading and swimming at beaches, and even hurled themselves
onto the sand. Never before nor since has orca-tuna predation on such a scale been reliably reported in the Gulf of Maine.[5]

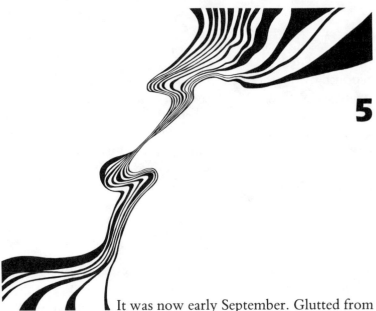

5

It was now early September. Glutted from their feeding orgy in Provincetown Harbor, the orcas ambled lazily northward, the direction most bluefins had seemed to take when they slipped through the blockade. Most likely the tuna would follow Stellwagen Bank up to Cape Ann, feeding as they went.

The littlest calf and her mother were swimming on the pod's east flank, a mile or so from shore. The calf had just spotted Race Point lighthouse a mile or two ahead when she heard a great crescendo of clicks and whistles coming from the south. She recognized the sounds of white-sided dolphins, but never had she heard so many at one time.

The sounds drew closer, and soon she saw whitesides porpoising all the way from shore to within fifty yards of her pod. There were nearly a thousand of them, swimming in an oblong pattern three thousand feet long and half as wide. The herd included very small calves riding their mothers' pressure fields. The dolphins did not appear to be hunting, for the young orca could see individual whitesides leaping and spyhopping, probably checking out her pod.

The whitesides widened their formation and began slapping their tails against the surface. Their whistling gave way to buzzing glissandos and sharp cracks of sound. The dolphins in front began porpoising in a flat arc some three thousand feet wide, clearing the water with all but their flukes and slapping their tails as they reentered.

Fascinated, the young orca broke a cardinal rule and wandered off, unnoticed by her mother, who was napping on the move. Within seconds the calf found herself plunged into a horde of white-sided dolphins. Some of them circled and sonared her as if uncertain what she was. Apparently satisfied that she posed no threat, they went about their business as though she were not even there.

She could see now that the great herd was actually composed of many smaller ones, which intermingled fluidly with each other in beautifully coordinated weaving patterns that were gradually concentrating all fish in their path into dense balls. When various schools of fish tried to break up and confuse their pursuers, the dolphins buzzed them with sound and frightened them with bubble bursts, much as the orca calf had seen humpbacks do. Her own pod did many of these same things while herding prey, but it was fascinating to watch a thousand dolphins coordinating these intricate maneuvers at such high speed.

Already the whitesides had gathered together several large concentrations of fish. Two of these formed disks about ten feet in diameter and half as deep. Another was shaped like a sea cucumber, and measured some six by thirty feet. Above it, scores of herring gulls were wheeling. As the orca calf neared the oblong shape she saw that the fish were so densely packed that tails stuck out of the writhing mass like the tentacles of some gigantic anemone. Whitesides were working both sides of the concentration, moving in opposite directions as they fed. While single feeders worked the sides, other dolphins used bursts of sound and bubbles to keep the fish tightly balled. The dolphins that had fed then helped contain the fish while others took their turns at feeding.[1]

Engrossed by the dolphins' skillfully coordinated efforts, the orca calf became swept up in the rhythm of their movements and tagged along as though she were one of them. Then, above the din of the hunt, she heard a distant cry. It was her mother's voice. The call was coming from the north, so the calf knew that she had fallen far behind the pod. She wended her way through the dolphins' ranks, answering her mother's calls as she went, then spyhopped and saw the pod hurrying in her direction. She made a couple of high jumps to show that she was coming, then porpoised quickly toward the pod, which had stopped and was awaiting her.

Minutes later she slipped back into position at her mother's flank and received a sharp flipper slap for her carelessness.

When the little calf was once again tucked safely between her mother and another adult, the pod leaders continued northward, sonaring the bottom as they went. Soon they heard the start of Stellwagen Bank, signified by a rapid halving of the depth to thirteen fathoms about five miles north of Race Point. They altered course slightly west to follow the bank.

Soon after the turn they heard, amidst the babel of fish sounds and dolphin whistles, the voice of a single orca. It rambled on and on, not communicating with other orcas as far as they could tell, but apparently talking to itself. Its voice was surrounded by the birdlike chirps and whistles of white-sided dolphins, which seemed to be approaching at the same speed as the orca.

The old cow coasted to a stop and called for silence. She and the old bull listened and exchanged click-whistle comments. The orca stranger's acoustic repertoire contained many phrases foreign to them. Its dialect was not that of any pods they knew, and its speech was peppered with sounds both human and machinelike.

The pod resumed its journey. The sounds of the stranger drew steadily closer, its frequent exhalations suggesting that it was swimming at the surface. When it sounded close enough to be seen, the old cow and bull reared back at the surface to take a look. They saw the orca a quarter mile away, traveling in the company of a dozen white-sided dolphins. The orca was about seventeen feet long and looked immature, as did the dolphins. It was not uncommon for the pod to encounter herds of young whitesides shifting for themselves because their mothers had new babies or because their herds had grown beyond optimum size, but solitary orcas are rare, and the sight of this one seemed to unnerve the elders.

All twelve pod members were spyhopping now, bobbing slowly, heavily in the swells. They felt the distant orca's sonar scan their bodies like a wash of fine bubbles, then the stranger reared back and stared at them. Its dolphin companions did the same. A few leaped high in the air to get a better look; then all the young dolphins quickly and quietly left the area.

Vocalizing excitedly, the orca stranger approached the pod. The elders let it come within fifty feet, and then the old bull fired off a gunshot clap of sound. The stranger veered away and circled the pod at the distance specified by the bull's warning. Now all could see as well as hear that the loner was an adolescent female about five or six years old. On her side were five parallel white scars apparently caused by the teeth of another orca.

The old cow approached the stranger from the side and sonared her from head to flukes. Nervous now, the stranger defecated as she continued to circle the pod. The old cow swam a short distance behind her and tasted her feces, then issued a strident command. The stranger stopped. The old cow pressed her rostrum against various parts of the stranger's body and listened to her vital signs. Apparently the stranger passed her test, for the old cow backed off, then permitted the other to approach and pay her respects. That was the cue for the rest of the pod to surround them with much vocalization and mutual inspection. It appeared that the stranger had been accepted.

The old cow barked orders and resumed the northward

journey. The others fell in behind her, but when the stranger tried to bring up the rear, she was rebuffed by two adult cows who bumped her hard and pushed her away.

The loner reared back at the surface and watched until the pod moved out of sight. Then she turned and scanned the surface all around, as though looking for her young whiteside companions. They were nowhere in sight. She sank back into the water and vocalized to herself for a while, then headed south.

Reaching Provincetown, she rode the stern wave of a vessel all the way into the harbor. There she proceeded to entertain crowds of people gathered on the wharves.

•   •   •

The pod's wariness toward the solitary stranger could have had several roots. The pod leaders may have been fearful of contracting disease, though it is unlikely that the stranger would have been cast out by her pod simply because she was physically ill. If she were an outcast, it may have meant that she was a rogue, which would make her a threat to any pod.

Another possibility is that some pods are simply too clannish to adopt a stranger. A pod is after all an extended family, and its members spend their entire lives in this closed society. To hunt or socialize, they may team up with other pods from time to time, but almost never does the pod's membership change except through births and deaths.[2]

Seen in this light, the pod's reluctance to accept the stranger is understandable, but the solitary orca is then all the more puzzling. How can such highly socialized animals ever end up as lone wanderers? Was she the sole surviving member of a pod decimated by whalers, fishermen, disease, or natural disaster?

The pod's rejection of the solitary stranger is fiction, but the stranger herself is based on fact, and her story is a fascinating mystery. Most of the sighting reports for 1982 in the Appendix relate to her.

This is not the first time the young female has visited the Provincetown area. She first appeared there on 16 May 1982, when she was sighted about nine miles off Race Point. Scientists from Provincetown's Center for Coastal Studies, working aboard a Dolphin Fleet whale-watching vessel, recorded the young orca's description, including the five parallel scars on her side. These scars would be mentioned in many sighting reports that summer.

The loner spent a few days around Provincetown and the southern reaches of Stellwagen Bank, then on 22 May was seen near Graves lighthouse outside Boston Harbor. A day later she was sighted off Marblehead, some ten miles north of Boston. Four days after that she spent time around Hingham Harbor, south of Boston, then returned to Boston Harbor, where she was seen on the first of June.

From there she apparently progressed steadily northward and was sighted at least six times during the month of June at various points along the coasts of New Hampshire and Maine. The captain of M/V *Northeasterner* reported seeing her feeding on mackerel about four miles off Hampton Beach, New Hampshire. She showed no fear of several fishing boats gathered there and approached *Northeasterner* close enough for the men to get good photographs. Within this same period, a lone orca — conceivably this same female — was seen swimming "companionably" with several white-sided dolphins near the Isles of Shoals off Portsmouth, New Hampshire. Then (order of appearances uncertain) she was sighted at various points along the Maine coast between mid-June and late August. Twice during this period, an orca matching her description was photographed near Mt. Desert Island. She also spent some time in Seal Harbor, again showing no fear of boats. Fishermen reported seeing her over Morton Ledge, then a week later over Coffins Ledge, where she followed one particular handline fisherman's boat more than any other boat in the area. (She may have liked the sound of his engine or the tickling wash of its propeller.) The last report from Maine was on 28 August, when she visited Somes Sound and was again very tolerant of boats.

Now she was back in Provincetown. Outside the harbor she intercepted a homeward-bound whale-watching vessel and rode its stern wave all the way into the harbor. She followed the boat to its berth, then entertained the people gathered on the wharves by lobtailing and standing on her head. For several days she hung around Provincetown Harbor, performing like a trained seal, much to the delight of crowds gathered on the waterfront.

One day she wandered behind some sandbars into an area that the locals knew would be left high and dry by the falling tide. Dr. Charles "Stormy" Mayo, director of the Center for Coastal Studies, who had already spent much time with the animal, waded into the water near her and tried to get her out of the shallows, but failed. Knowing how much the orca liked to follow boats, he got into a small boat and rowed near her. True to form, she followed his boat and he was able to coax her out of the dangerous shallows into deeper water.[3]

As suddenly as the mysterious young orca appeared, she dropped out of sight and was never seen again. The possibility was raised that she might be a former captive, perhaps a navy animal, but despite widespread publicity, no one ever laid claim to her.

•   •   •

The orcas were some twenty miles northeast of Provincetown, porpoising slowly about fifty feet apart and whistle-talking among themselves. The little calf was wandering throughout the family, visiting various adults and enjoying their attention, when she heard deep moaning calls and heavy, widely spaced clicks. She recognized the sounds; a pod of finback whales was approaching from the north. As if expecting violence, she darted back to her mother's flank.

The finbacks drew closer and closer. Soon she could see

them, seven in all, moving slowly at the surface like her kin. They seemed to show no fear. In fact, to her astonishment, they maintained their heading and passed right through the orcas' formation. Apparently not all whales were afraid of her kind. Equally amazing, her kin continued to whistle-chat, all but ignoring the finbacks as the two pods of whales threaded each other's ranks.

The calf resumed her wandering, seeking attention and getting it, for being the baby of the pod, she was pampered by all. For another three hours the pod continued its leisurely northwestward pace, following Stellwagen Bank. They saw many humpback whales, all of which tolerated their close approach, and the elders showed no more interest in them than they had in the finbacks. Only when a school of adult mackerel happened across their path did the orcas deviate from course, and even then only long enough to snack on a few dozen of the plump blue-silver beauties.

By midafternoon the little calf could see land ahead and to her left. This was a far cry from the low sandy shores she had been seeing around Cape Cod, for she was looking at the high, rocky shoreline of Cape Ann. Here, some parts of the coast soar two hundred feet above the sea, and for mile after mile she could hear surf booming against rocks. The natural underwater background noise here was like a continual roll of distant thunder, twice as loud as it had been around Cape Cod.

The elders maintained their northwesterly heading all the way to Thatcher Island, whose twin lighthouses they had for some time been using as their landmark. Passing on the seaward side of Thatcher, they continued on past Straitsmouth Island, swung left a bit, and swam to Halibut Point. They rounded the point and swam into Ipswich Bay, then paused to rest and reconnoiter.

The little calf spyhopped and looked around. All along the eastern horizon, clouds billowed and rolled like a giant mountain range. Above these and closer to her was another great sweep of flat-bottomed clouds. Between the two ran a broad band of deep blue sky, and though the upper cloudbank was closer, its flat bottom seemed to form the far bank of a sky blue river.

Nearby, the old bull was spyhopping too, but he was looking toward land. Heavy swells were running from the northeast, and he could see them piling up at the mouth of the Annisquam River. A storm was building. That explained why he saw so few boats in the bay. Sweeping his gaze northward, he saw smoothly rounded hillocks of forest surrounded by tawny salt marsh. North of that, Plum Island was a long gold line, and beyond the island gentle hills rolled red and gold nearly to the sound. The water near the island was light green, so shallow in spots that he could see it breaking white over sandbars. Just north of the island lay the mouth of the Merrimack River, and each time he rose on the crest of a big swell, he could see boats five miles away almost pitchpoling as they tried to enter the river. The big swells running from the northeast were bucking a strong outgoing tide and piling up huge waves at the river mouth. Farther still to the north, clouds soared over the land like snowy mountains.

Once again the old bull scanned the bay, noting the scarcity of vessels; then he conferred briefly with the old cow, and they led the pod north.

Outside Newburyport they paused awhile to watch boats negotiating huge rollers at the river mouth, then continued north to the Isles of Shoals, a group of nine rocky islets ten miles off Portsmouth, New Hampshire. By the time they reached the islands — which the orcas viewed as the high-and-dry summit of a sea mountain — big whitecapped rollers were breaking so hard against the rocks that spray was flying over the roof of the hotel on Star Island.

The light was fading. Normally this would be a good time to hunt, but most fish had apparently gone deep, for the upper waters sounded barren. The orcas headed east toward Jeffreys Ledge.

6

By sunset of that same day the orcas were swimming over a granite escarpment, four miles by twenty, that parallels the coast from northern Massachusetts to southern Maine. This submarine formation is known as Jeffreys Ledge. The depth at its top ranges from twenty-five to fifty fathoms. The surrounding water is as deep as one hundred fathoms. Though small compared to the Gulf's outer banks, Jeffreys Ledge supports a great abundance of life.

The sky to the east was mountainous with clouds, but in the west conditions were clear. The sunset's afterglow had left a narrow red band across the western horizon topped by a sapphire blue sky pierced with starlight. As color began to drain from the western sky, muscular clouds came thundering out of the northeast and a gale began pounding the Gulf of Maine.

The storm caused so much underwater noise that the orcas had difficulty sonaring well enough to hunt. Not that it mattered much. Most of their preferred prey fish had either holed up or abandoned the top of Jeffreys Ledge in favor of less turbulent depths.

The orcas dove to fifteen fathoms or so and cruised along

the ledge. On the western side they could hear the Cove, where scattered mushy echoes stood out from the hard, flat bounce of the rocky bottom, suggesting that the Cove might be harboring many big fish, such as adult bluefins sitting out the storm. But the Cove is fifty fathoms deep and the depth nearby reaches one hundred fathoms, so the orcas did not bother to investigate.

They tried riding out the storm at the surface, but a juvenile male with an ear infection became seasick, so the pod went deep again to escape the worst of the wave action. Even fifteen fathoms down, they were rising and falling some three fathoms in the storm surges, but the young male did stop vomiting. For the rest of the night they made long deep dives.

Toward dawn the gale blew itself out. As the storm noise subsided, the orcas heard the faint calls of other killer whales far to the east and south. They could not make out what was being said, but it sounded like two pods were entering the Gulf of Maine through Northeast Channel and Great South Channel. With the noisy shoals of Georges Bank between them, it was doubtful that the distant pods could hear each other. For their voices to reach Jeffreys Ledge, they must have been calling loudly and directing the sound ahead of them through the shipping channels. Maybe they were trying to find out if other orca pods were already inside the Gulf. Perhaps they hoped to join forces in a great hunt. Equally exciting, such a hunt would include much socializing.

Now that sea conditions were moderate, ships were once again heading out of Portland, and propeller noise from the first of the southbound vessels began masking the distant orca calls. The elders led the pod east and found a quieter spot where Platts Bank cut off most of the Portland traffic noise and where sounds from Northeast Channel and Great South Channel were unobstructed by banks. From here the distant orca calls were more audible, though still not understandable, for they were still about a hundred miles away.[1] Judging by the sounds of large ships coming from the same directions as the calls, the pods were definitely moving through the major eastern and southern shipping channels.

The orcas conducted a predawn hunt and by first light had filled their stomachs with short-finned squid. Noting a general lull in distant ship noise, they returned to the area east of Platts Bank and listened to the sounds coming from the two great shipping channels. Now they could hear the other pods clearly. Perhaps the younger adults recognized the dialects of the distant pods. Maybe they were just excited by the prospect of socializing. Whatever their reason, they began milling around the old cow, as if seeking her approval of something. She conferred briefly with the old bull, who turned and hurled his loudest calls into the distance, pitching his voice deep and facing first toward one shipping channel and then the other. Both pods replied.

The pod spent the rest of the day in the vicinity of Jeffreys Ledge and Platts Bank, preying on schools of short-finned squid that had come in to feed on sand lances.

Shortly after sunset, the pod from the east arrived. It was a group of sixteen, led by two big bulls who ventured ahead of the others. The old male with the ailing jaw, accompanied by the younger bull, swam out to meet them. As if expecting trouble, the bulk of both pods hung back. The bulls on both sides surfaced in unison, blowing and snorting as though about to charge each other, then slowly approached to within a body length. In a brief stand-off, the big bulls faced each other and exchanged calls, then the two pods merged and began to socialize, using much body play — some of it sexual, all of it joyful.

Just before nightfall the other pod arrived from the south. This group numbered seventeen and included three big bulls. Once again the senior bulls of each pod confronted each other in a ritual of snorting and loud vocalization, then the three pods combined and socialized. The youngest calves, clearly tentative about mixing with strangers, hugged their mothers' flanks.

Similarities in fin shapes and color patterns among the three pods suggested a common ancestry. Judging by the clear seniority of the old cow with the 1919 tag in her fin and the common deference shown toward her, it appeared that the newly arrived pods had at some point in the past spun off from hers.

The seven mature bulls led the combined pods for a time, then drifted off to one side and floated together at the surface, quietly vocalizing among themselves. The cows and juveniles, still busily socializing, moved on and left the bulls a hundred yards behind. The bulls spyhopped and stared at them, then caught up and moved into the lead.

While the group followed a generally southward course, individuals crisscrossed each other's paths, vocalizing and rubbing. With forty-five orcas meandering over a fairly wide area, submerging and reappearing at random, they gave the impression of being twice their number. They sounded like twice their number, too. The surrounding area reverberated with their calls.

All at once the bulls began to breach. One after another, the big males soared through the air and landed on their sides, as though trying to outdo each other with thundrous reentries. Soon cows and juveniles began to jump. Immediately the bulls stopped breaching. Some smacked their tails against the surface. Others rolled on their backs and waved their flippers in the air.

Although the three pods seemed to intermix freely, all maternal subgroups maintained their cohesiveness. These subgroups comprised cows with suckling calves and the calves' older siblings. Some included second cows, sisters perhaps, who had no dependent young of their own, but served as attentive nannies. Some of these childless cows were barren; others had lost their calves to illness or accident.

Six adults began swimming nose to tail in a tight circle, then came together, rubbing against each other and squealing. One big bull rubbed belly to belly against a cow, then they mated. This triggered mating activity among other adults and even among juveniles. The very young pursued more innocent pleasures.

Darkness fell, and the group set off on its evening hunt, making a lot of noise and moving twice as fast as any one pod normally travels when not in direct pursuit of prey. Their every movement seemed exaggerated, even to the way they smashed through the waves, and all creatures fled before them.

•   •   •

Long-term observations in the Pacific Northwest suggest that when an orca pod multiplies beyond a certain point, some members leave and form a splinter group. The reasons for division are unclear. Perhaps beyond some optimum pod size leadership breaks down, or the groups find it difficult to get enough food within given habitats. Cows and their accumulated young typically form subgroups within orca pods, so whatever the reasons for partitionment, maternal associations may mark the lines along which pods eventually divide.[2] Pods of ten to fifteen are average for orcas seen in the eastern North Pacific and the western North Atlantic.

Splinter pods sharing common ancestry appear to maintain clanlike associations, living in adjacent ranges and traveling through each other's territories with impunity. From time to time they join forces to socialize or hunt. Being related, they show similarities in appearance and vocal repertoires. Scientists refer to the vocal similarities as dialects. The closer the relationship between two pods, the more similar are their dialects.

The existence of orca dialects was suspected twenty or more years ago, when comparable sound recordings revealed vocal variations between individual captive orcas. Some thought the differences to be sex related, but more recent evidence shows them to be pod-specific dialects.

That recent evidence was supplied by Canadian zoologist John Ford, whose 1985 doctoral dissertation dealt with orca acoustics as indicators of social structure.[3] Ford found that many vocal exchanges within a pod seem to involve a dozen or so different calls repeated frequently. The degree of use depends on what the animals are doing. When they forage some distance from each other, ninety-five percent of their calls are discrete (that is, unique and recognizable to human listeners). When members of a pod come together and socialize, variable sounds increase by thirty percent.

Through spectographic analysis, Ford confirmed that stable kin groups of orcas use fixed repertoires of eight to fifteen discrete calls. The repertoires of any two pods differ in accordance with the degree to which the pods socialize, which in turn seems to reflect how closely they are related. Pods that frequently associate with each other tend to share discrete calls, while pods largely isolated from each other have entirely different repertoires. These repertorial differences are called dialects, and they are so distinct that scientists can use them to identify pods.

The emphasis here is on discrete calls because they are valuable research tools, but this is not meant to suggest that orcas meet all their communications needs with repertoires of only eight to fifteen calls. As Dr. Ford has written to me,

> The discrete call repertoire represents only a portion of the social signals produced by killer whales. Vocal output depends very much on context. When the animals are foraging, about ninety-five percent of their calling is restricted to discrete calls. When socializing, however, they also produce a wide array of "miscellaneous" pulsed sounds and whistles, which probably serve to communicate subtle information concerning the social interactions underway. Discrete calls are also fairly variable in structure, and likely these variations have meaning to the whales, especially excitement level, individual identity, etc. In summary, I don't think the actual call types carry much meaning beyond kin membership. The minor variations in the way they make those shared calls, however, are very important.[4]

Given the likelihood that new pods form as spin-offs from older pods, it follows that pods sharing discrete calls probably share a common ancestry. Ford has lumped the various British Columbia pods into acoustically unique groups that he calls clans. Pods within each clan have related dialects, whereas the dialects of the various clans are completely different. Based on the splinter-group hypothesis, he suggests that clans with more pods may have resided in the area longer than clans with fewer pods.

Orcas make a broad range of of sounds, including creaks, squeals, squeaks, squawks, trills, whistles, trumpet blasts, screams, roars, and bursts of "machine-gun fire." All consist basically of two types, pulsed signals and nonpulsed tonal signals.

Pulsed signals, by far the most common, fall into two major categories. One type is very short (less than twenty-five milliseconds) and very sharp (containing energy over a wide range of frequencies). These are the trains of clicks believed to function as echolocation signals.

The other category comprises the most characteristic orca vocalizations, rapidly pulsed or burst-pulsed emissions. These last anywhere from fifty milliseconds to over ten seconds, the average duration being about a second. Most pulsed-call energy is concentrated in the range of 1–10 kilohertz (1,000 to 10,000 cycles per second), clearly audible to people. These calls sound somewhat like echolocation clicks but are lower in pitch and often higher in pulse repetition rate (up to 5,000 pulses per second). Orcas can control both pulse repetition rate and frequency content of pulsed signals. By varying the two, they produce a wide variety of intense sounds having unusual aural qualities. Some listeners describe them as screamlike. Others say they have a strident or metallic quality.

You can demonstrate the simultaneous variation of pulse repetition rate and frequency content by humming and gargling at the same time. Note how you can change the pitch of your hum (frequency content) and/or the speed of your gargling (pulse repetition rate) to produce a wide range of sounds. To sound more like an orca, try whistling and gargling at the same time, then move the gargling pulsations from your throat to your lips.

The second type of orca sound comprises high-pitched tones or whistles with no pulsed structure. The pitch and duration of these whistles are highly variable.

Orcas can emit pulsed calls or whistled calls separately, or they can generate both simultaneously to produce very complex sounds. John Lilly observed much the same phenomenon in the signals of bottlenose dolphins.[5]

Orcas seem able to coordinate many individuals in complex activities well beyond visual range. Such coordination must involve fairly sophisticated communications, but we have no idea what form these take. It is highly unlikely that any species uses language as we define the term, but highly social mammals like orcas may have extremely complex signaling systems.

In my book *A Dolphin Summer* I sidestepped the issue of cetacean "language" by using the viewpoint of a naive juvenile dolphin. I did this because to my knowledge no one had (or has since) analyzed the phonations of Atlantic white-sided dolphins, so I lacked a basis on which to fashion even a wildly speculative model of dolphin communication.

Although this book uses adult viewpoints for the most part, my narrative again dances around the issue of how orcas communicate because so little evidence exists. Still, I have played with possibilities and devised a hypothetical model for orca "language," which I would like to share with you here.

When I learned that orcas use repetitive discrete calls, I was reminded of the signature whistles thought to be used by other dolphin species. In *A Dolphin Summer* I hypothesized that these call signs identify individuals, let others know where they are, enable others to call them by "name," and provide personalized echolocation/orientation signals whose echoes stand out from the crowd. What works for other dolphins should work for orcas, I reasoned. Their repetitive discrete calls, used so heavily while the animals hunt, seemed likely candidates for call signs or personalized orientation signals.

Were this the case, the number of discrete calls used by a pod should equal the number of orcas in it. To check this theory, I prepared the following table, which combines Ford's data on discrete calls with Bigg's data on pod size.[6] As you can see, there are some close matches and some severe mismatches.

Comparison of Pod Repertoires to Pod Sizes for
12 Resident British Columbia Pods

POD DESIGNATION*	NUMBER OF ORCAS	NUMBER OF CALLS
A1	14	14
A4	7	14
A5	12	13
B	8	13
C	9	11
D	10	10
H	6	8
I1	16 ± 1	11
I11	6	8
J	19	15
K	10	10
L	50 ± 1	15

*The pod designations were established years ago by Michael Bigg, Ian MacAskie, and Graeme Ellis of the Canadian Department of Fisheries and Oceans. These men photographically identified virtually every orca in British Columbia waters and established the makeup of thirty different pods. Ford's findings focus on twelve of these pods whose calls he was able to isolate.

Might extenuating circumstances explain the mismatches in my table? Where the number of orcas in a pod exceeds the number of the pod's calls, perhaps Dr. Ford's research overlooked a few pod calls. Where the number of calls exceeds the number of orcas, perhaps close ties with other pods are responsible for the additional calls. That is, call signs for friends or relations in other pods may be used often enough to become part of a pod's repertoire. This explanation might account for why some calls are common to two or more pods and why socially isolated pods seem to share no calls.

I suggested these possibilities to Dr. Ford, who replied that he does not think the discrete calls are signatures:

> Each whale seems to give the entire repertoire, and there is no clear correlation between pod size and repertoire size. Recently, we have begun to question the validity of the pod as a social entity. The most important social group is the maternal group, several of which may travel together for some time to form a pod. Pods actually may fragment quite frequently, with maternal groups spending considerable time on their own.[7]

That "each whale seems to give the entire repertoire" did not dissuade me. In fact, it suggested to me that the animals might call each other's signs as well as their own, thus supporting my call sign hypothesis. As for the correlation, granted it is not clear, but for eight out of twelve pods the numbers are close. And in seven of the eight, repertoire size is within two points of matching pod size.

Dr. Ford's doubts about the validity of pods as social entities came as a big surprise. If pods keep changing their make-up, it made little sense to attempt comparisons of pod size and repertoires. Still, these pods had been closely observed for seventeen years. Even the ± 1 deviation in size estimates for eight of the thirty British Columbia pods does not suggest a highly fluid situation.

Pet hypotheses die hard, so I took a broader look at the data and came up with the following comparison of mean pod size (all British Columbia pods considered) to mean repertoire size for pods reported by Ford.

- Mean pod size (all 30 B.C. pods):   8.70 orcas
  Mean repertoire size (all 15 pods
     reported by Ford):   9.87 calls

- Mean pod size (15 transient B.C. pods only): 3.13 orcas
  Mean repertoire size (3 transient pods
      reported by Ford):   2.0   calls
- Mean pod size (15 resident B.C. pods only): 14.27 orcas
  Mean pod size (12 resident pods
      reported by Ford):   13.9   orcas
  Mean repertoire size (12 resident pods
      reported by Ford):   11.9   calls

Now *this* seems a clear correlation between pod size and repertoire size. The discrepancies are not much worse than the uncertainties as to pod size. A slight additional deviation may stem from the difficulty of isolating pod vocalizations in coastal waters having high reverberation levels. This must have introduced question marks in Dr. Ford's data base.

When all is said and done, though, one fact remains to punch holes in my call sign hypothesis. In a 1982 International Whaling Commission paper, Ford and Fisher stated that certain common calls in a pod's repertoire often occurred in repetitious series and *overlapped each other*.[8] (Italics mine.) These signals had different intensities and reverberation patterns, so apparently they were not simply multiple echoes. This makes me question my hypothesis, for it seems unlikely that any animal's call sign would be repeated with overlapping rapidity by other pod members. It is possible, but improbable. So much for call signs, though the apparent correlations still intrigue me.

What other explanation might there be for these stereotyped calls? They could be fixed frames of reference around which orcas weave (or between which they sandwich) variable signals to convey information specific to given situations. The variable signals could take the form of sonar "images" or mimicry. (Ample evidence exists that orcas and other dolphins are very good mimics.) If each signal contained one variable signal sandwiched between two discrete calls, even a limited repertoire could make many permutations. In the following example, the discrete calls are italicized:

Listen! (mimicry of minke sound) *Hunt!*
If each signal contained three elements, arranged like the example, then with as few as ten discrete signals and twenty mimicries or sonar "images," orcas could build a vocabulary of 24,360 permutations ($30 \times 29 \times 28$). With more signals or larger arrangements, the possibilities soar.

Typical discrete signals might have meanings such as:

> *Silence!*
> *Listen!*
> *Hunt!*
> *Danger!*
> *Help!*
> *Hurry!*
> *Slow down!*
> *Come!*
> *Go!*
> *Left!*
> *Right!*
> *Ahead!*
> *Back!*
> *Up!*
> *Down!*

Even without structured arrangements or variables such as mimicry, ten repetitive contextual signals could by themselves yield 120 three-element combinations. With fewer signals than that, we used to voice-control two old draft mares on a Vermont dairy farm where I worked one summer. We seldom needed reins to control the mares because they understood a vocabulary of work commands such as *gee* (right), *haw* (left), *up* (go ahead), *back* (back up), *a step* (move one step), *easy* (slow), and *whoa* (stop). Whether we were pitching hay onto a wagon or skidding logs out of the woods, we could control the horses with compound commands such as the following:

"*Up gee,* girls." (go ahead, turning right)
"*Back haw,* girls." (back up, turning left)
"*Up easy,* girls." (go ahead slowly, as when taking the initial strain on a log)
"*Back a step,* girls." (The horses would back up one step.)

Using combinations of seven basic commands, from anywhere within earshot, we could put the horses through fairly complex backward or forward maneuvers.

When I suggested the possibility of compound orca calls to Dr. Ford, he replied: "Yes . . . , discrete calls can convey information beyond group identity, and they are often used in conjunction with variable calls, but I think not in the way you suggest here. The whales have specific signals that convey extreme excitement or agitation, but they don't mimic boat sounds or such."[9] For my example to him, I had suggested: "*Danger!* (mimicry of boat sound) *Dive!*"

Dr. Ford's recordings have apparently not detected any mimicry, but orcas have been heard mimicking sounds, both natural and unnatural. Erich Hoyt, who spent several summers recording orca sounds in British Columbia, tried to simulate their calls with a synthesizer. To his surprise, the orcas mimicked his mimicry.[10] Also he quotes Graeme Ellis, a skeptical researcher, as swearing that he heard a captive orca whistling a perfect rendition of the first two bars of "It's raining, it's pouring, the old man is snoring."[11] Another time, Hoyt whistle-mimicked a three-note call frequently used by orcas, and was answered by a female near his canoe. Hoyt describes her response as sounding like an echo of his whistled call.[12]

Dolphins in general (orcas being the largest dolphins) seem to be excellent mimics. Lilly's captive bottlenose dolphins proved so adept at mimicry that he and others swore the animals were speaking English.[13] Ford, in one of his articles, notes that dolphins are good vocal mimics and probably learn their natural acoustic repertoires (as opposed to genetically programmed vocal development).[14] Ford apparently did not mean to suggest interspecies mimicry, but it seems plausible to me that dolphins' repertoires might include mimicry of sounds made by other creatures important to their survival. Also, unnatural sounds heard often enough to have survival value could conceivably become part of their acoustic repertoires.

At any rate, that is my "sandwich" model for orca language. After reading it a friend asked, "If discrete calls were fixed semantic components, why would one pod use ten while another used fifteen?" I suppose the variations could be idiomatic, the "language" evolving somewhat as new pods spun off from older ones. On the other hand, if pods are but temporary amalgams of maternal associations, it may not be true that one pod uses ten discrete calls while another uses fifteen. All maternal groups may use roughly the same number of signals, but when groups intermix to form a "pod," the combinations may mislead listeners.

• • •

The next day was hot and humid, the air so laden with moisture that the horizon was a smoky blur. The dawn hunt had been unproductive, so the three pods of orcas prepared to make a major midmorning sweep.

The seven bulls waited quietly at the surface over Jeffreys Ledge. The others swam several miles south, making as little noise as possible, then spread out in a great parabola and headed back toward the north. As they swam, they smashed their chins against the chop and slapped the surface with their flukes. To this pulsing thunder they added their eerie hunting cries, which served both to frighten prey and to coordinate pod movements.

As they approached Jeffreys Ledge, they saw what appeared to be the face of a vast iceberg soaring blue-white out of the dark green sea. While they were gone, the tide had turned, and cold upwellings from the hundred-fathom depths east of Jeffreys Ledge were condensing the warm, moist air into a sharply defined bank of thick fog that extended for miles along the ledge.

Inside the fog the bulls waited silently at the surface. The old bull tuned out the noise of the approaching pods and listened for signs of prey being driven ahead of them. His surveillance was interrupted as a dragger completed a trawl along the ledge, turned east into deeper water to retrieve its net, and passed like a ghostly apparition within a hundred yards of the bulls. Its foghorn moaned and was answered by other horns within and beyond the fogbank.

Behind him, over Jeffreys Ledge, the old bull heard the calm surface quiver and the faint chuff of dolphins exhaling as they fed on what sounded like a mixed aggregation of menhaden, sand lances, herring, mackerel, and squid. Apparently the fish schools were thick, for the dolphins were catching their fill without using echolocation. Their silence no doubt stemmed from the noisy approach of the other orcas, who were now spread across a wide arc to the south.

Water riffled to the old bull's left, then he saw a school of several hundred bluefin tuna, all about two years of age and weighing twenty pounds or less, heading north. The young tuna were not spread out as they would be when hunting. Tightly massed, they moved with restless precision, changing direction with each loud sound.

The old bull led his group south until they could see clear water through the fogbank. The bulls reared back with their heads well above the surface and saw the combined pods several miles to the south. Kicking up a great arc of white water, they approached like a breaking wave.

Now a school of four-year-old bluefins, sixty-pounders, passed near the bulls. Like the others, they were tightly massed and heading north. Moments later the dolphins who had been feeding nearby were heard leaving the area, moving fast but breaking water very quietly each time they breathed.

Then an eight-foot bluefin, making forty knots, blundered

almost into the jaws of the waiting bulls, surprising them as well as itself. The big tuna tried to swerve, but one of the younger bulls darted into its path and rammed it headfirst. The stunned fish circled aimlessly, then the twenty-five-foot orca clamped his jaws around its head and surfaced. The eight-hundred-pound bluefin shook off the effects of the collision and put up a mighty struggle, but the orca held the fish high so that it could not dig its powerful tail into the water. The harder the bluefin fought, the deeper the orca's teeth sank through its gills. Blood streamed down the young bull's snowy chest, then his teeth penetrated the tuna's spine, and with a dull snap the great fish went limp. As the bull sank back into the water, another young male severed the tuna's tail to make doubly sure it could not escape.

Leaving the dying bluefin to sink, the bulls spread out and lay in wait. The rest of the orcas were much closer now, and the water between them and the edge of the fogbank was beginning to boil like a tidal rip as many large bluefins and incidental prey approached Jeffreys Ledge, urged on by the cries of the whales behind them.

As fish began darting among them, the bulls sprang into action, ramming the largest tuna and stunning medium-size ones with their flukes. As soon as they slowed one of the great fish, they crippled it by severing its caudal fins. Meanwhile their high-speed attacks and chilling cries turned the fish back upon themselves, causing even greater panic and confusion. Some tuna escaped, but most circled in confusion long enough for the rest of the orcas to sweep in from the south and close the trap. The older, more experienced bluefins tried to go deep, but a number of orcas, anticipating that maneuver, got below them and drove them back up against the surface. Having nowhere else to go, the fish took to the air.

It was a scene of dazzling beauty and massive slaughter. Everywhere the eye could see over an area of several acres, giant tuna were leaping high out of the water, pursued by or-cas. Some fish were intercepted in midair and had great chunks bitten out of them. Those that escaped the airborne mayhem bought themselves only a few more seconds of life, for other orcas pounced on them as they fell back into the water. Concentrating on the largest bluefins, the orcas worked in pairs, one attacking from the front to slow the tuna while another bit off its tail. Each crippled bluefin was left to sink, for the orcas were concerned with disabling as many fish as they could. Within fifteen minutes, they had cut down about ten tons of tuna, almost the daily requirement for this group of forty-five, which needed to consume at least five percent of their body weight each day to stay healthy.

First the orcas ate all the fish still at or near the surface, then they went deep and echolocated the ones that had sunk to the bottom. In some cases this entailed diving as much as a hundred fathoms, but the orcas showed themselves to be quite capable of deep dives.

Feeding continued for an hour or more, and the surface for miles around became coated with a multicolored sheen of blood and oil. The scene attracted thousands of sharks and gulls and other scavengers. Some sharks tried to get their share early but were driven off by the orcas. Feeding at their leisure, the orcas consumed all but the heads of every bluefin caught in their trap, then gathered at the surface and napped while scavengers cleaned up the offal from their kill.

•   •   •

Orcas have a reputation for killing far more than they can eat, but I have found no documented cases of wanton slaughter. I think the preceding scene may explain how orcas got this reputation. When hunting swift, powerful prey, such as adult bluefin, orcas cannot always take the time to kill each fish right away. If they did, the bulk of the fish would escape. It makes sense for them to cripple fish, then come back for them. Earlier observers may have misinterpreted such tactics as wanton slaughter.

Wanton killers or no, the very mention of orcas brings a

sour response from the average tuna fisherman. Even back in the early 1970s, when bluefin were caught strictly for sport and then hauled to the dump or perhaps sold for pet foot at $.10 a pound, fishermen had little love for orcas. Imagine their attitude now, with big bluefins worth up to $15.00 per pound at dockside. Since the early 1970s, Japanese market demands have driven bluefin tuna prices steadily upward. A single bluefin, dressed out, now fetches as much as $17,000 at the Tokyo fish market. Each large bluefin eaten by orcas represents thousands of dollars out of some fisherman's pocket, so the situation between killer whales and fishermen is more charged with tension than ever.

•   •   •

It was early morning on an overcast day. The three pods of orcas were hunting about ten miles east of Cape Ann. Quite a few big bluefins were in the area, but they seemed to be wiley old-timers who, as soon as they detected the orcas, headed deep so that their echoes were lost amidst bottom clutter. When the orcas went deep and tried to flush them out of hiding, the bluefins sprinted away at blinding speed. Even with forty-five orcas working together, the odds favored the bluefins. The big fish could stay deep indefinitely, whereas the orcas had to surface for air, and when they did, they often lost track of their prey. Even working in relays, taking turns surfacing for air, they still managed to catch only a few of the great fish.

Perhaps this is why, when the orcas came upon a dozen sport fishing boats anchored off Halibut Point, they chose to exploit them. The fishermen had been enjoying better luck than the orcas. Already, four of them had "hooked on," and one team had an eight-foot bluefin close aboard. As the gaffer leaned over the taffrail to secure the catch, a bull orca flashed out of the depths, seized the tuna, and nearly pulled the gaffer over the side. Ripping a hundred yards of line out of the screaming reel, the orca dragged the tuna well clear of the boat, then paused and decapitated the fish. When the line went slack, the fisherman reeled in, only to find that all he had left was the severed head, its jaws still snapping even as the light left its eyes.

While several orcas shared the tuna a hundred yards astern of the boat, the old bull noticed the men calling from boat to boat. Usually when the orcas stripped tuna off their lines, fishermen shook their fists and shouted a lot. These men seemed quite calm about the whole thing.

The old bull studied the fishermen for a time, then went deep and slipped in under a harpoon boat that was cruising slowly in a great circle around the anchored rod-and-reel fishing boats. Through the surface, he could see a man poised in the pulpit, balancing a long harpoon on his shoulder. As the old bull followed beneath the boat, he noticed a young male rising toward the surface just ahead of the vessel. Seeing the rippling image of the harpooner come to attention, the old bull snapped a warning. The young male went deep, and the boat passed harmlessly over him.

The bull heard angry shouts from a nearby boat as another hooked bluefin was snatched away, then the vessel he was shadowing maneuvered among the others. He dropped back and watched as the harpoon vessel moved from boat to boat. The harpoon men were passing out small boxes of some sort to men on the other boats.

Now orcas in all directions began lobtailing, making a thunderous commotion as they closed in on a point about half a mile south of the boats. Knowing they must have some tuna trapped, the old bull headed that way.

By the time he reached the scene, the combined pods had formed a semicircle measuring half a mile across and were trying to close ranks around a concentration of bluefins. Just then the old bull heard all the boats start their engines. Looking back, he saw them weigh anchor and move at high speed toward the orcas. He snapped a warning, then dove with the others and helped drive the bluefins up against a ledge.

While the boats circled overhead, the orcas crippled dozens of giant bluefins. Some, having swallowed air, rose to the surface and flopped about helplessly, their caudal fins severed. A slick of blood and oil began to sheen the surface, diffracting the sunlight into separate rays of color that haloed the undersides of the waves.

With their prey disabled and available for the taking, various groups of orcas rose for air. As they approached the surface, men on the boats began throwing small objects into the water, and the orcas were bombarded by explosions. The explosives being thrown by the fishermen were not powerful enough to injure the orcas, but the noise they made was painfully loud, and the younger orcas were thrown into a state of chaos. The orca elders were powerless to maintain order.

The old bull also saw dozens of white-sided dolphins darting about in total panic. Apparently they had been near the boats when the explosions started, and they too were caught up in the confusion. One whiteside calf, who must have been separated from her mother in the panic, streaked into view and nearly rammed the old bull. Turning aside at the last possible second, she grazed his flipper, just missed being struck by his big flukes, and went deep.

The old bull went deep too, for the explosions were concentrated near the surface, and each blast pierced his sensitive ears with a shaft of pain. Orcas were crisscrossing all around him, and white-sided dolphins darted between the orcas. The old bull tried to signal his kin, but the explosions made it difficult for them to understand each other, so he simply kept sounding his call sign as he swam westward away from the boats.

The next time he surfaced for air, he saw the top of Halibut Point some six or seven miles ahead. That seemed a good landmark toward which to direct the others. As he swam and continued to signal his kin, he was joined by a young bull and cow. Although not from his pod, they followed his lead.

They had left the boats about two miles behind them when the old bull heard a dolphin up ahead at the surface, panting and whistling for help. He scanned it with a stream of clicks.

It stopped whistling. The next time he surfaced to breathe, he saw a little white-sided female rear back and walk on her tail to look at him. As he sounded his call sign, the little dolphin flipped over backward and porpoised toward shore.

Off to his right the old bull heard his pod's calf of that spring, together with her mother and older sibling. A moment later he heard the little dolphin squealing in terror up ahead. He identified the source of her fear and heard it moving toward the mother-calf group. Flanked by his companions, he raced toward the dolphin.

Covering a quarter mile in about a minute, they came upon a dozen porbeagles pursuing the whiteside calf, who was leaping into the air and changing direction each time she reentered the water. She had the right idea, but she was getting tired and the sharks were getting closer. Fortunately for her, the sharks were also getting dangerously close to the mother-calf group from the old bull's pod. The old bull and his companions swept past the young dolphin and attacked the sharks.

Although the porbeagles were six-foot, heavy bodied sharks weighing about two hundred pounds, the old bull put two of them away on his first rush. While he bit one in half, he struck another with his flukes and sent it soaring twenty feet in the air. The other bull intercepted that one in midair and ripped out its belly. The cow accounted for two, and the bulls got three more. All told, the orcas killed or maimed half of the porbeagles. The rest went deep and escaped.

The orcas ate some of the sharks on the spot. The porbeagles' big livers were rich with oil, and their flesh had much the same texture and flavor as swordfish. The two bulls and the cow consumed three and took the others back to their kin.

As they headed toward the mother-calf group, they again heard the frightened young whiteside. Moments later she came porpoising back in their direction. Apparently she had encountered the mother-calf group and reversed direction. When she saw herself virtually surrounded by orcas, she seemed to go into shock. Apparently too winded to dive, she circled slowly and sounded her distress whistle. The orcas gathered around the young dolphin.

Urged on by her mother, the orca calf approached the little whiteside, who eluded her as best she could without getting too close to the adults. As the dolphin circled, the adults opened up a twenty-foot circle in which she could maneuver, then urged the calf to catch her. When the calf hung back, the old bull poked his big head into the circle and gave her a hard push. The calf caught the dolphin by the flukes. Although twice the dolphin's size, the calf was toothless, so the little whiteside escaped without injury. Round and round the two calves swam, bounded by the adults, who gave the dolphin as much swimming room as they could without letting her escape.

The dolphin was able to elude the inept calf fairly well. Bit by bit, the little whiteside extended her evasive maneuvers to the point where the adult orcas were leaving large gaps in their ranks when they moved out of her way. The dolphin's breathing had returned to normal, and she was eyeing the wide gaps between adults, as though getting ready to escape, when another dozen orcas joined the group.

The newcomers included two calves, who were immediately pushed into the circle by their adult guardians. Now the young dolphin found herself being pursued by three feisty orca calves. She tried to escape by going deep, but the calves mobbed her, tugging at her flippers and flukes and holding her underwater until she was on the verge of drowning. The old bull interceded and allowed her to surface for air.

The dolphin's right flipper was scratched and bleeding, for one of the older calves had needle-sharp teeth. The young whiteside convulsed a bit and retched, but she had nothing in her stomach to regurgitate. Her stomach growled with fear and hunger.

Again the orca calves rushed the little whiteside, and the game went on until the dolphin, exhausted, floated motionless at the surface while the calves mauled and butted her. Then all at once she snapped at the calves and butted them in turn. Surprised by her sudden aggressiveness, they backed away.

Perhaps amused by her pluck, the old bull called an end to the game. She might have become a meal for one of the others, but just then the whine of propellers turned their attention to the north. A hundred-foot vessel came into view, steaming at full speed directly toward the orcas. Perhaps still edgy from the bombing by fishermen, the elders sounded a warning. The cows collected their calves, the others formed a protective ring around them, and the group moved off at a brisk pace toward the south, calling to the rest of their pods as they went. The boat followed, and the young dolphin was left bobbing in its wake.

The old bull checked the vessel's heading and speed, then led his group deep, doubled back, and gave the boat the slip. Minutes later the three pods regrouped and set off at a leisurely pace toward Halibut Point, playing as they went.

7

For the next two weeks, the orcas remained in the general vicinity of Jeffreys Ledge, feeding on herring, hake, and the occasional bluefin tuna. So long as heavy concentrations of fish were available, the three pods stayed together. When feeding became spotty, the orcas divided into their respective pods and spread out to forage over wider areas. If one pod found enough food for all, the others were called in to share the catch.

One day when feeding conditions were poor in the Jeffreys Ledge area, the old matriarch and the old bull led their pod some thirty miles south to Stellwagen Bank. Conditions were even worse there. The schools of sand lances seemed a fraction of their former numbers, and that decline had impoverished all species dependent on the sand lances. The orcas saw no humpbacks over Stellwagen, and only a few minkes and finbacks.

About twelve miles south of Gloucester, the pod came upon a big barge dumping a mountain of gurry into the water. The orcas circled well clear of the barge and its tug, but nonetheless their mouths became defiled with the taste of rotten fish. Scanning the bottom with their sonar, they heard the area for miles around littered with gurry. That part of the bank was like a watery desert. Where once sport fishing boats and commercial fishing vessels had abounded, the orcas saw only sailboats. Compared to its former abundance of life, the northerly part of Stellwagen Bank seemed dead. The orcas headed back toward Jeffreys Ledge.

• • •

Gurry is the offal from fish processing plants. It has so little food value that even gulls largely ignore it.

Gurry used to be dumped offshore at various points along the coast, but beginning in May 1985, gurry from all Massachusetts seaports was trucked to Gloucester, then hauled by barge to a point twelve miles offshore and dumped on Stellwagen Bank. An average of 640,000 pounds of gurry was dumped in this area every week. By mid-1986, more than 66 million pounds had been dumped on Stellwagen. This action was approved by state and federal environmental protection agencies.

Some suspect that this concentrated dumping of gurry may be partly to blame for the lack of humpback whales on Stellwagen Bank during 1986. Be that as it may, many humpbacks that for ten years had been regular visitors to our inshore banks did spend the summer of 1986 far from our shores. Whales were still to be seen over other inshore banks, but a Boston newspaper article made it sound as if they had deserted us en masse, and that article's nationwide syndication dealt a body blow to our whale-watching industry.

What caused the whales to change their feeding habits? The same thing that drew them here in the first place. To explain that, I must go back about ten years.

I remember my surprise when, in the late 1970s, humpbacks began drawing droves of whale watchers to Massachusetts each summer. During all my time at sea before 1975 (when I was forced to sell my boat to support my writing habit), I had never seen humpbacks over the inshore banks. I used to see many finbacks and minkes, even a rare right whale now and then, but I could not recall seeing any humpbacks.

This stands to reason, for apparently they were not there to see. According to Provincetown's Center for Coastal Studies, humpbacks have a long history of visiting nearby waters every summer, but some knowledgeable sport fishermen I interviewed confirmed my suspicion that few humpbacks were feeding farther north over Stellwagen Bank and Jeffreys Ledge before 1975. And the reason they were not there is that sand lances were not present in sufficient numbers to attract them.

From about 1964 until the two-hundred-mile limit went into effect, foreign fishing fleets combined with our own to take a heavy toll of cod, haddock, mackerel, and other commercially valuable species. By the mid-1970s, with predatory pressure minimized by this overfishing, the sand lance population had exploded. The National Marine Fisheries Service estimates that the sand lance biomass peaked at one hundred thousand metric tons in the Gulf of Maine. So enormous did this resource become that a commercial fishery was being contemplated.

While fishermen and scientists contemplated the sand lances, the whales ate them. In 1975 humpbacks discovered this resource and started to extend their feeding range inward and northward over Stellwagen Bank and Jeffreys Ledge. For the first time in recorded history, hundreds of humpbacks were feeding within a few miles of shore all along the Massachusetts coast. A whale-watching business grew up around the humpbacks, and for ten years the whales and their watchers prospered.

By 1986 the sand lance biomass had fallen so far below its mid-1970s peak that many humpbacks abandoned the inshore banks. Needless to say, many species other than humpbacks had been preying on sand lances (including sand lances themselves, which have been found to cannibalize their own eggs and larvae). Also, the whales ate other species in addition to sand lances. Still, a few hundred humpbacks, each eating one or two tons per day eight months a year for ten years, appear to have played a major part in the collapse of inshore sand lance populations.

When the humpbacks appeared on Stellwagen Bank in early spring of 1986 and found the feeding poor, some went back out to Great South Channel, where sand lance schools were later reported to be ninety feet thick. Other humpbacks moved north, perhaps in search of herring. Many individuals that had been seen over Stellwagen Bank for ten years were sighted in 1987 near Brier Island off the southwest coast of Nova Scotia. Sand lances must be making a comeback, for humpbacks seem to be returning to the inshore banks of Massachusetts.

•   •   •

One evening the old cow led her pod on a hunt over Platts Bank. Already the pod's baby, though she was only six months old and would nurse for another year at least, was beginning to develop her sonar skills. By imitating her mother and other adults, she had learned how to generate clicks that returned sharp echoes, but she was only just beginning to interpret the echoes, and much more learning lay ahead of her.

Over the past few days, for example, she had come to understand that the adults changed the pitch of their sonar in accordance with the species being hunted. When they first made contact with a school of fish, they raised and lowered the pitch of their sonar until echoes from the fish took on a subtle ringing quality, then they locked onto that pitch. As they closed for the kill, they increased their click rate from a slow growl at long range to a rapid whine for close-up scanning, but they kept the tone contained within each click locked onto the key pitch for that type of fish. The calf did not understand why, but this ring-tone technique somehow caused the fish to mill about aimlessly, making it easier for the orcas to catch up with them.

During this period that the orcas were feeding on smaller prey, such as herring, the calf learned that the pod's sounds could be dangerous. From an early age she had noticed that the adults never raked each other with loud sound. When conversing at close range, they called softly, and should a sonaring orca pass close to another orca, it shut down its sonar until it passed clear. Much more than common courtesy, this was a matter of safety, for when a school of smaller fish came within visual range, the adults made *bang!* sounds so powerful that they stunned the fish and even made some of them bleed from the gills.

So now the calf understood how the adults caught smaller prey that might otherwise scatter like a bomb burst and escape them altogether. First they tuned their sonar to a frequency that made the fishes' ears ring so loudly that they became disoriented. Then, as the orcas drew close enough to see the prey, they suddenly increased their click rate from a *buzz* to a *zeee,* then each of them fired off an explosive burst of sound thousands of times louder and longer than any one click. It was as though all the energy of thousands of loud sonar pulses were packed into one big bang that blasted the prey senseless. The only noises she had ever heard that compared with these stun pulses were the explosive charges dropped by the tuna fishermen a few weeks ago.

The calf was too small and inept to stun prey with sound, but she practiced the ring-tone technique and began detecting a subtle resonance in her echoes when she locked onto a prey species' most sensitive hearing point. If she could watch the fish as she did this, the disorienting effect was apparent, but the ring-tone technique was usually used beyond visual range, so she had to master the art of hearing that nuance of resonance in her sonar echoes. Slowly, with much practice, she improved.

•   •   •

In the early 1970s, Kenneth S. Norris, now with the Long Marine Laboratory, University of California at Santa Cruz, suggested that some objects sonared by cetaceans may resonate as well as returning echoes. Dr. Norris speculated that this resonance or "ringing" might tell cetaceans something about the objects they sonar.[1] Underlying Dr. Norris's hypothesis is the demonstrated principle that objects tend to resonate when bombarded with sufficient energy tuned to their natural frequencies.

It was Norris who, together with Bertel Mohl of Aarhus University in Denmark, first proposed in 1981 that dolphins and larger toothed whales may be able to immobilize prey with intense sound.[2] By mid-1983 Norris and Mohl had assembled enough theoretical, observational, and anecdotal evidence to earn their hypothesis a hearing, but many of their peers remained skeptical.[3]

In September 1986, Norris's colleague Kenneth Marten reported that orcas seem to emit sounds in the 400-hertz (400 cycles per second) frequency range, exactly the range in which herring hear best. Because the herring probably rely on hearing for navigation, Marten speculated that orcas might use intense sound to overload the fish's aural systems.[4]

According to Norris and Marten, the clicks used by odontocetes for long-range sonaring can be "jet-engine loud." These scientists speculated that the clicks may disturb the prey's sensitive lateral lines, those organs in fish that detect waterborne vibrations. In support of this hypothesis, Norris and Marten cited cases of fish appearing to be stunned immediately before being eaten and of odontocete stomachs often containing seemingly undamaged fish. Still, Norris and Marten were not able to demonstrate experimentally that even very loud echolocation clicks affect prey.[5]

Recently their fish-stunning hypothesis was strengthened by the findings of Virginia L. Cass, formerly at the La Jolla Southwest Fisheries Center of the National Marine Fisheries Service. Cass found that wild bottlenose dolphins and orcas make banging noises while feeding. These bangs are much lower in frequency than sonar clicks (low enough to coincide with the hearing range of prey), much louder than sonar clicks, and about a thousand times longer. A typical recording is described as "an ascending trill of clicks followed by what sounds exactly like a gun firing or a stun grenade exploding."[6]

In this chapter I borrow from all three hypotheses cited in the foregoing. To these I add my own hypothesis, ring-tone scanning. It is conceivable that orcas could memorize the critical pitch for each prey species, but this pitch probably shifts as creatures grow and age. This being the case, orcas would have to scan, so I speculate that Kenneth Norris's "ringing" hypothesis might be used to determine the frequency at which prey hear best. Then the orcas could bombard the fish at that pitch and disorient them. This kind of bombardment could be accomplished with nonpulsed tone, but a sonar function is still needed to track the prey, so I further speculate that the orcas would pulse-modulate the tone. Thus, the 400-hertz tone ideal for herring would be transmitted as a series of pulses, with repetition rate varied according to range. (Higher repetition rate provides higher resolution.)[7]

It is also possible that the orcas could double the effect by synchronizing pulse repetition rate to ring tone, e.g., transmitting a 400-hertz tone at 400 pulses per second. (If the relationship between tone and pulse repetition rate confuses you, you can demonstrate it to yourself by whistling or humming at a constant tone while you gargle at various pulse repetition rates.)

Nowhere in the articles I cite is any mention made of distance, which is a critical factor. Granted, a dolphin can generate the same sound intensity as a blasting cap (about 230 db), and such bursts can stun or kill fish, but at what range? In the case of a burst from an unfocused source such as a blasting cap, its intensity would decrease as the square of the distance; that is, the intensity would be nine times greater one foot from the source than it would be at a distance of three feet. Obviously, to stun distant prey, cetaceans would have to be able to focus their sound bursts to some degree, or they would do more damage to themselves than to their prey.

Even with the inverse-square law repealed by focusing,

waterborne sound is so rapidly damped by absorption and scattering that I believe stunning would be limited to fairly short ranges. Cetaceans could probably use resonant-frequency (ring-tone) sound to confuse prey from quite a distance, but to stun prey I should think they would have to get well within visual range.

As far as I know, the acoustic research conducted by Erich Hoyt, John Ford, et al. in British Columbia shows no evidence of orcas stunning prey with sound or making sounds powerful enough to suggest the same. Perhaps salmon, the principal prey of British Columbia orcas, are too large to be stunned by sound. Or perhaps the high reverberation levels of British Columbia's coastal waters would make such intense sound levels unbearable for the orcas themselves.

•   •   •

During these first two weeks of September, dozens of humpback whales and hundreds of white-sided dolphins also were feeding over Jeffreys Ledge, and the calf noticed that they seemed not to fear her pod's approach. Perhaps because there were plenty of fish to eat, the orcas showed no interest in preying on cetaceans, and the other animals somehow knew this.

Some dolphins hunted in groups well away from the humpbacks, while others hugged the whales' flanks, feeding on injured sand lances and herring that dribbled from the whales' mouths. Large bluefin tuna often did the same, feeding right alongside the dolphins. Close behind each group of feeding whales, scores of herring gulls, black-backed gulls, and greater shearwaters skimmed the waves and picked up their share, while below the whales, various species of fish picked up any scraps that escaped the others. Predatory pressure on the sand lances and herring seemed greater than ever, and this at a time when they no longer had astronomical numbers in their favor.

Day and night, the raspy whistles of white-sided dolphins could be heard all over the area. Many of the dolphins seen by the orcas appeared to be juveniles that had left their maternal herds, as whitesides seem to do during their adolescent years. Few were over six feet long. Many were only about five feet. Their backs were dark gray or very deep brown, not black like those of adult whitesides, while the colors on their sides seemed not as bright or sharply defined as those of the babies seen in maternal herds. Whether feeding or seeking food, the young whitesides were always in a hurry. They seemed far less organized than the adults, but their speed and energy made up for whatever they lacked in terms of hunting skills. By the time they rejoined the reproductive herds when they were about six years old, they would probably be expert.

Now and then while the pod rested near feeding humpbacks, the calf was able to slip over and observe the whales. Some humpbacks, which were only about thirty-five feet long and may have been juveniles feeding on their own for the first time, seemed to waste energy by chasing fish in circles and slashing at them with their flippers. But the larger, older whales seldom wasted energy and seemed to have an endless variety of feeding techniques, one to fit every occasion. Sometimes they hovered motionless and waved their white flippers in front of themselves to frighten fish into the apparent dark safety of their open mouths. Other times they swam with their flippers extended ahead of them like the cephalic fins of a manta ray, directing swarms of krill and small fish into their mouths. She often saw whales scissor their flukes or smack them against the surface to stun fish. Still others combined many different methods, turning within their own lengths, using flippers and flukes to herd or stun fish, and blowing clouds of bubbles.

Their bubble-feeding techniques were especially impressive. The older humpbacks were so skilled at this that they made it seem easy to fill their big stomachs. In fact, they were as skillful in their use of bubbles as the orcas were with sound.

The orca calf saw many different bubble formations. Some whales blew large clouds of bubbles to force schools of fish against the surface, then with mouths opened wide, they surfaced inside the bubble clouds and captured their prey. Others formed nets of bubbles around schools, then rose inside the nets, forced the fish against the surface, and swallowed them. Some whales worked in groups, surrounding fish schools with several bubble-bursts, then surfacing together in their center to swallow the fish. Still other whales formed long, straight walls or curtains of bubbles, then lunged with mouths open to catch fish that gathered at the middle or end of the bubble formation. Variations included elliptical bubble-nets and curved bubble-walls. Some whales seemed to have favorite bubble structures that they used most of the time.

Each time a whale captured a mouthful of fish, it would plane along the surface with its head held high while it expelled water from its mouth and swallowed the catch. In the course of feeding, the whales trapped a lot of seaweed and debris in their baleen filters. To clean their baleen, the humpbacks swam along the surface with their mouths open and repeatedly dipped their heads to flush out debris.[8]

Many finback and minke whales fed near Jeffreys Ledge too, and one day the orca calf saw a curious thing, a scarred old finback cow that had a habit of blowing bubbles as she approached the surface. The young orca thought at first that finbacks must use bubble-feeding techniques, as humpbacks do, but this cow's bubble clouds seemed unrelated to her feeding behavior. She seemed more intent on avoiding several large power yachts that were in the area following various whales. Whenever one of the boats was within a hundred yards of her as she rose to breathe, she exhaled while her nostrils were still well below the surface. As a result, she left no visible blow, and the people aboard the boats never even noticed her.[9]

One day the orca calf ventured near a baby humpback to watch it nursing. Although she was still toothless and the humpback calf was twenty-four feet long, nearly three times her size, the baby's mother extended a flipper and gently pushed her away. The young orca returned to her mother and drank her fill of thick warm milk.

• • •

Only recently have we begun to understand the more subtle relationships between predators and prey. These subtleties are especially evident in habitats where prey and predator often come within sight of each other. On the planes of Africa, for example, game animals understand the body language of big cats, hyenas, and wild dogs well enough to know at a glance whether these predators are hunting or simply passing through an area. Marine animals also seem to know when they need not fear their predators, so they too must have visual or aural ways of interpreting the intentions of predators.

This ability to gauge predators' intentions has survival value for all concerned. If prey animals felt compelled to flee every time they saw predators, their feeding and nurturing behavior would be so severely disrupted that entire populations might be threatened. Were this to happen, both prey and predators would suffer.

But nowhere in the natural world are there interspecies relationships to compare with those between orcas and the marine mammals on which they prey, for as well as peacefully coexisting between hunts, predator and prey sometimes socialize like kindred spirits. In Chapter Five, I gave two examples of this behavior involving single orcas socializing with pods of white-sided dolphins. Orcas in British Columbia are known to prey on minke whales, yet researchers often see minkes swimming with impunity near or amidst pods of orcas. Similarly, orcas prey on Dall's porpoises, common near Vancouver Island, yet they are also seen swimming peacefully with them. Erich Hoyt and James Hunter once saw thirty-four Vancouver Island orcas foraging almost side by side with two minkes and twelve Dall's porpoises.[10,11]

From examining the stomach contents of harpooned orcas, Soviet whalers have concluded that minke whales are the principal prey of orcas in Antarctica, at least in some sectors and seasons. Yet an amazing thing happened in January 1981, while Antarctic researchers were studying twenty-five to thirty minkes near the entrance to Erebus Gulf. A pod of some twenty orcas approached, stopped, and milled about near the minkes, then mixed in among them. No sign of panic was seen, no indication that the minkes had even tried to avoid the orcas. The two groups appeared to accept each other. At one point, a big bull orca and a minke about the same size breached side by side and collided in midair, bumping each other away with no apparent concern shown by either animal. Most amazing of all, to me at least, the two groups intermingled for about *ninety minutes!* Eventually the orcas and minkes went their separate ways.[12]

Were those minkes nonchalant because they somehow knew the orcas were not in the mood to eat them? Did their hearing tell them the orcas had full stomachs? Whatever the case, why mix with such formidable predators? Why flirt with death?

One final fascinating anecdote: on the occasion of the largest reported orca sighting in the Gulf of Maine, a gathering of about one hundred in Ipswich Bay, a finback whale was seen traveling with the orcas.[13]

Can you imagine wildebeests or impala loping amiably along in the company of lions or Cape hunting dogs? Can you picture caribou gamboling across the tundra with wolves? Why is it, then, that cetacean species preyed upon by orcas are sometimes seen swimming peacefully with them?

One possibility is that some pods of orcas are strictly piscivorous. This is thought to be the case in British Columbia, where fifteen "resident" pods appear to eat only fish, while fifteen "transient" pods seem to prefer marine mammals. Still, when we try to impose such clear-cut distinctions on nature, we usually find that the exceptions far outweigh the rule. Especially now, with food stocks impoverished the world over, why should orcas anywhere elect to restrict their diets? My guess is that when the salmon are far at sea (which coincides with seasons when British Columbia's weather discourages observation), orcas thought to be strictly piscivorous resort to preying on marine mammals. They may do so even when the salmon are inshore. In August 1980, John and Deborah Ford found a 50-pound chunk of minke flesh floating in the midst of a resident pod. The meat was so fresh that the Fords were convinced the minke had been killed only a short time before they arrived on the scene.[14]

Dietary preferences seem an even less likely explanation of the anecdote from Antarctica, where minkes appear to be orcas' preferred prey. Using that anecdote to illustrate my point, I should like to offer a scenario that may explain many of these peaceful encounters.

Either caught unawares by the orcas or well aware that they could not outswim them, the minkes saw no hope for escape, so they simply stayed together (defensive schooling behavior). When the orcas peacefully mixed in among them, the minkes felt so profoundly relieved that they engaged in exuberant behavior. I liken this to the range of emotions that many hostages show toward captors who deign to spare their lives — viz., fearful gratitude, identification with their captors, and (in some cases) behavior bordering on collusion.

The other side of the question is, Why would orcas bother to interact peacefully with potential prey? To the best of my knowledge, they do this only with fellow cetaceans, so therein may lie a clue. Cetaceans frequently demonstrate interspecies affinity, even to the point of altruism.[15] Another possible reason for species mixing is that, when hunting certain piscine prey, orcas may find other cetacean species helpful because they possess certain specialized abilities.

At any rate, cetaceans show unusual interspecies tolerance, so perhaps when orcas do not need fellow cetaceans for food, they occasionally find their company a pleasant diversion. The other cetaceans may not always be enthusiastically in favor, but I imagine that when orcas want to be friendly, the others are smart enough not to press their luck.

Another possible explanation for orca "chumminess" is that some dominant animals like to lord it over their subordinates from time to time. They seem to enjoy seeing abject fear and the fawning behavior that ensues when they remove or minimize their threat. This sort of behavior — often seen within groups of social primates and canines — may cross interspecies lines between cetaceans.

8

It was now mid-September. The orcas had enjoyed two bountiful weeks, but feeding conditions were beginning to change. As often as not now, the three pods went their separate ways, extending their hunts ever farther from Jeffreys Ledge, where the herring schools were thinning and large quarry, such as bluefin tuna, were few and far between. Sometimes the members of each pod spread out to forage far and wide, the first to find food alerting the others, who would hurry in from various directions.[1] Also, the three pods stayed in touch with each other acoustically, ready to join forces should a major food source be discovered.

This was one of those days when the pod headed by the old cow went its own way. At daybreak the sky was sullen and the sea surly, but a few hours after sunrise, wind and tide began moving in concert, which gentled the sea considerably. The sky remained solidly overcast, encouraging planktonic animals to stay in the upper part of the water column. Thousands of Wilson's storm petrels fluttered and dipped over the waves, seeming to walk on water as they used the bright orange webs between their toes to startle copepods and other tiny prey into telltale movement. Behind each orca tiptoed a flock of the little birds, feeding on organisms stirred up by the whale's flukes. Others picked their way through the moving pod, sometimes passing within a few feet of the whales.

The orcas had not fed at daybreak, and nothing substantial was to be found near the surface now, so over Platts Bank they began making long, deep dives. At a depth of some thirty fathoms they managed to catch a few pollock, haddock, and cod, but most of the groundfish scurried into small gullies and holes. Winded by the exertion of many long dives, the orcas swung southward.

They swam slowly, engaged in leisurely play. The old bull and the two juvenile males performed slow rolls and rubbed against each other. The suckling calf turned spirals around her mother. Two cows swam with flippers touching. Others swam belly to belly, then side by side, and back again.

At a depth of fifteen fathoms on Ammen Rock, the shallowest part of Cashes Ledge, they caught some rosefish and cunner. Over the deeper, southerly end of Ammen Rock, they jumped a school of silver hake feeding on sand lances and took a dozen of the hake, which were only a foot long and not very plump. Still hungry, the orcas completed a rather unproductive circuit of the mid-Gulf ledges and banks, then headed westward.

Over Fippenies Ledge, they came upon an extensive windrow of floating kelp and other marine plants. Most of the orcas swam around the windrow, but the juvenile males chased each other into the thick of the plants. Moments later a loud thud was heard, then one of the thirteen-foot males flew into the air and landed heavily on his back. Squealing for help, the other male darted to his side. The others hurried over and found the young male semiconscious, struggling to regain control of his breathing.

Then, from beyond the windrow, they heard the low susurration of a big whale trying to breathe without being heard. The bulls approached the windrow and, scanning it with their sonar, heard a right whale cow and calf hiding in the plants. The

baby was about twenty-two feet long. Its mother measured
a good fifty feet and sounded like she weighed well over sixty
tons.

The bulls immediately plowed into the windrow and tried
to attack the right whale calf, but the mother rolled under her
baby and lifted it high and dry on her belly, then fought off
the bulls with thundrous blows of her flippers and flukes. Again
and again the bulls tried to break through the right whale's
defenses, but the thick plants hampered their movements and
the right whale cow was powerful. Somehow keeping the calf
safely balanced on her belly, she fought savagely.

Bruised and bleeding, the bulls backed off and waited for
the right whale cow to roll over and breathe. But she simply
arched her body until her nostrils were clear, took a deep breath,
and resumed her defensive posture.[2]

The bulls were about to resume the attack when they heard
propellers and saw a hundred-foot vessel approaching at high
speed. It looked like a research or whale-watching vessel. Men
on the bridge were peering through binoculars. As the vessel
drew closer, the men waved their arms and shouted, then the
vessel's horn began blasting repeatedly. Perhaps fearing they
might once again be bombarded with explosive charges, the
orcas slipped under the windrow and headed westward.

The vessel slowed and hove to near the windrow. Cameras
clicked and whirred as excited scientists recorded the rare
presence of the right whale cow and calf. For ten or fifteen
minutes the scientists took photographs and made notes, then
the vessel backed down, came about, and quietly left the area.
The right whale spyhopped and scanned the surface all around,
then with her baby at her flank she headed eastward, skim-
feeding as she went on copepods and the larvae of benthic
animals.

•   •   •

Midmorning, and still the orcas were hungry. Despite solid overcast, the sky had grown increasingly bright and the zooplankton had gone deep, so the surface waters were relatively quiet. The elders called to the other pods and received lackluster replies. They were having no better luck at finding food. The old cow led her pod toward Cape Ann.

While halfway across Wilkinson Basin, the orcas heard the raspy whistles of many white-sided dolphins. The sounds were being rapidly punctuated, as though the dolphins were leaving and reentering the water at high speed. The dolphin herd was moving from north to south. Maintaining silence, the orcas gauged the herd's speed, then headed southwestward to intercept it.

Ten minutes had passed, and the sounds of the whiteside herd were growing louder when two orca juveniles, distracted by a flight of gannets diving on their right, collided and buzzed angrily at each other. Immediately the whitesides' bearing became constant and their sounds slowly faded. The dolphins had heard the quarreling juveniles and were heading directly away. The old bull turned and gave the guilty juveniles a blasting reprimand. They hid behind their mothers.

The other two pods could be heard approaching from the northeast and southeast. Knowing it would take them some time to catch up, the old bull and cow slowed to a crawl and the family rested. The juveniles who had so carelessly alerted the dolphins sidled up to the old bull and rubbed against him. He petted them with his flippers. Again they rubbed against him, then did the same to the old cow. Now everyone began to make intimate contact. Tightly clustered, the twelve orcas continued slowly westward, intertwining as they caressed each other with various parts of their bodies. It was a ritual of affection observed several times daily, with the senior animals receiving more than they gave.

Soon the other pods joined up with them, and the gentle familial caresses gave way to spirited play. Preadolescents nipped and chased each other, adolescent females teased males of all ages, and adult males courted any females who showed the slightest interest. Foreplay seemed to observe no boundaries, but consummation was restricted to a few mature cows who were receptive. Their favors were hotly contested by the big bulls, who snorted and bellowed and shouldered each other aside in their attempts to mate. The competition stopped short of actual fighting, though. The cows showed definite preferences based only in part on size and strength, for smaller bulls sometimes succeeded where larger ones failed.

Courtship continued off and on for the better part of an hour, then was replaced by general frolic. Churning the sea white as they played, the forty-five orcas continued inshore toward Cape Ann.

As land came into view, the elders stopped and called for silence, then everyone spyhopped. The old bull scanned the shore. Mist shrouded distant hills. A shaft of sunlight poked through the overcast like a colossal spotlight, illuminating some herring seiners that were operating unusually close to land. Toward Halibut Point the old bull could see many tuna boats at anchor, spread out for miles. Conditions sounded quiet aboard the boats, but from their general vicinity he heard much whale talk. He headed toward the boats, and the others followed him.

About half a mile from the tuna boats, the orcas once again stopped to check the signs. A current flowing their way bore the taste of herring and whale feces mixed with bloody, oily chum from the boats. They heard the gulping sounds of feeding whales and felt rather than heard the subsonic moans of their calls. The orcas poked their heads above the surface and saw nine or ten finbacks maneuvering among the boats.

The strong taste of chum suggested that the tuna fishermen were still trying, but the orcas heard no strum of taut lines, no whine of big reels, so apparently the fishermen were not getting much action. That came as no surprise, for tuna stay low while the sun is high. Most bluefins in the area were probably in the deepest water they could find, hiding in trenches where they would be safe from predators while they rested from their dawn feeding.

Anchored about half a mile from the whales was a ninety-foot vessel. It was a charter fishing boat, but the two brothers who operated it had no customers aboard.[3] They were after bluefin tuna, worth several dollars a pound to Japanese whole-salers, and this part of Middle Bank had always been a good spot for bluefins. It was an overcast, hazy day, but the brothers could see about seven miles to Halibut Point, where tailings from the old granite quarry littered the high cliff like the aftermath of an avalanche.

Their boat was one of about forty vessels anchored at half-mile intervals over an area of several square miles. The assemblage included sport fishing boats, charter fishing vessels, motor yachts, and outboard motorboats. Many schools of herring, mackerel, squid, and sand lances had been running close inshore this day, and herring seiners were operating well inside Ipswich Bay.

It was a typical day of bluefin fishing. A dozen or so big tuna had been caught early that morning. Since then the fishermen had been taking one here and there. The brothers were still marking bluefins on their fishfinders, but the tuna were not feeding as actively since the sun was high. Still, each big bluefin represented thousands of dollars to the man who caught it, so as long as even a few giant tuna remained in the area, the men kept fishing.

The fishermen were occasionally entertained by the sight of finbacks skim-feeding amongst the boats. A few humpbacks had also been feeding close inshore this summer, sometimes only four or five miles off Plum Island. No humpbacks were in sight now, but quite a few finbacks were in the area. The brothers noticed three of them clustered motionless within half a mile of their boat.

Then beyond the finbacks the brothers saw some forty killer whales approaching from the east.[4] A month earlier they had seen one killer whale, then later a pair of them inside Jeffreys

Ledge, but never had they seen killer whales this close to shore. And never had they seen this large a pod.

The old bull floated head-down and without making a sound, listened to the bottom. It was about fifty fathoms deep here in Scantum Basin, and the bottom was littered with sunken boats, snagged nets, and human junk. Ideal hiding places for fish, less than ideal hunting conditions for orcas.

He could hear many stomachs rumbling. The other two pods were as hungry as his. They were all too hungry to wait until evening when worthwhile numbers of bluefins and other fish would again venture near the surface.

His matriarch moved slowly past him, swimming just below the surface and listening intently to something. With a single thrust of his big flukes, the old bull caught up with her and searched the spectrum of sounds reaching him. Immediately he knew what had caught the old cow's attention. A cavernous gurgling sound, which he had thought to be a distant humpback blowing bubbles, seemed instead to be coming from one of the finbacks.

Swinging their heads from side to side as they listened, the old cow and bull led the combined pods toward the boats, then stopped and faced a group of three finbacks about half a mile away. All the orcas heard and understood. One of the three finbacks ahead was very ill. Every time it drew a breath, it sounded as though thousands of big sea clams were blowing bubbles through mud. Apparently the whale's lungs were so congested with mucus that it could scarcely breathe.

Still silent, the orcas moved to within a quarter mile of the finbacks. Now they could see the whales' backs breaking the surface. The signs were clear. The ill whale was so weak that two others were pressing against its sides, holding it up to keep it from drowning. The two on the outside looked to be about sixty feet long. The sick one—probably suffering from pneumonia or diphtheria—was no more than forty feet in length. This group no doubt comprised a female and her calf, escorted by the female's mate.[5]

The old cow exchanged very high pitched signals with the other pod leaders, then the combined pods sprinted toward the three whales. Although the orcas were now mute, the urgency of their movements seemed to signal their purpose, for one moment the area was a tranquil scene of feeding whales and circling gulls and lazily rocking boats, then the orcas were detected and Scantum Basin seemed to crackle with fear. Most finbacks in the area went deep and fled north or south at twenty knots, but the two adults with the sick calf chose to stay with their charge. They even tried to shield it with their bodies, but the forty-five orcas divided into their three respective pods and each pod surrounded one of the whales.[6]

As far as the brothers could see, the finbacks made little or no attempt to escape. The three groups of killer whales used the same tactics. There were two orcas behind each finback, two in front, and several on each side. Those on the sides took turns diving, at least three at a time going under each whale. The finbacks' bodies shook as the orcas tore at their flesh. As the orcas surfaced, they rolled, and the brothers could see great slabs of flesh in their mouths.

The orcas at the finbacks' heads and tails appeared to be holding the whales in place, while those at the sides did all the feeding, diving under the whales and biting off mouthfuls, then surfacing on the opposite sides. After a while the orcas changed positions so that those who had been keeping the finbacks in place could take their turn at feeding. Those restraining the finbacks did not seem to be gripping them with their teeth, but merely staying close so that the finbacks could neither move ahead nor dive.[7]

The old bull with the missing teeth and one of the younger cows moved to the head of the seventy-foot female and floated at the surface facing her. The oldest cow and the younger adult bull took up similar positions at her tail and immediately chewed off her flukes. The rest of the pod lined up on either side of the whale, then those on the left dove and began ripping open her belly. The finback moaned and tried to roll over, but the old bull and his companion clamped their jaws on her snout, while those at the rear seized her tail. The combined strength of the four largest orcas was enough to prevent the whale from rolling belly-up to protect her vitals.

In groups of three, the orcas at the sides took turns diving beneath the whale and biting out great chunks of blubber and flesh. As one team surfaced to eat, the other dove and took its share. Removing several hundred pounds of flesh with each dive, they soon ate their way into the finback's body cavity. Her intestines, some four hundred feet long, spilled out and dangled in a massive snarl. The water became clouded with feces and blood. The finback's breathing, until then a rapid wheeze, took on a strangling sound. Her moans and those of the other two whales, so low in pitch that the orcas could scarcely hear them, rolled through the bay like the muted aftermath of a great explosion.

The orcas changed places. The old bull, together with the cow who had helped him hold the whale's head, moved alongside the finback, then dove and began to enlarge the abdominal wound. The old cow and younger bull, who had been at the tail, took up positions on the other side. With the largest orcas at the sides now, those at the head and tail had difficulty restraining the whale, even though her flukes were shredded. Perhaps because they knew how dangerous the death flurry of a fifty-ton finback could be, the older orcas decided to get it over with and go for the vitals rather than simply feeding on the whale's flesh.

The old bull ripped open the finback's stomach pouch, which disgorged a ton of krill into the water. Pushing his way past the collapsed stomach, the bull went for the whale's thundering heart. The ribs of finbacks and other baleen whales are not attached to the sternum, so despite the bull orca's thickset build, he was able to force his way inside the whale's thorax. He sank his teeth into the finback's wildly beating heart, a mass of muscle weighing as much as the pod's youngest calf, then twisted and shook until at last the great blood vessels tore loose.

Enveloped in a cloud of blood, he ripped out the still-beating heart and gave it to the cow on his right. While she shared the heart with other cows, the old bull began biting mouthfuls from one lobe of the huge liver.

Even now, with the finback all but totally eviscerated, a spark of life seemed to linger in the widened eyes. While two adult cows propped open the whale's fifteen-foot mouth, the other females and the juveniles bit off chunks of her tongue, which yielded several tons of succulent meat. The young orcas were encouraged to sample various parts of the whale; some flesh, some blubber, a bit of tongue. The toothless calf tried to munch on some liver, but ended up swallowing such a large piece that she nearly choked.

Blood was now staining the sea for miles around, yet despite the mammoth scale of the slaughter, the brothers heard scarcely a sound. The attack continued for an hour or more, and throughout this time the finbacks were visible at the surface. At no time did the finbacks roll belly-up, and the brothers noticed little or no fluke movement or thrashing. It was as though the finbacks were drifting motionless while the killer whales ripped them apart.[8]

Since the appearance of the killer whales, the brothers had marked no tuna or bait on their fishfinders. Except for the three finbacks under attack, there was not a baleen whale in sight. For some time it seemed that even the seabirds had fled the area, but when chunks of finback flesh began floating about, many gulls returned to feed. The brothers made no attempt to get closer to the attack scene. Having baits in the water, they stayed on their anchor.

Two Down-Easter "stick boats" happened by, and the men in the high spotting towers noticed the killer whale attack. The boats approached the finbacks, which by now were half-dead masses of torn, bloody flesh. The harpoon fishermen, though accustomed to death and dying, had never seen slaughter on so grand a scale. They shook their heads and exchanged grimaces. "Good gawd," said one man, and that seemed to sum it up for all of them. They took a few pictures, then left the killers to their gory work.[9]

Their stomachs filled to bursting, the orcas released their prey. Although the last signs of life had left the finbacks' eyes, they stayed wide open as the whales' remains sank slowly into Scantum Basin. Settling to the bottom, the cow, calf, and mate came to rest nearly as close in death as they had been in life.

The three orca pods rejoined and swam away.

·   ·   ·

Were it possible to kill whales quickly, orcas would probably do so because a large whale, thrashing about, can seriously injure its attackers. But a fifty-ton whale does not die easily. Orcas might drown whales if they could force them under-water and take turns keeping them there, but being weight-less in water, orcas would be hard pressed to keep large prey underwater long enough to drown them, especially whales that can hold their breath for thirty minutes to an hour. There seems no alternative but the fang, and even a badly mauled whale could take the better part of a day to die, so orcas prob-ably have little choice but to eat large prey alive. Perhaps, to minimize risk of injury to themselves, they can hurry death along by going for the vitals, as the old bull did in this scene. It is likely that the orcas ate only preferred portions of their prey, for three whales this large would probably yield at least forty tons of meat and blubber, far more than forty-five orcas could eat.[10]

9

The three pods were swimming a few miles off the New Hampshire shore. It was a clear autumn morning, and their breath floated white on windless light. Since the finback kill some days ago they had been moving steadily northward, hunting herring along the ten-fathom curve.

Throughout the day they maintained an easy pace and by nightfall were passing Portland, Maine. The western sky was red, the shoreline black. Pairs of lights, some white, some red, moved swiftly through the dusk. The pods were very close to land. Too close. The leaders changed course to the northeast. The lights fell away behind them. The sky went from red to black. On the shore a building burned, sending showers of sparks to drift among the stars and then wink out.

Just before moonrise, clouds moved in and blanketed the area. The sea began to fire, marking the orcas' every move with blue-green light. Their breaths sparkled on the night. For hours the sky remained overcast, then the clouds parted and moonlight burst through like the rays of a cold, white sun. The silvery path laid down by the moon coincided with their course.

They took turns napping on the move. Those not resting

probed the bottom with sound, keeping the pods on a track that approximated the ten-fathom curve, for this habitat interface had been proving productive. Throughout the night they continued northeastward along the coast, exploiting whatever feeding opportunities presented themselves.

Daybreak found them passing between Monhegan Island and Muscongas Bay. Mist swirled low over flat black water and hugged the shoreline of Monhegan. The island appeared to float above the sea. The rising sun was an indistinct blob, glistening on swells that heaved so slowly they made the sea look gelatinous. Monhegan, rocky and furred with spruce, stood black against a sky pink as salmon flesh. Then the sun, red-gold in thinning haze, cleared the horizon, and the sea shone like polished copper. A lobster boat chugged past the pod, its deck and wheelhouse heaped high with traps. When the boat dipped behind a swell, it looked like some lumpy sort of whale.

Later that morning the orcas passed Metinic Island on their left. The mainland coast was thinly veiled by distance and sea-level haze. Far to the northwest, mountains rose smoky blue. Sharply etched against this soft background, a nearby piney point stood out in dark contrast. Along the waterline of the point stretched a thin ribbon of silver sunlight, and in the light many dolphins made dazzling leaps. Just this side of the light band, a minke slowly threaded the surface. Closer still a gray seal surfaced, turned its horsey head this way and that, then sank nose-up with nary a ripple. Scoters skimmed flat water.

The elders turned east and spread out across a two-mile front, swimming zigzag and opening their mouths every few minutes to gauge the water temperature. The old cow and bull were swimming at the northern end of the line, and their pod was spread out behind them. On one of his more northerly excursions, the old bull found what he and the others had been seeking, a sharp temperature gradient. South to north over a distance of half a mile or less, the sea temperature fell four or five degrees. The old bull signaled the others. They gathered about him, then the entire group of forty-five set off toward

Nova Scotia, swimming in great zigzags to keep themselves on the cold side of the temperature gradient.

For the rest of that day and night they swam, feeding opportunistically. About midnight they passed Mount Desert Rock. From there they swung south about eight miles to place themselves directly over the hundred-fathom curve. Now and again they sonared the bottom to keep themselves positioned over submarine escarpments, but temperature and taste differences were so well defined above the steep slopes that it was generally possible to follow the hundred-fathom curve without making a sound. This enabled them to take prey by surprise.

Twice during the night the old cow with the 1919 fin tag had minor collisions with floating debris. Toward dawn she suffered a painful bump from a large log she failed to sense. She seemed to be having trouble generating precisely controlled sonar clicks, and her hearing was apparently not up to its usual acuity.[1] Well aware that she had a problem, she began hugging the old bull's flank and following his lead.

Until now the feeding had been spotty, but once the orcas picked up the hundred-fathom curve, the abundance of prey rose sharply. At a point about two-thirds of the way to Yarmouth, Nova Scotia, the curve swung north and then sharply south, and from that point on the orcas began encountering enormous schools of shad. Most of these were adult fish, fifteen to twenty inches long, that had been spawning in the Bay of Fundy's many rivers and were now returning to the sea's mid-depths for the winter. Having spent months in cold water, the shad were acclimated and had a strong aversion to temperature increases of more than a few degrees. Accordingly, they tended to stay on the colder side of the temperature gradient that the orcas had been following. When attacked, some fish escaped into warmer water, but most simply went to the bottom. Near Cape Sable, the temperature gradient curved close to shore, crowding the shad into shallower water where the orcas could more easily trap them against ledges and in small coves.

Traveling with the shad were hordes of herring and other

freshwater spawners on their way back to sea, so the orcas enjoyed heavy feeding. Their most productive hunts came during the darkness hours, when the fish followed their principal food, zooplankton, closer to the surface.

· · ·

The American shad (*Alosa sapidissima*) is an anadromous fish that lives in the ocean for its first several years, then returns to its river of origin to spawn. At one time the species ascended all major rivers along the entire Atlantic coast of North America, but by 1900 pollution and dams had destroyed so many of the spawning grounds that the American shad fishery all but ceased to exist. Since 1960, pollution controls and the installation of fish ladders have enabled the species to stage a recovery. Our good neighbors to the north seem to be enjoying a remarkable shad recovery,[2] but the U.S. fishery has virtually collapsed. Whereas the total 1896 commercial catch for the U.S. Atlantic coast alone was 22,680 metric tons (50 million pounds), the total 1983 commercial catch for all regions, including the Pacific coast, was down to 1,585 metric tons (3.5 million pounds).[3] This figure does not even approach the recreational catch, which in 1970 totaled 2,180 metric tons (4.8 million pounds) for just the coastal waters from Cape Hatteras to Maine.[4] As of 1987, the U.S. recreational catch was continuing to equal or exceed the commercial catch.

Shad spawn as early as mid-November in Florida and as late as July in some Canadian rivers. In the upper reaches of the Bay of Fundy, shad are present in great numbers from early spring through most of the summer. According to research conducted by Mike Dadswell of the St. Andrews Biological Station, Nova Scotia, as much as a third of the entire Atlantic coast shad population may participate in this annual Fundy migration.[5]

Unlike some anadromous species that spawn once and die, shad can spawn a number of times in the course of their lives. The incidence of multiple spawning increases south to north,

with shad in North Carolina rivers dying after a single spawning, while those native to the Miramichi River (Bay of Fundy)
are known to return and spawn as many as eight times.[6,7]

Millions of shad still can be found in the Gulf of Maine each
summer and autumn, but their numbers are small compared
to the volume of water through which they move, so it is more
important than ever for the orcas to be smart hunters. Their
use of temperature gradients is speculation on my part, but
the existence of sharp gradients is well established. The one
mentioned in my narrative is caused by extensive mixing in
the Bay of Fundy. This mixing stirs cold water from the bottom to the surface and is doubtless due largely to the enormous tidal range in the Bay of Fundy.[8]

The cause of this extreme tidal range, typically thirty-seven
feet and sometimes more than fifty feet, remains a mystery.
One theory holds that the bay's dimensions and shape cause
it to resonate and amplify incoming tidal waves. If this theory
is valid, and if proposed tidal power dams were to change the
bay's resonance characteristics, the effects could be felt all over
the Gulf of Maine. Computer simulations have shown that a
tidal power dam in the Bay of Fundy would raise tide levels
as far away as Boston.[9] With global warming already causing
the sea to reclaim some 65 acres of Massachusetts coastline each
year, the last thing we need is a higher tidal range.

Our planet's tides are caused by interactions between the
gravitational and centrifugal forces of earth, sun, and moon.
These forces create a "bulge" that moves across the ocean like
a very slow wave. In the open sea, tidal movement is fairly
straightforward, but its effects along the coasts are highly complex. Local factors such as continental shelf width, water depth,
bottom contours, and shoreline contours not only come into
play but are major determinants of tidal range and currents,
even more so than astronomical forces. These local factors bring
about great differences in tidal range at various points along
the coast. If you travel south along New England's coast, measuring the tidal range in various harbors, you will find it steadily

decreasing. Maine's Passamaquoddy Bay tides range about twenty-five feet. On Cape Ann in Massachusetts, the tidal range averages ten to twelve feet. Continuing south to Cape Cod, you will find some ports where the tidal range is so small that marinas do not need floating docks. The first time I took my boat down to Falmouth, I was surprised to learn that the tidal range there is only about six inches.

• • •

Over the next two days, the oldest cow's breathing became abnormally rapid. She was now taking ten breaths for every one the others took. The old bull and the rest of her kin stayed closer than usual to her.

Arriving off Yarmouth, Nova Scotia, on a moonless night, the combined pods paused to rest. They napped at the surface, backs awash and aglow, their every exhalation a display of light and color, for the sea was firing.

For an hour or so they rested in slack water, then the tide turned and began carrying them north. The other pods became active and showed signs of wanting to move on, but the oldest cow was not ready to travel, and her pod would not leave her. After some lengthy vocal exchanges, the other two pods headed south toward Browns Bank.

For the next six hours the oldest cow and her pod drifted in the current. Her breathing continued rapid and labored. Toward daybreak they found themselves approaching Brier Island near the tip of Digby Neck. The tide went slack, and in the distance they could hear large whales breathing. The orcas milled about restlessly, touching the old cow and listening to her vital signs. The pod all rubbed and stroked her affectionately, but she seemed scarcely aware of the contact.

From the shallows came the shivering sound of small fish leaving the water in great numbers. When the old bull reared back to look, he saw in the distance dazzling arcs of biolumin-escence sprout from the surface like fiery marsh grass. Could those be smelt he saw leaping? Smelt did not interest him, but whatever was making them jump might be food for orcas. What predators pursued them?

Leaving the old matriarch in the care of the nursing cow, whose calf was then at the teat, he led the rest of the pod toward the area where he had seen surface activity. The little fish had stopped jumping, but he managed to locate them by the whispery sounds of myriad tails beating the water. Soon the orcas were encountering large schools of smelt, virtual rivers of the small slender fish. Taking mouthfuls whenever they could, they followed the smelt around the tip of the island into St. Mary's Bay, at one point swimming so close to shore that the big bull's belly scraped bottom, but they never did find out what had been making the bait fish leap.

The sun was well above the shoreline when they headed back to find those they had left behind. As they once again rounded the tip of Brier Island, they encountered dozens of humpback whales. Most of them looked and sounded familiar to the older orcas, for they had encountered these individuals in years past over Stellwagen Bank near the Massachusetts coast. Apparently the whales had changed their feeding grounds.

The old bull led the pod several miles northwest of the island, but the cows and calf were nowhere to be found. He called and called until at last he heard a faint reply coming from far behind him, from the direction of the island. It was the nursing cow's voice. Then, from somewhere to the left of the cow's position, he heard gunshots. Quickly he led the pod back in the direction from which the cow had called.

He could not see the island yet, only hilltops on the mainland beyond it, hills glowing red and gold in the sunlight, and beyond them clouds that loomed like high snowy mountains. When at last the island came into view, the old bull and the others reared back on their tails and scanned the area. Sunlight from behind a nearby cloudbank laid down a bright band of light along the island's shoreline. At a break in the light band they saw the entrance to a cove, and it was from there that the cow's voice was coming.

They swam to the mouth of the cove and looked inside. The water was glassy calm and clear all the way to a lofty point where wisps of fog were forming near shore. Something inside the fog sent ripples radiating toward the orcas. A seal barked and was answered by another near the opposite shore. Patches of gold and russet foliage, set among evergreen conifers, reflected on the surface as soft washes of color.

They heard the old cow's rapid breathing but could not see her. Her blows echoed sharply from the opposite shore. The nursing cow had fallen suddenly silent.

The old bull was about to enter the cove when a movement on the far shore caught his attention. A man had appeared at the edge of the trees. He had a rifle slung over his shoulder. Following the bull's lead, the orcas submerged. The bull rolled to keep his big dorsal fin out of sight, then slowly rose to the surface and watched with one eye barely awash. The man paused and looked across the cove, then walked out along a rickety old dock made of sapling trunks and weathered, twisted planks. Unslinging the rifle, he took aim at a point some distance to the orcas' right. The rifle kicked and smoked. The blast reached the bull's ears, followed a moment later by the old cow's distress call.

The old bull buzzed at the others, then sounded and headed toward the rifleman. Within three of four beats of his flukes, he was driving his big body across the cove at motorboat speed.[10] The others submerged, entered the cove, and swam toward the point at which the man had aimed his rifle.

About to squeeze off another shot, the rifleman glimpsed a lofty dorsal fin and saw a three-foot mound of water racing toward him. He swung the rifle around and began firing at this new target. The old bull felt one bullet nick his fin, then a second round hit his back just ahead of the fin. Although partially spent by the water, the bullet struck with sufficient force to penetrate the skin and lodge in his blubber.

The man never got off a third shot. Pushing an increasingly high wave ahead of him as he sped into shallow water, the old bull banked to the left, made a sharp turn, and slammed his flukes against the end of the dock. Pain shot through his tail, but he heard the dock snap and felt it crumple. A solid wall of water enveloped the man, catapulting him into the shallows amidst a hail of heavy timbers. Fortunately for him, he landed in water too shallow for the orca to reach him. The rifle, torn from his grasp by the wave, sank in deep water.

Stunned and bleeding, the man heard a gunshot blast of air and vaguely discerned an enormous apparition towering over the spot where the end of the dock once stood as the old bull reared back on his tail. The orca paused long enough to see that the man no longer had his weapon, then submerged and hurried back across the cove.

The others had found the missing cows and calf at a shingle beach a short distance inside the cove. The old matriarch was lying in the shallows with her back awash. Too weak to swim, she had elected to strand herself rather than drown.

The old bull pushed his way through the milling pod and examined the old cow. She had a bullet hole in her fin, but he saw no sign of a body wound. Her breathing was more labored than ever, and she was beginning to sound heavily congested, like the young finback whose mother they had eaten. He examined the nursing cow and her calf. They were uninjured.

The two bulls gripped the old cow's flukes in their teeth, then paddled backwards with their big flippers and pulled her off the strand. Supporting her between them, they bore her out of the cove. When they reached open water, they moved well away from the coast and headed south.

For the rest of that day they continued southward. Not until they reached German Bank did the bulls stop to rest. The tidal current here had a southeasterly set, the direction they wanted to take, so with the old matriarch safely supported between the bulls, the orcas rested and let the current carry them toward Browns Bank.

Six hours later, some twenty miles southeast of German Bank, the orcas once again began encountering large numbers of shad on the colder side of the temperature gradient that all three pods had been following earlier. While the bulls stayed with the old cow, the others followed the gradient northeasterly toward Cape Sable, feeding on shad that were bunching up against the headland. They brought back fish for the matriarch, but she could not keep anything in her stomach. When she vomited, it sounded as though she might strangle on mucus.

Leaving her in the care of two cows, the bulls went off and caught their fill of shad, then rejoined the pod. Once again they rode the current, drifting along between Browns Bank and Bacarro Bank. The bulls and adult cows took turns supporting the old matriarch between them. Just north of Browns Bank, in a broad belt of cold water, the orcas saw shad flowing out to sea like a blue and silver stream.

Cold upwellings, tidal currents, and a brisk opposing wind combined to make the sea very choppy all that night. From somewhere east of the pod came the pops, creaks, and snapping sounds of many sperm whales. Despite the garrulous whales and noisy surface chop, the old bull slept through much of the night, for the incident in the cove had left him sorely tired.

By daybreak, surface conditions were much calmer. The orcas could hear hard bottom one hundred fathoms below them. Beyond that yawned an echoless abyss. The current had carried them out over the continental shelf break. The water was deep blue and warm.

Now that the orcas were over the shelf break, the vocalizations of sperm whales sounded louder than ever. Most of the whales seemed to be very deep, but at the surface a quarter mile from the orcas a cow was nursing her calf. Mother and calf were accompanied by a bull about sixty feet long. They seemed unaware of the orcas.

As the orcas spyhopped to look at them, a juvenile bull breached near the other sperm whales and landed on his side with a great splash. Six times the male breached, totally ignored by the others, then he took several deep breaths and sounded.[11]

Time passed. The baby sperm whale finished feeding and began to play with its mother's tail. Its mother and her big bull escort appeared to be napping. Perhaps hoping for a chance to separate the sperm whale calf from its guardians, the young orca bull and two cows moved toward the cachalots. Was this wise? With the matriarch ill, the orca pod could not move quickly, and many sperm whales were in the area. The old bull showed signs of restlessness. Supporting the ailing matriarch with the help of the remaining adult cow, he listened closely to the sperm whales below him. He had been listening to them for over an hour and knew by their voices that the dozen or more whales feeding far below him had been down there all that time. That meant they had been diving deep for well over an hour, and would probably surface for air soon.[12]

No doubt well aware that feeding sperm whales usually surface in roughly the same area from which they dive, and that these were likely to come up as a group, the old orca recalled the young bull and the two cows. Even under the best of circumstances it would be unwise to let the pod be surrounded by surfacing cachalots, and with the matriarch nearly helpless, circumstances were far from ideal.[13] When the others returned, the old bull led his pod a safe distance from the sperm whale cow and calf, whose escort bull was already spyhopping to get a good look at the orcas.

From directly below him, some five hundred fathoms deep, the old bull heard such a cacophony that it sounded as if human divers were hammering and riveting on the sea bottom. Then the banging sounds gave way to a loud creaking noise, and he heard the thud of big bodies colliding. Minutes later, large bubbles broke the surface nearby. When the old bull swam over there, he tasted blood and oil and saw scraps of blubber floating about.

Now he heard a sperm whale, its heartbeat growing rapidly

louder, rising toward him out of the darkness. He circled back toward the pod and turned to watch. A patch of surface swelled, then a sixty-foot sperm whale breached, its head and body entwined by the tentacles of a squid as long as itself. The whale rolled puffing in the sun, chomping ineffectually on the squid's body, too winded by its long dive to make a swift kill.

While the whale gasped for breath and struggled to get a killing hold on its prey, the squid's tentacles frantically explored the whale's head. The squid thrust one tentacle into the whale's blowhole and blocked it. With other tentacles it searched out, and tried to *gouge* out, the whale's eyes. Rolling violently from side to side in an effort to shake off the clinging tentacles, the whale managed to protect its eyes, but could not clear its blowhole. The squid's barbed suction disks were leaving scores of circular white scars on the whale, and its powerful beak— capable of cutting heavy wire—was inflicting deep wounds on its attacker's boxy head.

At last the whale managed to seize the squid's head in its jaws and delivered a killing bite. The squid's limbs writhed and flailed like so many serpents, then the animal went limp. The whale, starved for oxygen, delayed its meal long enough to catch its breath.

That was when the orcas struck. While the bulls guarded the old cow and youngest calf, the others flashed in from all directions and chopped away at the dead squid's tentacles. The surprised sperm whale spat out the squid's body and struck at the orcas with its teeth and flukes, but by that time the orcas had severed eight of the tentacles and escaped with them.

The bulls were already pushing the old matriarch along with all possible speed. The pod cleared the area none too soon, for the rest of the sperm whales had surfaced and were hurrying to the scene. Three of them surrounded the bull who had made the kill and were allowed to share what remained of the squid. Of the two tons that the bull sperm whale had brought to the surface, over half had been stolen by the orcas.

When they were several miles away and heard no signs of pursuit, the orcas stopped and ate the squid tentacles. Bite-size chunks were carefully fed to the old cow, who managed to hold down about fifty pounds of food. It was an encouraging sign.

10

Making just enough headway to avoid drifting apart, the orcas napped and digested their meal. The old cow was still managing to hold down the squid meat. Her breathing, though far from normal, had slowed somewhat, and she seemed more aware of the others.

It had been a risky venture, stealing a sperm whale's kill with so many other cachalots about, but the orcas dared not overlook any feeding opportunities, for their mobility was severely restricted. Two adults were needed to keep the old matriarch afloat, and at least two more—usually the bulls—to protect her from sharks. With their youngest still a dependent suckling, this meant they could field no more than six at a time for the hunt. To make matters worse, the old cow's noisy breathing was alerting nearby prey, yet the pod's hunters could not range too far in case they were needed to help defend the ill matriarch from a mass shark attack.

With so many factors going against them, the hunters faced a daunting task. And their hunting parties would not only be weak in numbers, but without the bulls and the old cow, they would lack experience and killing power as well. This all but ruled out the taking of large whales, a few of which might have seen them through the old cow's crisis.

In the great depths outside the continental shelf, where prey can hide beneath plankton layers that scatter sonar pulses, the orcas could well find their hunts failing more often than not. Accordingly, they kept pretty much to the shelf break, where at worst they might have to dive one hundred fathoms to herd prey against escarpments.

For the balance of that day and through the night they maintained an easy pace, deploying hunters whenever signs of prey were heard or tasted. Pickings were lean until just before daybreak, when they enjoyed a great stroke of luck. They came upon a longline, adrift near the surface, its miles of baited hooks holding hundreds of large fish. Most of the hooked animals were still alive, and their struggles were causing the longline to whip about, brandishing many big hooks already stripped of their bait. Undeterred, the orcas made their way along the full three-mile length of the line and ate a few dozen swordfish, bluefin tuna, porbeagles, and mako sharks, leaving only their heads on the hooks. Still hungry, they worked their way back along the line and topped off the meal with some species of sharks they would normally overlook.[1]

With less and less weight on the longline, it whipped about all the more, and the empty hooks became increasingly dangerous. At last, as several orcas advanced on a fourteen-foot white shark, the inevitable happened. Literally shattering teeth as it tried to bite through the hook and defend itself, the shark thrashed about so violently that it drove an unbaited hook into a cow's side. Even though the cow's blubber was three to four inches thick, the big hook penetrated well into the underlying muscle tissue. She had the good sense not to thrash about, but the shark's continuing struggles threatened to rip her open nonetheless. The two younger orcas with her disemboweled the shark, but the animal continued to thrash about and inflict painful damage on the hooked cow.

Attracted to the scene by the cow's distress calls, the old bull immediately severed the auxiliary line, then led the injured cow a safe distance away and examined the big hook. The shark's struggles had ripped an eight-inch gash in the cow's side. The point of the hook had worked through her flesh and was projecting outside her skin all the way to the barb. The old bull chewed off the rest of the line attached to the hook eye, then carefully grasped the barbed end between his teeth and pulled the hook free. Though bleeding heavily, the cow frolicked and rubbed against the old bull as he headed back to guard the matriarch.

As daylight swelled along the horizon, the orcas were still in the process of stripping the longline. The sun had not quite risen when they heard the swish of propellers just south of them, then the hollow straining sound of a big winch. The sun rose, bright gold amidst scattered clouds, and in its light loomed a large fishing vessel flying a white flag with a red circle. The vessel had retrieved the northernmost marker buoy and was moving southward, taking in the longline as it went. When the men aboard the vessel began seeing many hooks with only the heads of fish on them, they sounded a chorus of shrill cries. Two men with rifles slung over their backs scurried aloft to the crow's nest.

The old bull had already gathered the others, and with the aid of the younger bull, was pushing the matriarch southward with all possible speed. Bullets began whining overhead and spanking the surface. Geysers of white water danced all around the orcas. Most of the pod went deep, but the bulls were forced to stay at the surface with the old cow, for she could not hold her breath very long. The younger bull took a bullet through his dorsal fin and the old one was wounded in the left flipper, but no one was seriously injured.

•　　•　　•

As the orcas drifted southwest of Browns Bank, the cavitation from many ships' propellers joined the spectrum of natural sounds coming from the continental shelf and beyond. Most of the propeller sounds were those of surface vessels, but some came from submarines patrolling the great depths outside the shelf break. The orcas seldom saw submarines, but they often heard them, and they knew that the deep-diving types were faster even than the fleetest whales. Some were whisper-quiet. Others could be heard from many miles away.

These mysterious vessels usually stayed very deep and well outside the shelf break, but the orcas could hear one of them now, ascending the continental slope toward Northeast Channel. It sounded like it was gaining on, and rising toward, an inbound surface vessel that had noisy propellers and squeaky drive shafts.

By the time the two vessels reached the channel approach, the orcas had drifted within sight of the shipping lanes and could see that the noisy surface vessel was a rusty old freighter. Below it cruised the submarine, its depth now only a few hundred feet and steadily decreasing. This was one of the noisier submarines, but its sounds were becoming masked by those of the freighter. When the submarine rose to within fifteen fathoms of the surface, the two vessels sounded almost like one.

The freighter and its covert submarine escort had moved a few miles into Northeast Channel when the orcas saw a twin-engine military jet approaching from the north. It circled the freighter and dropped listening devices into the water. A short time later the orcas heard high-speed ships approaching the area. There came a subtle change in the sounds from the channel. The submarine was descending quietly toward the bottom. The noisy freighter continued westward through the channel.

Two sleek gray warships flying flags with red leaf-emblems hove into view and began sweeping the area with powerful pulses of ultrasound that just happened to be pitched at a particularly sensitive point in the orcas' hearing range. Each time the sonar beams were directed toward the orcas, their heads seemed to ring like bells and they became disoriented. Loudly expressing their discomfort, they turned to leave the area. One of the destroyers headed their way and scanned them directly for some time. So intense was the sonic bombardment that the suckling calf vomited. No doubt she was suffering much as herring and other fish do when bombarded with ring tone sound by the orcas.

Slowed by the need to push their ailing matriarch, the orcas took the better part of an hour to move well clear of the destroyers. They were still within earshot when a great explosion shook the area, echoing and re-echoing in the deep, wide channel. As the last booming reverberations faded, the orcas heard the submarine moving at high speed toward the shelf break. The destroyers followed, but no more explosions came.

Free at last of the deafening sonar beams, the old bull stopped to check his matriarch's condition.

She was dead.

The bull snorted, then pressed his jaw against her side and listened. Her old heart was silent, its final beat having gone unnoticed amidst the sonar noise from the naval vessels. Again he snorted, then thumped her with his head. There was no response. Her eyes were half open, but they saw nothing. Her nostril, agape as though still seeking her final breath of air, freely admitted the rolling sea.

The entire family crowded around, touching her, listening to her body, softly vocalizing among themselves. This continued for fifteen minutes or more, then the bulls once again began pushing the old cow along between them. Barely moving their flukes, they headed slowly southwestward along the shelf break.

•   •   •

For the rest of that day the bulls bore the dead matriarch along, and in all that time the only pod member to take nourishment was the suckling calf. She did not understand what had happened, but the others were very quiet and no one would play with her. For one long day and night they swam slowly and quietly, and even with her mother at her side, the calf began to feel lonely.

On the following day the sea looked like a smoothly undulating plain of dull gray. The sky too seemed drained of color, and the October air felt unseasonably hot and humid. The calf found herself taking two breaths where one would normally suffice, and those pushing the dead matriarch had to be relieved frequently so that they could dive and cool themselves. After a summer of heavy feeding, the orcas' bodies were encased in thick blankets of blubber, and they could quickly overheat.

By afternoon a squall line was moving in from the south. As the calf watched one big dark cloud pass nearly overhead, she saw a funnel grow out of its base and descend toward the sea. Long before the funnel touched down, the water beneath it flew into turmoil and a cloud of spray began to form. Merging with the spray, the funnel took on the shape of a tube extending all the way from the surface to the base of the cloud. The waterspout seemed to drag along the surface, falling behind the cloud until its tube stretched out, bent and twisted, for nearly half a mile. Sweeping a great cloud of spray along with it, the waterspout whipped this way and that along the surface, sucking up so much water that its tube became darkly visible. At one point it skipped so quickly across the water that it caught a large raft of phalaropes unawares. A cloud of feathers burst into the air, and dead birds were flung in all directions.

The waterspout lasted for about fifteen minutes, then became so bent and elongated that it broke off about a third of the way up from its base. Immediately the surface spray disappeared, and the rest of the tube was sucked back into the cloud.

An hour later the sky grew dark as slate, then was splintered by a double fork of lightning. Like great blue blood vessels, lightning branched between clouds, then flashed between clouds and sea. No longer could the young calf conceal her fear. She voiced it loudly. Her mother and the other cows took the youngsters down to a safe depth, but the bulls could not dive without abandoning the dead cow, for her body was becoming bloated with gas and would not sink. They stayed at the surface with the corpse.

A great wind began to howl. Waves mounted. At the storm's worst, the waves soared thirty feet high. Sometimes when the suckling surfaced with her mother for air, she saw two or three waves merge into a single mountainous mass, its dark slopes snowy with foam, its peak capped in clouds of spindrift. Through it all the bulls swam slowly at the surface, supporting their dead matriarch between them.[2]

By late afternoon the storm had left the area. The sun set fiery red, and all around it clouds seemed to radiate as if from an explosion. Soon after nightfall the moon rose golden full, and across its broad disk passed a southbound flight of geese.

Still edgy, the suckling calf continued to hug her mother's flank. Whenever they happened to swim behind the long-silent cow, the calf tasted death. Why did the old matriarch taste this way? And why was everyone in the pod so quiet?

Following her mother and escort, she dove to avoid floating debris. Riding high and white now, the moon seemed to race behind low scudding clouds. Seen from swimming depth, its elongated silver disk rippled flounderlike along the surface.

Later that night, after moonset, they sky came alive with streaking lights. Like unswerving bolts of lightning, scores of meteors burned their way across the night sky. Swimming at the surface, the suckling watched the meteor shower until, as suddenly as it had started, it stopped. Sometimes she saw darting lights in the black depths below her, too, but they did not move as quickly as these long streaks in the sky.

For three days and nights the orcas kept their dead matriarch with them, then at sunset on the fourth day, by which time the corpse was so swollen that it looked ready to burst, the old cow was released. As if to make absolutely certain that no spark of life remained, each member of the pod touched the dead one with head or flipper, then they all swam away and left the bloated corpse wallowing in the swells.

The suckling glimpsed an exotic long-tailed bird hovering overhead, then the pod sounded and sea shut out sky.

• • •

Scanning blue slope water for signs of food, a tropicbird[3] wheeled easily in the long, red light of sunset. Some ninety miles southeast of Nantucket, the bird overtook the orca pod while the dead cow was being released. As the rest of the orcas continued on, the tropicbird hovered high above the corpse.

Tacking stiff winged into the wind, the bird watched and waited. Soon the dead orca was surrounded by swarms of small fish and crustaceans gathering to scavenge. Before long, thousands of short-finned squid were darting to the surface to feed on the small fish. Plunging ternlike from forty feet and cleaving the water as cleanly as an arrow, the tropicbird began feeding on squid and fish.

Now half a mile away, the great orca bull thrust himself straight up out of the water and looked back as if to get a final glimpse of his matriarch. One after another the orcas thrust their long black-and-white bodies high out of the water and looked back toward the dead cow. Then displaying their flukes in unison, they slipped out of sight. Their vapor trails drifted raggedly on the wind, and soon were gone.

APPENDIX
ORCA SIGHTINGS AND STRANDINGS IN THE WESTERN NORTH ATLANTIC

When I set out to write this book, I found that little was known about populations, distribution, and migratory ranges for *Orcinus orca* in the western North Atlantic. What *was* known discouraged me. Even though the Canadian Maritimes and the Gulf of Maine boast some of the world's richest fisheries, there seemed to be few reports of orcas sighted in these waters. In fact, while conducting extensive aerial surveys of continental shelf waters from Cape Hatteras to Cape Sable, environmental impact study teams associated with the Cetacean and Turtle Assessment Program (CETAP), University of Rhode Island saw a total of only eighty-five orcas in twelve sightings. As a result of this assessment and the prior history of the species, prevailing scientific opinion held that orcas constitute a fairly regular but insignificant component of western North Atlantic fauna.

Still convinced that I wanted to write about orcas, I considered setting the book in the Pacific Northwest, but that would have wasted years of study specific to the Gulf of Maine. Also, Pacific Northwest orcas are harassed from dawn to dusk by observers and film-makers. I would not feel right there.

It puzzled me that orcas could be insignificant in this, one of the world's richest marine habitats. Few were reported, to be sure, but did this necessarily mean that orcas are rare in this area, or were many people simply not reporting their observations? If, like humpbacks and right whales, orcas were the focus of intensive scientific study, the number of sighting reports would no doubt increase dramatically. But orcas seem to range widely in this habitat, and the weather is unruly, so ongoing field studies pose a daunting challenge. As a result, most orca sightings are opportunistic and are made by observers not prepared to file scientifically valid reports. Many sightings, especially those made by commercial fishermen, go unreported because people see nothing to be gained.

I knew from interviews conducted for my previous natural history, *A Dolphin Summer,* that sizable pods of orcas were seen in the western North Atlantic, but I soon learned that their apearance one year was no guarantee that they would reappear the next. This unpredictability can lead to costly frustration for researchers. In 1980 Earthwatch mounted two expeditions to Newfoundland's Avalon Peninsula for the express purpose of studying orcas. Historical precedent told scientists they should find orcas there, yet two expeditions spanning a month failed to see a single orca. When a species has a track record like this, scientists are discouraged from giving it more than incidental attention.

Drawing from various sources, I compiled all existing orca sighting data, then ran notices in commercial fishing periodicals. I also interviewed fishermen at random. The efforts with fishermen generated a number of new reports, enough to convince me that many orca sightings do go unreported.

This appendix includes 191 sighting reports spanning a century and the entire East Coast. It is a thin data base with many redundant entries, but I believe the following inferences will stand the test of time.

About eighty percent of the orca sightings fall between Cape Hatteras, North Carolina, and Cape Sable, Nova Scotia

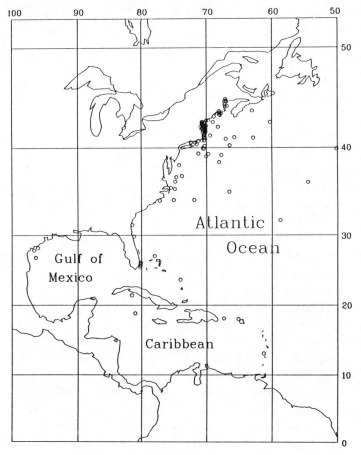

Figure 1. Sightings of killer whales *(Orcinus orca)*, Bay of Fundy to Equator, 1817–1987. [Source: *Rit Fiskideildar* (1988) 11: 205–224.]

(See Figure 1). Of these, about eighty percent occur in or near the Gulf of Maine during the summer months, peaking between 1975 and 1983 (See Figure 2). This peak coincides with the onset of the humpbacks' inshore feeding activity, which began in the mid-1970s, but it does not appear that the orcas come here primarily to prey on humpbacks. The data show only two lethal attacks by orcas on baleen whales in the Gulf

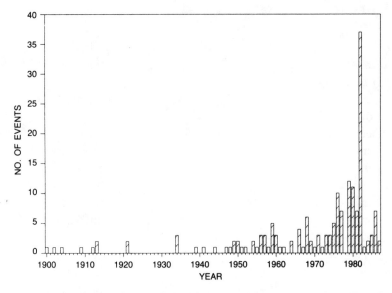

Figure 2. Distribution of killer whale *(Orcinus orca)* sightings or strandings, Bay of Fundy to the Equator, 1900–1987. [Source: *Rit Fiskideildar* (1988) *11:* 205–224.]

of Maine, and in only one of those was a humpback reportedly the prey.

Seasonal peaks of orca sightings and adult bluefin tuna catches coincide in the Gulf of Maine, so it appears that bluefins are one major reason orcas have historically visited the Gulf of Maine. It has been suggested that western North Atlantic orcas may prey primarily on bluefins, following the tuna along their migration route, as wolves do caribou. Were this the case, though, I should think predation would occur in the bluefins' Gulf of Mexico spawning grounds, yet I find that orcas are rarely reported from the Gulf of Mexico. Besides, it seems unlikely that one large orca pod ranges the entire East Coast, since mean reported pod size seems to increase with latitude, peaking in or near the Gulf of Maine and suggesting that the orcas seen south of forty-one degrees north latitude are not the same ones seen north of forty-one degrees north latitude.

All things considered, it appears that the annual occurrence of giant bluefin tuna has historically been a major reason orcas visit the Gulf of Maine. Further, it seems likely that the orcas come from far offshore, perhaps from continental slope waters, to feed in the Gulf.

Additional records of orca sightings in various parts of the North Atlantic can be found in *North Atlantic Killer Whales,* a special issue of *Rit Fiskideildar* (Journal of the Marine Research Institute, Reykjavik, Iceland) II (1988). One of the papers in *North Atlantic Killer Whales,* Katona et al., "Killer Whales from the Bay of Fundy to the Equator," incorporates my sighting data, and this appendix includes some of the data and figures from that paper. The two data bases are so similar that the figures can apply to either.

The data in *North Atlantic Killer Whales,* drawn from nine nations, suggest that North Atlantic orcas are less numerous now than in the past. The fifty or so sighted in the Gulf of Maine may be the bulk of the U.S. East Coast population. Possible reasons for the apparent decline in numbers include exploitation by whalers, lethal reprisals by fishermen, declining food stocks (due to overfishing), pollution, and disease.

In a separate study of the orca's global status, I am finding evidence that populations have been overstated and exploitation understated. Nearly seven thousand orcas have been reported killed by whalers over the past fifty years. Perhaps as many more have been harpooned but lost, and untold numbers have been shot and killed by fishermen. Furthermore, such factors as clannishness, low birth rates, and high proportion of adult males killed may make orcas especially vulnerable to human predation. Except for the waters around Iceland and Antarctica, orca populations the world over may be impoverished. Some genetically isolated populations may even be endangered.

Orca Sightings and Strandings in the Western North Atlantic

SOURCES KEY

CCS—Center for Coastal Studies, Provincetown, Mass.

CETAP—Cetacean and Turtle Assessment Program, University of Rhode Island, Graduate School of Oceanography, Narragansett, Rhode Island. Numbers shown (e.g., #H099480-1) designate files in CETAP computer.

GMWSN—Sighting reports published by the Gulf of Maine Whale Sighting Network, College of the Atlantic, Bar Harbor, Maine, prior to 5-22-86. Numbers shown (e.g., #75250) designate files in GMWSN computer.

GMWSN*—special printout supplied to me on 5-22-86 by College of the Atlantic.

MICS—Mingan Island Cetacean Study, C.P. 159, Sept-Iles, Quebec, Canada.

MMEP—Marine Mammal Events Program, a cooperative program of the Smithsonian Institution and the Cousteau Society, Washington, D.C. Numbers shown (e.g., #STR00664) designate files in MMEP computer.

NEWWI—New England Whale Watch, Inc., P.O. Box 825, Hampton, N.H. 03842.

NMFS—National Marine Fisheries Service (various locations, as specified).

USNM—U.S. National Museum of Natural History, Washington, D.C.

Shown in boldface at the beginning of each entry are the sighting number, date, and location of the sighting (including latitude and longitude where known). A summary of the sighting is followed by an abbreviated source notation (see Sources Key, above, and Bibliography for full citations).

Part 1   Chronological Listing of Sightings for Which Dates are Known

#1. July 1867 / Cape Elizabeth, Maine / 43°40′ N, 70°00′ W
Two orcas seen "in a terrific battle with a swordfish." Norton , "Mammals of Portand, Maine."

#2. 2-27-02 / Eastport, Maine / 45°50′ N, 67°00′ W
Two male orcas stranded. One 25 feet, 4 inches long. Letter in USNM files. MMEP #STR00664.

#3. March 1902 / Eastport, Maine / 45°50′ N, 67°00′ W
Two males, each about 25 feet long, stranded alive and shot. Photo of one in Katona et al., *Field Guide to Whales,* 112. CETAP.

#4. 11-14-04 / Harpswell, Maine / 43°50′ N, 70°00′ W
One male orca stranded, 25 feet long. Letter in USNM file says this

animal was 24 feet long and was stranded at Pennellsville, 4.5 miles from Brunswick, Maine. MMEP #STR00665.

#5. January 1909 / Barnegat, N.J. / 39°45′ N, 74°10′ W
Bones of stranded orca found. Animal estimated to have been 35 feet long. MMEP #00238112.

#6. 1912 / Bull Island, S.C. / 32°50′ N, 79°35′ W
Scientists obtained skull of one stranded orca from local resident. MMEP #CM037.58.

#7. 1921 / Florida / 24°30′ N, 81°30′ W
One juvenile orca (no measurements given) captured in the Gulf Stream off Florida Keys. MMEP #STR04968.

#8. 12–26–21 / Holloway Creek, Fla. / 25°41′ N, 81°26′ W
Orca tooth found near Everglades. MMEP #00238119.

#9. 1926 / Waterlily, N.C. / 34°–36°40′ N
Subfossil stranding. Number unknown. MMEP #00241401.

#10. 1934 / Hollywood, Fla. / 26°00′ N, 80°00′ W
One orca sighted off Hollywood. Estimated length 30 feet. Attempted capture. Photos taken. MMEP #STR00671.

#11. March 1934 / Palm Beach, Fla. / 26°40′ N, 80°00′ W
Two orcas sighted several times in Gulf Stream. MMEP #STR00672.

#12. March 1934 / New River Inlet, N.C. / 34°30′ N, 77°30′ W
One orca sighted off New River Inlet. MMEP #STR01041.

#13. 1939 / Florida / 26°32′ N, 79°55′ W
One (?) orca sighted at western edge of Gulf Stream. MMEP #STR00674.

#14. 1–27–41 / Wildwood Crest, N.J. / 38°55′ N, 74°50′ W
Vague—auditory ossicles retrieved from an 18- to 21-foot stranded orca (?). MMEP #AN020722.

#15. 1–11–44 / Orient, N.Y. / 41°10′ N, 72°20′ W
One orca stranded alive. No further data. MMEP #STR01033.

#16. March 1945 / Palm Beach, Fla. / 24°45′ N, 80° W
Frank J. Mather III of Woods Hole Oceanographic Institute photographed one male orca and eight to ten females or immatures off Palm Beach. At the same time, he also photographed what appeared to be a single orca. Personal correspondence from Dr. Frank Mather to author, 10–14–86.

#17. February 1947 / Boca Raton, Fla. / 26°20′ N, 80°00′ W
Three orcas sighted in Gulf Stream, 2 miles off Boca Raton. MMEP #STR00676.

#18. March 1948 / Summerland Key, Fla. / 24°30′ N, 81°30′ W
One orca stranded and died. Skull in Key West Municipal Aquarium. MMEP #STR00677.

#19. 1–4–50 / Minas Basin, east of Bay of Fundy, Nova Scotia, Canada / 45°10′ N, 63°30′ W

One orca stranded. Sergeant and Fisher, "Smaller Cetacea of Eastern Canadian Waters."

#20. January 1950 / Cape Cod Bay, Mass. / 42°00′ N, 70°10′ W
Unknown number of orcas mentioned in report on stranded *Delphinus*. Report in USNM *Delphinus* file. MMEP #STR01949.

#21. 2-19-52 / St. Augustine, Fla. / 29°30′ N, 81°10′ W
Six to eight orcas seen in a group, moving south off Marineland. MMEP #STR00678.

#22. March 1954 / Nantucket Island, Mass. / 41°15′ N, 70°00′ W (approx.)
Unknown number of orcas stranded on Nantucket Island. No further data. MMEP #UM102494.

#23. 3-23-54 / Mashpee, Mass. / 41°30′ N, 70°30′ W
One 9-foot orca stranded on Poponesset Beach. Photo of live animal on beach in USNM files. Orca left overnight on beach and towed out to sea still alive next day. MMEP #STR02626.

#24. 3-21-55 / Nantucket Island, Mass. / 41°20′ N, 70°10′ W
One orca stranded at Tom Nevers Head. Little and Andrews, "Drift Whales at Nantucket," 17. MMEP STR02065.

#25. 5-27-56 / East Pass, Fla. / 30°20′ N, 86°30′ W
One orca sighted 6.5 miles east of East Pass, Okaloosa County, Fla. Possibly shot. Skull at University of Florida. MMEP #STR00679.

#26. 4-27-57 / New Melbourne, Newfoundland, Canada / 48° N, 52° W (approx.)
Nineteen or more orcas stranded in Trinity Bay. Lengths 12 to 24 feet. Several large females examined on 5-16-57. Dearden, "A Stranding of Killer Whales in Newfoundland," 166-67. MMEP #STR02737.

#27. 12-14-57 / Tenants Harbor, Maine / 44°00′ N, 69°15′ W
One orca stranded alive. MMEP #STR00680.

#28. 1957 / Bay of Fundy, Canada / 45°00′ N, 67°00′ W
One orca stranded. Sergeant and Fisher, "Smaller Cetacea of Eastern Canadian Waters."

#29. July 1958 / Montauk Point, N.Y. / 41°00′ N, 71°45′ W
One orca, apparently a large male, followed boat to within 15 miles of shore. MMEP #STR01034.

#30. July 1958 / near Montauk Point, N.Y. / 41°00′ N, 71°40′ W
One probable orca sighted from vessel. No further data. CETAP #HO99480-1.

#31. 2-6-60 / St. Augustine, Fla. / 29°30′ N, 81°10′ W
One orca sighted a half-mile off Marineland. MMEP #STR00681.

#32. Late February 1960 / Newfoundland, Canada / 51°22′ N, 56°34′ W
One specimen, dead, at Green Island Cove, Strait of Belle Isle. Identification based on reported length of 24 feet, presence of teeth in both

jaws, and a seal in the stomach. Strait of Belle Isle open (free of ice) at the time. Sergeant et al., "Inshore Records of Cetacea for Eastern Canada," 1910–11.

#33. **4-25-68 / east of Bahamas / 23°42′ N, 74°00′ W**
Six probables sighted from vessel. No further data. CETAP #HO68501–75.

#34. **4-29-68 / 45 nautical miles southeast of Halifax, Nova Scotia, Canada / 41°12′ N, 62°47′ W**
Unspecified number of probables sighted from vessel. No further data. CETAP #HO68501–78.

#35. **6-25-68 / Prince Edward Island, Gulf of St. Lawrence, Canada / 46°53′ N, 64°14′ W**
One specimen stranded dead at Cape Wolfe, P.E.I. Probably a female; 19 feet, 11 inches long. Identified from color slides by characteristic color pattern of ventral surface. Sergeant, Mansfield, and Beck, 1970.

#36. **8-13-68 / 1.25 miles off St. John's, Newfoundland, Canada / 47°42′ N, 52°30′ W**
Sure sighting of four orcas from RV *Trident*. Group included one adult male. CETAP #HO68444–50.

#37. **1971 / Cutler Harbor, Maine / 44°39′ N, 67°10′ W**
One very large orca seen in this area. Came close to boats and made people nervous. GMWSN* #75250. See also sighting #56.

#38. **1-25-71 / oceanic / 43°40′ N, 41°00′ W**
Five probables sighted from vessel. No further data. CETAP #HO71501–2.

#39. **7-17-71 / off Bauline, Conception Bay, Newfoundland, Canada**
Two orcas killed by whaling catcher *Iversen*. One a 21.5-foot male, the other a 19-foot female. MMEP #00504925.

#40. **August 1972 / Williamsport, Newfoundland, Canada**
Five live orcas photographed by Ken Balcomb of Friday Harbor, Washington. Photos in USNM files. MMEP #STR02627.

#41. **3-17-73 / oceanic / 36°05′ N, 53°50′ W**
Three probables sighted from vessel. No further data. CETAP #HO73501–2.

#42. **Summer 1974 / Isles of Shoals, N.H. / 42°59′ N, 70°36′ W**
One orca sighted.GMWSN #74158.

#43. **9-19-74 / Kill Devil Hills, N.C. / 36°00′ N, 75°40′ W**
One 23-foot orca stranded on beach. Photo of live animal on beach in USNM files. Towed out to sea, still alive, by U.S. Coast Guard. MMEP #STR02629.

#44. **7-21-75 / 5 nautical miles south of Isles of Shoals, N.H. / 42°51′ N, 70°34′ W**
Fifteen probables sighted. No further data. This report probably based

on sighting #47. See also sighting #46. CETAP #HO75551–9.

**#45. 7–21–75 / 5 nautical miles south of Isles of Shoals, N.H. /
42°51′ N, 70°34′ W**

Ten possibles sighted. No further data. This report probably based on
sighting #48. CETAP #HO75551–84.

**#46. 7–21–75 / 5 nautical miles south of Isles of Shoals, N.H. /
42°51′ N, 70°34′ W**

A group of fifteen to twenty orcas, 15–18 feet long, seen 5 miles south
of the Isles of Shoals, was almost certainly a pod of killer whales,
according to sketches made by observer Peter Barleigh. Apparently
same event as sightings #44 and #47. GMWSN #75083.

**#47. 7–21–75 / 5 nautical miles south of Isles of Shoals, N.H. /
42°51′ N, 70°34′ W**

Fifteen to twenty orcas seen at 1335 hours on a clear day, 5 miles south
of Isles of Shoals, heading NNW at about ten knots. Estimated length
of animals, 15 feet. One pair of these whales crossed bow of observers'
boat within 10 yards. Animals sketched on sighting form. Observers
called them "killer whales." See also sightings #44 and #46. GMWSN★
#75009.

**#48. 7–21–75 / 5 nautical miles south of Isles of Shoals, N.H. /
42°51′ N, 70°34′ W**

Ten orcas seen 5 miles south of Isles of Shoals at about 1400 hours
on a clear day with four-foot seas and wind from SW, heading NW.
Distance between observer and animals ranged from 30 feet to 200
yards. At least one tall dorsal fin and white on back noted. Estimated
length of orcas, 12–18 feet. Field sketch available. See also sighting
#45. GMWSN★ #75083.

#49. 7–27–75 / mid-Gulf of Maine / 42°50′ N, 68°15′ W
Nine probables seen from RV *Westward*. CETAP #HO75412–1.

#50. 7–28–75 / mid-Gulf of Maine / 43°15′ N, 69°12′ W
Nine probables seen from RV *Westward*. CETAP #HO75412–2.

#51. 9–15–75 / Mount Desert Rock, Maine / 43°58′ N, 68°05′ W
One sure orca sighted. No further data. This report probably based
on sighting #53. See also sighting #52. CETAP #HO75551–224.

#52. 9–15–75 / Mount Desert Rock, Maine / 43°56.7′ N, 68°12′ W
Male orca about 30 feet long seen about 3 miles east of Mount Desert
Rock. Very tall dorsal fin and white spot over eye noted. Was swimming quickly behind a small school of "blackfish." (By "blackfish,"
observer may have meant pilot whales.) This report apparently the same
as sightings #51 and #53. GMWSN (unnumbered).

#53. 9–15–75 / Mount Desert Rock, Maine / 43°58′ N, 68°05′ W
One orca sighted about 3 miles east of Mount Desert Rock. Large dorsal

fin and white spot on head noted. With five cetaceans (blackfish). See also sightings #51 and #52. GMWSN★ #75215.

#54. 12–31–75 / Cutler Harbor, Maine / 44°39′ N, 67°10′ W
One sure orca sighted. No further data. This report probably based on sighting #56. CETAP #HO75551–258.

#55. 12–31–75 / Cutler Harbor, Maine / 44°39′ N, 67°11′ W
Large male orca seen near harbor. Had been seen frequently in that area for the previous three months. Schools of large herring also present. A Cutler fisherman who often saw the whale said that a killer whale had also been in Cutler area in about 1971. March 1902 (sighting #3) stranding of two males occurred just 20 miles northeast of Cutler. This report apparently the same as sightings #54 and #56. GMWSN (un-numbered).

#56. 12–31–75 / Cutler Harbor, Maine / 44°39′ N, 67°10′ W
One orca, about 25 feet long, with 4- to 6-foot dorsal fin and obvious white markings behind head and on sides, stayed in area of Cutler Harbor for three months. It avoided boats. Many large herring in area. Orca was seen by bird group led by Rev. Charles Dorchester of East Machias. In 1971, a very large orca was seen in this same area. (See sighting #37.) It came close to boats and made people nervous. This one avoided boats. See also sightings #54 and #55. GMWSN #75250.

#57. 15–75 (*sic*) (1–5–75?) / Isles of Shoals, N.H. / 42°59′ N, 70°36′ W
One sure orca sighted. No further data. This report probably based on sighting #58. CETAP #HO75551–338.

#58. 15–75 (*sic*) (1–5–75?) / Isles of Shoals, N.H. / 42°59′ N, 70°36′ W
One orca followed in wake of 38-foot trawler-type boat *Final Edition* while cruising. Definite ID by Red Marston, outdoors editor, *St. Petersburg Times* (Florida). This sighting description is located in a letter filed as #76577. See also sighting #57. GMWSN★ #75158.

#59. 13–76 (*sic*) (1–30–76?) / Bakers Island, Maine / 44°15′ N, 68°12′ W
One probable sighted. No further data. This report probably based on sighting #60. CETAP #HO76551–552.

#60. 1–30–76 / Bakers Island, Maine / 44°15′ N, 68°12′ W
A man from Salisbury Cove, Maine, reportedly had a killer whale "in" his lobster trap near Bakers Island during winter 1976. We (College of Atlantic) have not been able to verify this. (Author's note: I know of no lobster traps large enough to hold even a newborn orca. Perhaps the lobster fisherman was referring to his pound, a large floating enclosure in which lobsters taken from many traps are kept alive until taken to market.) See also sighting #59. GMWSN #76574.

#61. August 1976 / Cape Ann, Mass. / 42°42′ N, 70°38′ W
Shipmaster Mike Neelon of New England Whale Watch saw orcas four

times in two weeks. Six orcas one time, two to three the other times. All close to Halibut Point, Rockport, on Cape Ann. NEWWI.

#62. 8–20–76 / Cape Ann, Mass. / 42°42' N, 70°38' W
Thirty probables sighted. No further data. CETAP #HO76551–400.

#63. 8–20–76 / Cape Ann, Mass. / 42°37' N, 70°41' W
Thirty probables sighted from vessel. No further data. CETAP #HO99480–16.

#64. 8–20–76 / Cape Ann, Mass. / 42°37' N, 70°41' W
Thirty orcas sighted off Halibut Point by tuna fisherman. (Given coordinates intersect near Gloucester Harbor, not Halibut Point.) MMEP #SEAN1180.

#65. 8–20–76 / Cape Ann, Mass. / 42°42' N, 70°38' W
Thirty orcas sighted. Two mating. Traveled from Halibut Point (Cape Ann) to Race Point (at north tip of Cape Cod). No field marks reported. This same general southerly movement from Cape Ann to Cape Cod was observed in a pod of ten orcas from 9–8–76 to 9–12–76. See also sighting #72. GMWSN* #76421.

#66. 8–21–76 / Cape Ann, Mass. / 42°37' N, 70°41' W
Five probables sighted from vessel. No further data. CETAP #HO76551–406.

#67. 8–21–76 / Cape Ann, Mass. / 42°37' N, 70°41' W
Five to six orcas sighted off Eastern Point by Testaverdi family of Gloucester. Orcas not large — possibly juveniles. Orcas seen swimming south to southwest about 2 miles off breakwater. (Testaverdi brothers later recall at least one fin looking as big as a sail, suggesting the presence of at least one adult male.) MMEP #SEAN1182.

#68. 8–21–76 / Cape Ann, Mass. / 42°35' N, 70°38' W
Six sure orcas sighted. No further data. CETAP #HO99480–18.

#69. 8–21–76 / Cape Ann, Mass. / 42°35' N, 70°38' W
Six orcas sighted near Gloucester breakwater (Eastern Point, apparently), heading southwest. Identified by trained observer as six males. GMWSN* #76427.

#70. 8–26–76 / north tip of Cape Cod, Mass. / 42°03' N, 70°11' W
One probable sighted from vessel. No further data. CETAP #HO99480–22.

#71. 8–26–76 / north tip of Cape Cod, Mass. / 42°03' N, 70°11' W
Estimated ten orcas seen 1.5 miles west of Herring Cove Beach, heading inshore. Reported by U.S. Coast Guard, Provincetown. MMEP #SEAN1162.

#72. September 8–12, 1976 / Cape Ann, Mass. / 42°37' N, 70°41' W
Small group of orcas (number unknown) sighted several times 8–12 September, first off Gloucester, then farther south with each sighting. See also sighting #65. MMEP #SEAN1184.

#73. 9-8-76 / Cape Ann, Mass. / 42°37′ N, 70°40′ W
Ten sure orcas sighted. No further data. This report probably based on sighting #74. CETAP #HO76551-452.

#74. 9-8-76 / Cape Ann, Mass. / 42°37′ N, 70°40′ W
Ten orcas sighted heading south. Four males, 20-25 feet long. Six females, 6-16 feet long. Sightings made by fisherman at close range. Pod moved from Gloucester (Cape Ann) to outer Brewster (Cape Cod), then Barnstable (Cape Cod). Sightings made during "first week of September." See also sightings #73, #76, #78. GMWSN #76473.

#75. 9-8-76 / north end of Stellwagen Bank, Mass. / 42°25′ N, 70°25′ W
Ten sure orcas sighted. No further data. CETAP #HO76551-456.

#76. 9-8-76 / north end of Stellwagen Bank, Mass. / 42°25′ N, 70°25′ W
Ten to thirty orcas sighted. Probably same orcas as in sightings #73 and #74. Ollie Brazer sent three verbal reports to GMWSN of ten to thirty killers over Northern Stellwagen (8 September) to off Race Point, Provincetown, Mass. (12 September). (See sighting #78.) Col. E. S. Clark wrote to GMWSN that killers probably were feeding on tuna. GMWSN★ #76477.

#77. 9-12-76 / north tip of Cape Cod, Mass. / 42°04′ N, 70°16′ W
Ten sure orcas sighted near Provincetown, Mass. No further data. CETAP #HO76551-457.

#78. 9-12-76 / north tip of Cape Cod, Mass. / 42°02′ N, 70°16′ W
Ten to thirty orcas seen off Race Point, Provincetown, Mass. No photos. See sighting #76. GMWSN★ #76478.

#79. 9-12-76 / Cape Ann, Mass. / 42°37′ N, 70°41′ W
Five probables sighted from vessel. No further data. (Given coordinates would intersect on west shore of Gloucester Harbor. To my knowledge, orcas have not been reported inside Gloucester Harbor.) CETAP #HO99480-24.

#80. 9-16-76 / Boston Harbor, Mass. / 42°22′ N, 70°53′ W
One probable sighted from vessel near Graves Light, Boston. No further data. CETAP #HO99480-25.

#81. 9-16-76 / Boston Harbor, Mass. / 42°22′ N, 70°53′ W
One orca attacked small boat near Graves Light, Boston. Damage photographed and New England Aquarium, Boston, notified. Length of orca estimated at 13-14 feet. MMEP #SEAN1181.

#82. Summer 1977 / Newfoundland, Canada / approx. 50° N
One adult male photographed off Newfoundland coast by Peter Cohen of Ocean Research and Education Society (formerly in Gloucester, Mass. — now defunct). Katona, et al., *Field Guide to Whales*, 117 (photo).

#83. August 1977 / Mattituck, Long Island Sound, N.Y. / 41°00′ N, 72°30′ W
Several fishermen reported one or more orcas in both the ocean and

Long Island Sound. Numerous bluefish also in area. Newsclipping from B. Porterfield in USNM files. Reported in *Newsday,* 8-14-77. MMEP #STR02631.

#84. August 1977 / south end of Stellwagen Bank, Mass. / 42°10′ N, 70°15′ W

Twelve to eighteen orcas in the area for 5–10 days. Mayo, *Observations of Cetaceans.*

#85. 8-24-77 / Orleans, Mass. / 41°47′ N, 69°58′ W

Orca cow and calf stranded at 1300 hours on Skaket Beach. Driven off beach. Restranded on Lasallette Beach in Brewster, Mass. (41°46′ N, 70°05′ W). Put out to sea again. Last seen 2000–2400 hours about 3 miles offshore. Estimated lengths: cow, 20–21 feet; calf, 6–9 feet. Reported by Sealand of Cape Cod (Brewster, Mass.) and New England Aquarium (Boston, Mass.). Same as sighting #86. MMEP #SEAN2332.

#86. 8-24-77 / Orleans, Mass. / 41°47′ N, 69°58′ W

Orca cow 23–25 feet long with female calf 8–10 feet long stranded 1.5 miles off Orleans. Even at low tide, cow could have reached deeper water but did not try. Calf was swimming around cow all the while. Tide came in; still cow did not swim away. At last orcas swam away, then again came ashore in 4–5 feet of water at Brewster, Mass. Orcas then headed back toward Orleans, then returned to same spot at Brewster, where they drove hard toward beach and for first time were truly grounded. On two occasions, cow rolled belly-up. Men righted her, pushed her away from shore, and used boats to herd orcas out to sea despite orcas' repeated efforts to return to shore. Orcas finally disappeared. Same as in sighting #85. Bob King's detailed report in author's file. (Appears that female knew she was seriously ill and was trying not to drown. Questionable whether humans should interfere.) Personal interview with Bob King at Sealand of Cape Cod, Brewster, Mass.

#87. 8-26-77 / Barnstable, Mass. / 41°48′ N, 70°15′ W

Two sure orcas sighted. No further data. CETAP #HO77552–146.

#88. 8-26-77 / Barnstable, Mass. / 41°48′ N, 70°15′ W

Two orcas sighted north of Barnstable Harbor. No photos. GMWSN★ #77687.

#89. 8-26-77 / near Brewster, Mass. / 41°45′ N, 70°10′ W

Commercial fisherman reported to Sealand of Cape Cod that he saw about twenty-five orcas near Brewster. Group included at least one cow-calf pair. Sealand of Cape Cod.

#90. 3-24-79 / east of Va./N.C. border / 34°05′ N, 71°52′ W

One sure orca sighted from USCGC *Tamaroa.* CETAP #P179072–20.

#91. 5-20-79 / Tampa Bay, Fla. / 27°32′ N, 82°46′ W

One orca, 22 feet long, sighted 1.5 miles offshore. Orca was observed from boat for about fifteen minutes. Reportedly made two passes at boat, one under and one near the side. Was caught in haul seine and died. MMEP #SEAN420.

#92. July 1979 / southeast of Georges Bank / 41°05′ N, 67°00′ W
Five possibles seen. No further data. CETAP #0179176–5.

#93. 7-25-79 / south of Nantucket Island, Mass. / 40°19′ N, 70°15′ W
Six possibles sighted from vessel. No further data. CETAP #0279182–2.

#94. August 1979 / Ipswich Bay, Mass. / 40°19′ N, 70°15′ W
Orcas seen twice over the course of the summer: a singleton and a pair. Personal interview with shipmaster Bill Neelon of New England Whale Watch, Inc., 5–19–86.

#95. August 1979 / Jeffreys Ledge, N.H. / 43°10′ N, 70°05′ W
Three sightings, forty-three orcas total, mean group size of fourteen. GMWSN (unnumbered).

#96. August 1979 / Halibut Point, Cape Ann, Mass. / 42°40′ N, 70°30′ W
Twelve to thirty orcas in area for fiive to ten days. Attacked three finbacks. Mayo, *Observations of Cetaceans.*

#97. 8-6-79 / 2 nautical miles east of Isles of Shoals, N.H. / 42°59′ N, 70°34′ W
Observer reported one killer whale (tall dorsal fin, black-and-white coloring) leaving water vertically with tuna in mouth. GMWSN★ #79769.

#98. Late summer 1979 / near Jeffreys Ledge, N.H. / 42°45′ N, 70°30′ W
Several unconfirmed reports of orcas attacking three finback whales. No photos. Following report published by GMWSN in 1981: "A group of 40–50 killer whales broke up into three groups as they approached three finback whales. Each group began attacking a different finback. The killer whales dove under the finbacks and bit off pieces of meat, pushing the finbacks up out of the water a little during the attack. Feeding continued for over two hours and when it was over the water was full of pieces of meat and blood. The whales were not observed after the attack. If they were killed, the carcasses would have sunk." This report attributed to Jay Neeland. It should be Bill Neelon. See sighting #99. Stone et al., *Whales in the Gulf of Maine,* 15–16.

#99. August 1979 / a few miles from Halibut Point, Cape Ann, Mass. / 42°42′ N, 70°39′ W
Time: midday. While fishing for bluefin tuna, Captain Neelon saw twenty-five to thirty orcas approach from the east in a fairly tight grouping. Orcas "made a beeline" for three finbacks about ¾ mile from Neelon's boat, then split into three equal groups and attacked. As far as Neelon could see, finbacks made little or no attempt to escape. Eight

to ten orcas surrounded each finback—two in back, two in front, and two to three on each side. Those on one side dove under finback and came up on other side with big mouthfuls of flesh. Then those on other side would dive under and tear away pieces of flesh. It seemed to Neelon that orcas at finbacks' heads and tails were simply keeping finbacks in place, while orcas at sides did all the feeding. Then side orcas seemed to change places with orcas at front and back, taking turns feeding and keeping finbacks in place. Those restraining finbacks didn't seem to grip finbacks with their teeth—merely stayed so close to them that they couldn't move ahead or dive. No photos, but observer is considered reliable and experienced. See also sighting #98. Personal interview with shipmaster Bill Neelon of New England Whale Watch, Inc., 5–19–86.

#100. 9–5–79 / Ipswich Bay, Mass. / 42°43′ N, 70°37′ W
Forty sure orcas sighted near Cape Ann. Group included one calf. No further data. CETAP #0179552–338.

#101. 9–5–79 / Ipswich Bay, Mass. / 42°43′ N, 70°37′ W
Forty to fifty orcas sighted just north of Rockport and Halibut Point. Calves 6–8 feet long sighted with orcas. Seen rolling onto backs; observed under bow pulpit of boat. After feeding, split into two groups; one group of fifteen to twenty headed east, then northeast; other group headed north. Blues (bluefish) and mackerel being fed on by tuna; squid in area. Two finbacks sighted within 50–70 feet of orcas. GMWSN★ #79602.

#102. 9–15–79 / 3 nautical miles east of Mount Desert Rock, Maine / 43°58′ N, 68°05′ W
One orca sighted. No further data. GMWSN (unnumbered).

#103. 9–16–79 / Halibut Point, Cape Ann, Mass. / 42°42′ N, 70°38′ W
Experienced observer Scott Mercer (NEWWI) reported an unspecified number of killer whales attacking a humpback. (Scott Mercer did not actually witness this. He heard about the incident and reported it to GMWSN.) Sighting made in afternoon. Second report of this sent to GMWSN by Gerry Beekman who heard on CB radio that a large number of killer whales were in area. Heard detailed report of killer whales tearing a small humpback to pieces. One fisherman reported twenty-pound chunks of meat floating in water. No photos. GMWSN★ #79767.

#104. 10–19–79 / Great South Channel, Mass. / 41°25′ N, 69°24′ W
One probable sighted from RV *Albatross*. CETAP #P179288–5.

#105. 4–17–80 / off Currituck Beach, N.C. / 36°16′ N, 75°46′ W
Four sure orcas, one male and three others, sighted from RV *Evrika*. CETAP #P180106–3.

#106. 5–5–80 / some 60 nautical miles east of Virginia Beach, Va. / 36°46′ N, 74°38′ W

Five orcas seen. No further data. GMWSN (pers. comm. from T. Rumage).

#107. 5-8-80 / some 30 nautical miles northeast of Cape Hatteras, N.C. / 35°22′ N, 74°54′ W
One probable sighted from USCGC *Cherokee.* CETAP #P180123-24.

#108. 5-14-80 / Mouth Block Canyon, shelf break, 90-100 nautical miles east of Atlantic City, N.J. / 39°29′ N, 71°13′ W
One possible. U.S. Coast Guard thermography. CETAP #F180133-41.

#109. 5-19-80 / some 60 nautical miles southeast of Georges Bank / 38°30′ N, 68°00′ W
At least four orcas sighted. One solo, one with several females or subadults. GMWSN (pers. comm. from K. Balcomb).

#110. July 1980 / near northeast tip of Stellwagen Bank, Mass. / 42°30′ N, 70°20′ W
Five or more orcas seen. No further data. GMWSN (pers. comm. from T. Rumage).

#111. 7-26-80 / a few miles south of Boon Island, Maine / 43°10′ N, 70°30′ W
One orca seen. No further data. GMWSN (pers. comm. from T. Rumage).

#112. 8-19-80 / some 8 nautical miles southeast of Cape Porpoise, Maine / 43°21′ N, 70°25′ W
One orca seen. No blow visible. Surfaced and went down. Observer sure of ID; female orca dorsal fin (could have been subadult male) circled on report form. GMWSN★ #80101.

#113. September 1980 / Machias, Maine / 44°30′ N, 67°30′ W
Four orcas seen. No further data. GMWSN (pers. comm. from T. Rumage).

#114. 10-16-80 / 160 nautical miles south of Grand Banks, Newfoundland, Canada / 40°00′ N, 50°00′ W
Two orcas seen. No further data. (Given coordinates would place sighting more like 300 miles southeast of Grand Banks.) GMWSN (pers. comm. from T. Rumage).

#115. 5-23-81 / some 5 nautical miles east of Cape Ann, Mass. / 42°40′ N, 70°30′ W
One orca seen. No further data. GMWSN (pers. comm. from T. Rumage).

#116. 5-26-81 / some 16 nautical miles southwest of Cape Hatteras, N.C. / 35°11′ N, 75°48′ W
Four probables sighted from vessel. No further data. CETAP #0181705-2.

#117. 5-26-81 / Hatteras Inlet, N.C. / 34°03′ N, 75°03′ W
Three orcas sighted bearing 170 degrees from Hatteras Inlet: male,

28 feet; female, 22 feet; calf, 6 feet long. MMEP #MME00038.

#118. 5–26–81 / Hatteras Inlet, N.C. / 35°11′ N, 75°48′ W

Three to five orcas sighted bearing 170 degrees from Hatteras Inlet in 300 fathoms of water. Animals swimming northeastward. Photographed by Chip Shaefer, captain of *Temptress*. Lengths estimated at 26, 20, and 6 feet. MMEP #SEAN6204.

#119. 6–19–81 / some 100 nautical miles due south of Nantucket Shoals / 39°24′ N, 69°41′ W

One sure orca seen by U.S. Coast Guard fishery patrol. CETAP #F281170–32.

#120. July 1981 / Grand Manan Island, New Brunswick, Canada / 44°30′ N, 66°50′ W

One orca sighted. No further data. GMWSN (pers. comm. from T. Rumage).

#121. 9–22–81 / some 10 nautical miles southeast of Block Island, R.I. / 41°03′ N, 71°25′ W

Twenty sure orcas sighted from vessel. No further data. CETAP #0181107–109.

#122. 10–5–81 / near shelf break, some 80 nautical miles south of Martha's Vineyard, Mass. / 40°01′ N, 70°23′ W

One probable seen by U.S. Coast Guard fishery patrol. CETAP #F281278–5.

#123. 10–17–81 / south of Georges Bank, 35 nautical miles south of Bear Seamount / 39°18′ N, 67°40′ W

Two to four orcas sighted. No further data. GMWSN (pers. comm. from T. Rumage).

#124. 1–5–82 / Ocean City, Md. / 38°12′ N, 74°13′ W

Ron Naveen of NMFS, Washington, D.C., and others sighted seven orcas and got their boat close enough to get photos of four, including one mature male. Lengths of five (females or subadult males) estimated at 18–20 feet. Other two (adult males) estimated at 28 feet. Notation added: "This is the first official record for this species in Maryland waters." MMEP #SEAN7634.

#125. May 1982 / Cashes Ledge, Maine / 42°50′ N, 69°00′ W

James Tripp, a fisherman out of Spruce Head, Maine, saw two orcas at Cashes Ledge (about 70 miles equidistant from Portland, Maine; Rockland, Maine; and Boston, Mass.) "breaching and bellyflopping and moving fast (about eight knots) toward trawlers, probably chasing herring. The orcas were 40–50 feet apart, and both had high dorsal fins (4–5 feet)." White body markings not noted. When last seen, orcas were heading south-southeast, as if toward Georges Bank. Photograph taken. Telephone interview with Mr. Tripp by author, 1–16–87.

#126. 5–15–82 / Stellwagen Bank, Mass. / approx. 42°15′ N, 70°10′ W
Breaching orca (appears to be female or subadult male) photographed
by Lyda Phillips. Katona et al., *Field Guide to Whales,* 115.

This was the first of at least twenty-one sightings of this particular
orca during 1982. See sightings #127–136, #139, #141, #144, #146–
148, #152–153, and #155–157. The orca was photographically identified on several occasions by five parallel raised scratches on its left
flank behind the saddle patch. In all but one sighting (#132), the orca
was alone and appeared curious about boats and people, frequently
approaching them closely. The orca was seen between Provincetown
and Gloucester, Mass., during May and June; at several locations
around Mount Desert Island, Maine, in mid-June; near St. Andrew's,
New Brunswick, in early June; then back at the Mount Desert Island
area in mid-August. On 13 August, an orca that was probably this
same animal was disentangled from lobster fishing gear between
Frenchboro Long Island and Swans Island, Maine. The animal was
seen near Lubec and Eastport, Maine, in the third week of August;
near Mount Desert Island, Maine, on 25 August; at Hingham Mass.,
on 2 September; at Boston on 4 September; and at Provincetown from
mid-September through mid-October. While at Provincetown, the
orca accepted food thrown into the water or dangled on lines from
piers and boats. Photographs taken at Provincetown on 16–17 October
showed that the teeth in the lower jaw were worn to approximately
half their normal length; teeth on the left side of the upper jaw were
worn to the gumline, and several teeth were apparently misaligned.
On two occasions people guided the orca to the sea after it entered
shallow water. At Wellfleet, Mass., people forced it out of a tidal creek.
At Hingham, Mass., a boat "led" it around a sandbar. The last sighting
of an animal that could have been this same orca occurred on 20
November 1982 at Dipper Harbor, New Brunswick. Katona et al.,
"Killer Whales from the Bay of Fundy to the Equator," 223–24.

**#127. 5–16–82 / 9.5 miles off Race Point, Provincetown, Mass. /
42°09′40″ N, 70°15′ W**
Jim Stone and others observed one orca for an hour on 5–16–82. Also
observed (same animal?) at various times through 5–20–82 (at Stellwagen Bank, Mass., on 5–20–82.) Photos taken by many aboard
whale-watching vessel. Notation: "Although killer whales occur in
Cape Cod Bay and the south Gulf of Maine for a short period of
time during their migration each year (and are occasionally reported
by fishermen), this is the first time in four years that they have been
observed in this area by a whale-watching vessel. (Author's note:
These boats are out regularly each year from April until the end of
October.) MMEP #SEAN7636.

#128. 5–22–82 / **Graves Light, Boston Harbor, Mass.** / **42°18′ N, 71°01′ W**

Lone orca estimated 18 feet long seen near Graves Light for two days (5–21 and 5–22); near Aranes Light and off Marblehead on 5–23; south again at Hingham Harbor 5–27 and 5–28; north again at Boston Harbor on 6–1. Photos thought to have been taken. MMEP #SEAN7604.

#129. 5–26–82 / **Gloucester, Mass.** / **42°35′ N, 70°40′ W**

Two orcas sighted, one of them the animal sighted frequently in the Gulf of Maine during 1982. See also sighting #126. GMWSN (pers. comm. from W. Weinrich).

#130. 5–28–82 / **Hingham, Mass.** / **42°15′ N, 70°53′ W**

One orca sighted, circling and following fish schools. *Quincy Patriot Ledger* (Quincy, Mass.).

#131. June 1982 / **4 nautical miles off Hampton Beach, N.H.** / **42°55′ N, 70°38′ W**

Young female orca sighted from M/V *Northeasterner*. Orca was apparently feeding on schools of mackerel and moving around three or four local party boats fishing for mackerel. It closely approached *Northeasterner*, and good quality photographs were obtained. NEWWI.

#132. June 1982 / **Isles of Shoals, N.H.** / **43°00′ N, 70°35′ W**

Lone orca seen swimming "companionably" with several white-sided dolphins. Gormley, *A Dolphin Summer,* 77–78.

#133. June 1982 / **Mount Desert Island, Maine** / **44°20′ N, 68°15′ W**

Shows one orca photographed by Bob Bowman. Katona et al., *Field Guide to Whales,* 116–17.

#134. June 1982 / **Mount Desert Island, Maine** / **44°20′ N, 68°15′ W**

Katona et al., *Field Guide to Whales,* 110–11. Shows one orca photographed by Scott Marion.

#135. 6–12–82 / **Seal Harbor, Maine** / **44°20′ N, 68°15′ W**

Lone orca sighted. Quite tolerant of boats. GMWSN (unnumbered).

#136. Summer 1982 / **Provincetown Harbor, Mass.** / **42°05′ N, 70°10′ W**

Lone orca (17–18 feet long—sex uncertain, but most think it was female) hung around Provincetown so much during the summer of 1982 that it put a dent in the whale-watching business. People could stand on wharves and watch the orca performing like a trained animal (lobtailing, standing on head, etc.), so why pay to go out on boats? Charles "Stormy" Mayo, Ph.D., first saw the orca sometime in May, the first day it was sighted in New England waters. He was heading into harbor on a fast whale-watching vessel (17 knots), and the orca was "ghosting" along on the port quarter, under and to one side of them. Stormy was sure it wasn't getting the benefit of a stern-wave thrust but was pacing them and didn't even seem to be working hard.

He said it was surfacing for air about every two minutes or so. It seemed an easy pace.

The orca hung around Provincetown for two days, then went all the way up the coast to Eastport, Maine. (Some controversy as to whether the same animal accounted for both these sightings.) Stormy found it a very peculiar animal. He spent a lot of time with it, and one time when it was in danger of stranding, he got into the water with it. A daunting experience, he said. The orca had wandered behind sandbars into an area that goes dry at ebb tide, so he lured it out by getting it to follow him in a small rowboat. It "ghosted" along beneath the boat, much the way it had followed their high-speed boat. It loved to follow boats. In late September or early October it was back in Provincetown, then left and was never seen again, to his knowledge.

I asked Stormy if he thought it might have been a navy animal, or at least an animal held captive and trained by someone. He said that possibility had been raised by others, and it wasn't out of the question, but no one ever claimed the orca. Personal interview with Charles Mayo III at the Center for Coastal Studies, Provincetown, Mass., 5-7-86.

Patricia Fiorelli at the New England Aquarium, Boston, Mass., collected all movement data on this animal and submitted same for publication. Nature/date of publication unknown, but the orca's movements are summarized in sighting #126.

#137. 6-29-82 / 40 nautical miles southeast of Montauk Point, Long Island / 40°32′ N, 71°29′ W

Three orcas sighted. No further data. GMWSN (pers. comm. from S. Sadove).

#138. 7-4-82 / Newfoundland, Canada / 44°28′ N, 50°04′ W

Ten to twelve orcas were seen attacking twenty to thirty humpbacks on Southeast Shoal of the Grand Bank of Newfoundland. Orca pod included three adult males 17–22 feet long, and seven to nine smaller ones. Orcas rushed humpbacks, which were seen to turn bellies toward attacking orcas and thrash with flukes. Turning and rolling were also common responses to attack, together with loud "wheezing" blows. Attacks observed for several hours. Open wounds seen on three humpbacks. Many lumps of stringy blubber with bits of attached flesh seen floating in water. Whitehead and Glass, "Orcas Attack Humpback Whales," 183–85. See also sighting #161.

#139. 7-7-82 / Colson's Cove, New Brunswick, Canada / 45°05′ N, 67°04′ W

One orca followed boat. Curious. GMWSN (pers. comm. from R. Reeves).

#140. 7-13-82 / well east of Jeffreys Ledge, N.H. / 43°10′ N, 69°50′ W

Eight orcas reported to me by Scott Mercer, but Scott has never seen orcas himself, so this must be a secondhand report. NEWWI.

#141. 7-20-82 / Tenants Harbor, Maine / 43°58′ N, 69°11′ W
One orca sighted. Curious, circled boats. GMWSN (personal communication from A. Fuller).

#142. 8-12-82 / Stellwagen Bank, Mass. / 42°25′ N, 70°10′ W
Two pods sighted, one with ten, the other with twenty orcas. One included a cow with calf. GMWSN (from CCS).

#143. 8-12-82 / Stellwagen Bank, Mass. / 42°20′ N, 70°05′ W
Two to three orcas sighted. No further data. GMWSN (from CCS).

#144. 8-13-82 / between Frenchboro, Long Island, and Swans Island, Maine / 44°08′ N, 68°22′ W
One orca sighted, entangled through mouth with rope from lobster gear. Rope removed by two lobster fishermen who said orca lifted its head onto the side of their boat, making it easier for them to cut the line from its mouth. The rope left an abrasion on the skin around the orca's mouth. GMWSN (pers. comm. from S. Grierson).

#145. 8-13-82 / Stellwagen Bank, Mass. / 42°10′ N, 70°05′ W
Two pods sighted, one with fifteen, the other with twenty orcas. No further data. GMWSN (from CCS).

#146. 8-20-82 / Lubec, Maine / 44°53′ N, 67°01′ W
One orca sighted. No further data. GMWSN (pers. comm. from S. Kraus).

#147. 8-20-82 / Head Harbor Passage, New Brunswick, Canada / 44°55′ N, 66°55′ W
One orca sighted. Small dorsal fin. Could be female or subadult male. Photos taken. GMWSN (from NEA).

#148. 8-25-82 / between Bear Island and Suttons Island, Maine / 44°17′ N, 68°16′ W
One orca sighted. No further data. GMWSN (pers. comm. from R. Bowman).

#149. Summer 1982 / Head Harbor Island, New Brunswick, Canada / 44°57′ N, 66°54′ W
A handline fisherman, brother of Reid Wilson (see sighting #151), reported to Bruce McInnis that he had seen four orcas at Head Harbor Island, which lies off the northeast tip of Campobello Island, near East Quoddy Head. Personal communication, Bruce McInnis to author, 12-9-86.

#150. Summer 1982 / Morton Ledge, Maine / 44°48′ N, 66°59′ W
A day or so (no more than a week) prior to sighting #151, Bruce McInnis "saw what I took to be this lone female (the orca reported in sighting in #151) at Morton Ledge." Personal communication, Bruce McInnis to author, 12-9-86.

#151. Summer 1982 / Coffins Ledge, Maine (almost in Canadian waters) / 44°55′ N, 66°58′ W
Lone orca sighted by handline fishermen. Bruce McInnis estimates length at 25 feet. Sickle-shaped dorsal fin. Saddle. Thought to be female. Orca came "so close you could touch her" and followed one of Reid Wilson's boat more than others. Mr. McInnis later checked a book to confirm that it was an orca he had seen. "Lots of fish on the ledge that day. Mackerel and cod and pollock, I think. That was the last year there was any fish on the ledge, as a matter of fact, except for a few mackerel. . . . All this happened in 1982, I think. It was summer time . . . June, July, or August. Although there are numerous whales around here in the summer, I had never seen a killer before or since." Personal communication, Bruce McInnis to author, 12–9–86.

#152. 9–2–82 / Hingham, Mass. / 42°15′ N, 70°53′ W
One orca sighted. Circled around boat. *Quincy Patriot Ledger* (Quincy, Mass.)

#153. 9–4–82 / Boston Harbor, Mass. / 42°20′ N, 71°01′ W
One orca sighted next to New England Aquarium Discovery barge. (Author's note: The aquarium's dolphins are kept in the barge; their vocalizations may have attracted the orca.) GMWSN (pers. comm. from S. Kraus).

#154. mid–September 1982 / Jeffreys Ledge, N.H. / 42°55′ N, 70°10′ W
Three orcas seen moving southwestward across southern third of Jeffreys Ledge. Observer: Captain Jack Hilton of M/V *New Englander.* NEWWI.

#155. 9–23–82 / Frenchman's Bay, Maine / 44°26′ N, 68°12′ W
One orca followed boat. Occupant(s) fed it lobster bait. GMWSN #82025 (pers. comm. from Mrs. B. Jones).

#156. October 1982 / Provincetown, Mass. / 42°03′ N, 70°10′ W
Robert Lamarche from Malibu, Calif., was able to pat the young orca that hung around the Provincetown pier and harbor areas for a week or more in October 1982. Personal communication from Robert White, Provincetown harbormaster, to author, 12–9–86.

#157. 11–20–82 / Dipper Harbor, New Brunswick, Canada / 45°05′ N, 67°04′ W
One orca sighted. Followed boat, acted "friendly." GMWSN (pers. comm. from B. Scott).

#158. 11–24–82 / 120 miles east of Vero Beach, Fla. / approx. 27°40′ N, 78°20′ W
Four orcas photographed. Three adults with calf. At least one male. (By this, I presume observer meant mature male with high dorsal fin.) MMEP #MME00907.

#159. **1983 / 10 miles east of Newburyport, Mass. / 42°50′ N, 70°40′ W**
One orca sighted near Hampton Shoal Light. NEWWI.

#160. **3-30-83 / Topsail, Newfoundland, Canada / approx. 46°40′ N, 53°30′ W**
One orca entrapped in ice on Avalon Peninsula. Data collected by Jon Lien, Memorial University of Newfoundland, St. Johns, Canada. MMEP #STR05496.

#161. **6-25-83 / some 22 miles northwest of Southeast Shoal, Grand Bank, Newfoundland, Canada / 44°49′ N, 50°10′ W**
Observers saw about seventeen orcas (three large males, two small calves, and about twelve medium-sized animals) attacking humpbacks, which defended themselves with vigorous fluke thrashes. No lumps of floating flesh sighted. Only one small flesh wound seen. Orcas did not appear intent on killing, but merely obtaining mouthfuls of flesh or perhaps testing whales for weakness. (This attack took place within 22 miles of the place where a similar event was seen by the same observers one year earlier. See sighting #138.) See also sighting #162. Whitehead and Glass, "Orcas Attack Humpback Whales," 182–85.

#162. **6-26-83 / some 22 miles northwest of Southeast Shoal, Grand Bank, Newfoundland, Canada / 44°49′ N, 50°10′ W**
Observers saw about seventeen orcas (three large males, two small calves, and about twelve medium-sized animals) attacking humpbacks. Attacks less vigorous than on 6-25-83 (see sighting #161), and humpbacks' defensive measures almost leisurely. No lumps of flloating flesh sighted. Only one small flesh wound seen. Orcas did not appear intent on killing, but merely obtaining mouthfuls of flesh or perhaps testing whales for weakness. Whitehead and Glass, "Orcas Attack Humpback Whales," 183–85.

#163. **Summer 1983 / Hampton Shoal Ledge, N.H. / 42°50′ N, 70°40′ W**
Captains Bill and Mike Neelon saw one orca about 2 miles off Hampton Beach, near Hampton Shoal Ledge. They followed it for an hour. Bill thinks it was in June. Mike thinks it was in August. They agree on the year. Personal interview with shipmasters Bill and Mike Neelon, NEWWI, 5-19-86.

#164. **9-16-84 / Mingan Islands, Quebec, Gulf of St. Lawrence, Canada / 50°07′ N, 63°53′ W**
Richard Sears, founder and director of the Mingan Islands Cetacean Study, saw three orcas attack and eat a minke whale. When Sears first noticed the attack, the minke was alive and struggling. By the time Sears's boat reached the scene, the minke was dead. Chunks of blubber and flesh weighing up to fifty pounds were floating about the area. At one point, an orca surfaced with the entire minke in its jaws.

A finback passed nearby, unmolested and apparently unperturbed. Personal interview with Richard Sears, MICS, in Tadoussac, Quebec, 10-1-86.

#165. Summer 1985 / Jeffreys Ledge, N.H. / 43°11′ N, 69°58′ W
Tuna fisherman anchored on the extreme northern end of Jeffreys Ledge reported seeing a group of small whales with visible blows coming into the area. He remarked that they had extremely large back fins. Mercer, *Observations of Cetaceans on Jeffrey's Ledge.*

#166. 10-23-85 / New Scantum Ledge, N.H. / 42°50′ N, 70°22′ W
0730 hours. While towing gear and watching two finback whales, Captain D. Goethel of the sterndragger *Ellen Diane* from Hampton, N.H., saw a lone killer whale approach at high speed directly out of the sun glare from the east. The orca moved directly toward the finback whales and came very close to the smaller of the two finbacks. The killer whale sounded and apparently moved off. Captain Goethel did not see the killer whale again and reported that the finback whales seemed undisturbed. Mercer, ibid.

#167. 3-22-86 / about 50 miles due south of Martha's Vineyard Island, Mass. / 40°04′ N, 70°31′ W
1000 hours. Sunny, two-foot seas. Water temperature 9° C (48° F). Nearest landmark, Long Island, N.Y. Depth 80 fathoms. Eighteen-foot male killer whale seen at distance of 200 feet, feeding on over-flow of squid from net of Spanish trawler. No photos. Gannets and gulls seen near orca. Reported by NMFS observer (Steve Cadria?) stationed aboard Spanish trawler. NMFS/Gloucester.

#168. May 1986 / Gulf of St. Lawrence, Quebec, Canada / 50°00′ N, 64°00′ W
Normand Dupuis, a fisherman from Long Point, Quebec, told MICS that he saw about ten orcas between Longue Pointe de Mingan and Anticosti Island (both located in northern part of Gulf of St. Lawrence) in May 1986. MICS.

#169. 7-25-86 / Gloucester Harbor, Mass. / 42°40′ N, 70°40′ W
One juvenile orca sighted, 12-14 feet long. (Given coordinates inter-sect some 4 miles north of Gloucester Harbor, in Ipswich Bay, Mass.) GMWSN (pers. comm. from M. Weinrich).

#170. 8-6-86 / Nomans Island (small island just south of Martha's Vineyard Island), Mass. / 41°15′ N, 70°50′ W
One orca sighted. No further data. MMEP (unnumbered).

#171. 8-14-86 / Stellwagen Bank, 15 miles northeast of Provincetown, Mass. / 42°15′ N, 70°00′ W
"@2015; 7 to 9 Orcas at loran location 13714/44157; they were travel-ing at the surface and occasionally lobtailed." Personal communica-tion from Sharon Pittman, CCS, to author, 10-6-86.

#172. 8–14–86 / Stellwagen Bank, 12 miles northeast of Provincetown, Mass. / 42°10′ N, 70°00′ W

A pod of twelve orcas and another pod of seventeen orcas were seen breaching and traveling. GMWSN (from CCS).

#173. 8–14–86 / Stellwagen Bank, 4 miles northwest of Race Point, Provincetown, Mass. / 42°07′ N, 70°15′ W

"@ 1745; 7 Orcas were sighted at loran location 13844/44139 and their behavior was surface traveling and short dives." See also sighting #175. Personal communication from Sharon Pittman, CCS, to author, 10–6–86.

#174. 8–26–86 / Cape Cod Bay, Mass. / 41°50′ N, 70°20′ W

"On the morning of Aug. 26, 1986, myself and crew left Barnstable harbor for day of tuna fishing in Cape Cod Bay. Once reaching 80 ft. of water northwest of the Barn [stable] Bell, I sighted a pod of whales splashing around [breaching]. There were 2 cows, 2 calves, and one large bull 20–25 feet in length. Once I reached them, they started traveling north at approx. 10 kts. After going north for about 3 miles you could see another pod of whales coming west as [if] to intercept the pod moving north. The group moving west consisted of 2 adult whales and about 50–75 *tuna* which they had corralled and would not let dive. The tuna were from 600–700 lbs. The two pods of whales then met up and they really had the tuna corralled up. At this point one of the other boats that was following the whales went right in amongst them and harpooned a tuna. Once I saw that I did the same thing. Several other boats did the same. All in all 6 fish were stuck as the whales kept them up. The whales kept this up as I understand for another couple of miles to the north. I do not know what happened because as soon as I stuck my fish it sounded and went due south. From what I understand the orcas lost the fish." Personal correspondence from Frank Budges, East Sandwich, Mass., to author, 10–10–86.

#175. September 1986 / Plymouth, Mass. / 42°00′ N, 70°30′ W

While in Newburyport, Mass. one day, I happened to encounter John B. Heiser, Ph.D., director of the Shoals Marine Lab (Appledore Island, Isles of Shoals, New Hampshire). Aware of my interest in orcas, he told me that some had been sighted near Plymouth. These may be the same ones in sighting #173. Personal interview with author, early September 1986.

#176. 10–1–86 / Mingan Islands, Gulf of St. Lawrence, Canada / approx. 50°00′ N, 64°00′ W

Richard Sears, director of MICS, told me that personnel at his Mingan Islands research station saw three orcas with a calf of the current year that morning. Personal interview with author at Tadoussac, Quebec, 10-1-86.

#177. 3-7-87 / north of Cape Hatteras, S.C. / 35°30′ N, 75°30′ W
Three orcas sighted. One adult male with distinctive notch (presumably dorsal fin). One humpback also sighted (presumably near orcas). No further data. GMWSN (pers. comm. from D. Lee).

#178. Summer 1988 / Mingan Islands, Gulf of St. Lawrence, Quebec, Canada / approx. 50°00′ N, 64°00′ W
Judith Beard, Ph.D., College of the Atlantic, Bar Harbor, Maine, mentioned seeing dramatic slides showing a minke being killed and consumed within ten minutes by a pod of ten orcas. Photos were taken by Richard Sears of MICS. Sears said the orcas immediately ripped out the minke's throat pleats. (These grooves may provide an ideal grip and enable orcas to tear into a minke's vitals.) Sears noted that the speed with which the orcas consumed the minke may explain why more such incidents are not reported. An observer would have to be in the right place at the right time. Telephone interview with Judith Beard, GMWSN, 5-2-89.

Part 2   Sightings for Which Dates Are Unknown or Uncertain

#179. Date unknown / Ipswich Bay, Mass. / 42°40′ N, 70°50′ W
Tudor Leland, a sport fisherman, saw more than one hundred orcas in Ipswich Bay. Cows and calves swam abreast of each other in a rank, with an adult male at each end of rank. Calves quite young, about 6–8 feet long. Most amazing, a finback was traveling with them. Tudor says orcas generally show up around Cape Ann about once a year, but he hasn't seen any in last couple of years (1984–1985). Telephone interview with Tudor Leland, Beverly Farms, Mass., 5-11-86.

#180. Date unknown / 5 miles off Brandt Point, Scituate, Mass. / 42°10′ N, 70°30′ W
Tudor Leland has heard that on two occasions orcas have attacked humpbacks near "H" buoy, 5 miles off Brandt Point, between Plymouth and Scituate, Mass. Telephone interview with Tudor Leland, Beverly Farms, Mass. 5-11-86. Captain Francis, Scituate harbormaster, knows nothing of these attacks. Nor does Ralph Savery, assistant Plymouth harbormaster.

#181. Date unknown / northern tip of Cape Cod, Mass. / 42°05′ N, 70°20′ W

Captain Charles Mayo (father of Dr. Charles "Stormy" Mayo III) has seen orcas surface with tuna weighing 500 pounds or more in jaws. Sometimes other orcas would surface either side of first, trying to get their share of tuna. While orcas fed below, he has seen chunks of tuna flesh floating about, being eaten by gulls. Has seen pods of ten orcas patrolling Truro coast, often in groups of two. Has seen similar-size pods off Race Point, Provincetown, Mass. Used to see orcas every year, at peak of tuna run, mid- to late July. (This agrees with Cape Ann sightings, most of which historically occur in late July, August, and early September.) And this concurrence agrees with Bigelow and Schroeder (*Fishes of the Gulf of Maine*), who cite tuna as historically appearing at Cape Ann, Cape Cod, etc., at about the same time each summer and showing little north-south movement within the Gulf of Maine. Personal interview with Captain Charles Mayo, Provincetown, Mass., 5–8–86.

#182. Date unknown / northern tip of Cape Cod, Mass. / 42°02′ N, 70°10′ W

Captain Charles Mayo recalls that one of the most spectacular orca-tuna attacks occurred just outside Long Point, near bell buoy. Mayo had been fishing patches of tuna here and there. One school of two-hundred-pounders (about two hundred to three hundred of them) was "cartwheeling" at surface in a perfect circle, so he trolled his baits, but tuna ignored them. Then Mayo saw two orcas about 1.5 miles south, so he backed his boat off 50–75 yards and watched. Orcas swam swiftly within 100–150 yards of tuna, then slowed and approached like stalking cats, scarcely blowing when they surfaced, being very quiet. Tuna maintained a tight circle, swimming with fins breaking water. Orcas dove. For a time, no sign of them. Tuna still tightly circling. Then, like an explosion in center of tuna, orcas struck. Tuna scattered in all directions, trying so hard to escape that their tails were half out of water and they couldn't get enough thrust to reach full speed. They swam to Mayo's boat and huddled against it (Mayo also has seen mackerel do this when pursued by tuna). The two orcas went off in two different directions.

One year, Provincetown harbor was choked with giant tuna for two to three days because orcas were patrolling just outside harbor. In addition to tuna, orcas prey on mackerel when abundant.

Personal interview with Captain Charles Mayo, Provincetown, Mass., 5–8–86.

#183. 1950s / northern tip of Cape Cod, Mass. / 42°06′ N, 70°15′ W

The largest group of orcas Captain Charles Mayo ever saw was fifteen to twenty, in the 1950s, about 5 miles north of Race Station. Hard to judge how many, because orcas surfaced in relays, eight to nine at a time, coming up nearly underneath boat. But within a mile or so of boat, Mayo thinks there may have been fifteen to twenty animals. Difficult to count them because they can move so quickly when they want to, and they keep exchanging positions or surfacing in respiratory groups. Captain Mayo told everyone to reel in and remove hooks, then troll hookless baits to see what orcas would do. Orcas stayed with boat for a good hour, rolling onto their sides to look up at people. (Mayo mentioned in passing that 1948 was a big year for tuna. No Gulf of Maine orca sightings for 1948 in my data base as yet.) Personal interview with Captain Charles Mayo, Provincetown, Mass., 5–8–86.

#184. 1960 / northern tip of Cape Cod, Mass. / 42°02′ N, 70°10′ W
Captain Charles Mayo of Provincetown, Mass., saw orcas outside the Long Point bell buoy, probably in July or August. Personal interview with Captain Charles Mayo, Provincetown, Mass., 5–8–86.

#185. 1946–1986 / coastal waters, New Jersey to Massachusetts
Frank Cyganowski, former owner of M/V *A. A. Ferranti* and pioneer of local bluefin purse seine fishery, either saw orcas or heard about them every fall (mid-August thru September), but usually in Massachusetts Bay and the "back side" (southeast side) of Cape Cod off Chatham, Mass., where he fished for the big tuna, not off Long Island and New Jersey, where he fished for the smaller ones. When he did see orcas, they were in the area of bluefins, but they could have been feeding on anything. He himself has never seen an orca with a bluefin in its mouth. Telephone interview with Frank Cyganowski, New Bedford, Mass., 6–10–86.

#186. Sometime between 1966 and 1971 / Provincetown Harbor, Mass. / 42°02′ N, 70°10′ W
Harpoon tuna fishermen Sonny McIntyre and Dana Kangas both recall that orcas trapped tuna in Provincetown Harbor one summer and drove them among bathers. Tuna were leaping sandbars, stranding themselves, etc. Beaches red with blood. Orcas reportedly continued feeding orgy for days. Dana Kangas recalls that this occurred in September, because he had to go back to school while it was happening. Telephone interviews with Sonny McIntyre, Ogunquit, Maine, and Dana Kangas, Gloucester, Mass., 6–10–86.

#187. 1960–1986 / coastal waters of Massachusetts
Sonny Avalar, captain and owner of M/V *Ruth & Pat* says that he and his spotter pilot have never seen orcas inside Cape Cod Bay or around Cape Ann, except for one time near Provincetown. (Strange. Seems to contradict most other sources.) Usually saw orcas south of

Nomans Land (a small island 3 miles south of Martha's Vineyard, Mass.) and up on Georges Bank. Avalar has been working with spotter planes for twenty-five years and has seen orcas more in swordfishing waters (colder) than in school (subadult) bluefin waters (warmer). About 35–40 miles south-southwest of Nomans Land seems popular with orcas. Telephone interview with Sonny Avalar, New Bedford, Mass., 6–10–86.

#188. Early 1980s, probably in June / Isles of Shoals, N.H. / 43°00′ N, 70°35′ W

Pod of orcas reported close to rocks on Duck Island, Isles of Shoals, N.H., perhaps hoping to prey on newly weaned harbor seal pups. Followed by a vessel, orcas headed easterly toward Jeffreys Ledge. Gormley, *A Dolphin Summer,* 72.

#189. 1980s / northern tip of Cape Cod, Mass. / 42°06′ N, 70°15′ W

Dr. Charles "Stormy" Mayo III recalled a day when, at sea near Provincetown, he saw a group of finbacks and a pod of orcas approach each other. Expecting a bloodbath, he had an associate videotape the scene. To his surprise, the orcas and finbacks passed through each other's ranks like cards being shuffled and went their separate ways with no sign of trouble. No evasive maneuvers by the finbacks. Personal interview with Dr. Charles "Stormy" Mayo, CCS, Provincetown, Mass., 5–9–86.

#190. Sometime in 1980 or 1981 / Boon Island, Maine / 43°08′ N, 70°30′ W

Harpoon tuna fisherman Sonny McIntyre saw fifteen to twenty orcas spread out in groups of two to three outside Boon Island off York, Maine. Telephone interview with Sonny McIntyre, Ogunquit, Maine, 6–10–86.

#191. July or August of 1980 or 1981 / Isles of Shoals, N.H. / 42°58′ N, 70°38′ W

Harpoon tuna fisherman Dana Kangas, skipper of M/V *Coot,* saw four to five groups of a dozen orcas each (total of forty-five to sixty animals), coming out of northwest and "going like hell" southeastward. There had been plenty of bluefin tuna in area all morning, but long before orcas showed up, tuna disappeared. That was largest number of orcas he had ever seen. He hasn't seen orcas very often, but recalls seeing them now and then in Ipswich Bay, Mass. Telephone interview with Dana Kangas, Gloucester, Mass., 6–10–86.

NOTES

For complete references, see Bibliography.

CHAPTER ONE *(pages 1–19)*

1. Heezen and Johnson, "Alaskan Submarine Cables." A dead orca was found tangled in a submarine cable at a depth of 563 fathoms (3,378 feet). If the animal dove this deep and entangled itself, this is the deepest orca dive on record. In fact, it rivals the deepest recorded dives for sperm whales. This makes me suspect that the orca was dying, sank to the bottom, and became entangled.

2. As described in Mitchell and Baker, "Age of 'Old Tom,'" the Eden Museum in New South Wales, Australia, displays a killer whale skeleton thought to be that of "Old Tom," one of the orcas that maintained a symbiotic relationship with generations of whalers around Twofold Bay. The old whalers there swear that "Old Tom" was about ninety years old when he died and washed ashore. Some scientists think he was much younger (see note 7). Whatever this orca's age at death, its teeth are certainly the worse for wear. Half a dozen are blackened and worn so flat that they look like blunt pencil leads. Two teeth are missing from the upper jaw, front right, where there is evidence of an abscess. The authors cite five other references documenting dental abscesses in killer whales.

3. Cousteau and Diole, *Whale,* 86. A sperm whale seemed to feel no pain when stuck with a harpoon too short to penetrate beyond the blubber.

4. "Wolves of the Sea," 46; Hancock, "Killer Whales," 341–42; Hoyt, *"Orcinus orca,"* 25; Hoyt, *Whale Killed Caller,* 43.

Both Hoyt citations recount the incident reported by biologist David Hancock. In May 1964, on the west coast of Vancouver Island, British Columbia, Hancock saw a pod of orcas slaughter a minke whale. The next day he found the carcass minus lips and tongue, neatly stripped of its skin, but with the blubber and flesh intact. Hancock described the appearance as "being that of a freshly peeled orange." Two months later, in the same general area, Hancock found another minke that had apparently met a similar fate — i.e., stripped of its skin.

While I was on a research expedition in Canada's Gulf of St. Lawrence in 1986, Richard Sears, founder and director of the Mingan Island Research Center, told me he had seen three orcas attack and eat a minke whale in the Gulf of St. Lawrence two years earlier (1984). When Sears first noticed the attack, the minke was alive and struggling. By the time Sears reached the scene, the minke was dead. Chunks of blubber and flesh weighing up to fifty pounds were floating about the area. At one point, an orca surfaced with the entire minke in its jaws. A finback passed nearby, unmolested and apparently unperturbed.

Erich Hoyt in *Orca,* p. 72, writes: "Russian studies of orcas' stomach contents in the early 1970s had revealed that minke whales were the main and sometimes exclusive food item for orcas at certain seasons and in certain sectors of the Antarctic."

5. Whitehead and Glass, "Orcas Attack Humpbacks." This paper is summarized in appendix sightings #138, #161, and #162.

6. Many of these parallel scars appear on the humpbacks' flukes, or at least are more noticeable there because scientists use fluke photographs to identify individual humpbacks.

When I interviewed Dr. Charles "Stormy" Mayo at the Center for Coastal Studies in Provincetown, Mass. (9 May 1986), he expressed skepticism about these scars being caused by orcas. He finds it hard to believe that if orcas seized humpbacks by the tails, they would merely leave rake marks. More likely, he thinks, they would shred the whale's flukes or bite them off altogether. Also, he cited evidence that many of these scars are inflicted neither at the humpbacks' northern feeding grounds nor at their tropical mating/calving grounds, but somewhere in between. Believing the scars to be caused by false killer whales (*Pseudorca crassidens*) encountered during the humpbacks' midocean migrations, he had students compare typical pseudorca tooth spacing to scars visible in humpback photographs. According to Dr. Mayo, the spacings matched. Pseudorcas have revealed themselves to be fierce predators undeserving of the name "false" killer whale, but many scientists disagree with Dr. Mayo's pseudorca hypothesis.

Soviet whalers in southern oceans have reported many orca bite marks on fins of large whales, but few remains of such whales in orca stomachs. In *Orca,* p. 164, Hoyt reported that eighteen percent of gray whales examined at a California whaling station during the 1960s showed signs of having been attacked by orcas, but that accounts of successful attacks were rare.

Thus it seems that orcas often attack large whales but do not often kill them. Still, this does not necessarily mean that most such attacks are unsuccessful, for orcas may not always try to kill. Depending on appetite or mood, they may sometimes simply sample favorite parts of large prey.

7. In *A Natural History of Marine Mammals,* p. 101, Dr. Victor Scheffer states, "A male killer whale with peculiar markings was seen along the Australian coast for more than 90 years. He was known as Old Tom." Apparently favoring an orca life span of more like thirty years, Dr. Scheffer added, "Almost certainly, though, there were several 'Old Toms' of the same bloodline, separated by a generation or more." That there were several "Old Toms" is, of course, no more certain than that one could have lived for ninety years.

Mitchell and Baker (see note 2) concluded from a count of dentinal growth layers in a tooth thought to be from the skeleton of "Old Tom" that the bull lived for about thirty-five years, not the fifty to ninety years previously reported. Still, the authors admit that much subjectivity and interpretation is involved in this aging process. In "Toward Calibrating Dentinal Layers," Myrick, Yochem, and Cornell concluded that new methods for estimating age in orcas older than twenty years should be explored.

8. Michael Bigg, personal communication, June 1986.

9. Bigg, "Killer Whale Stocks off Vancouver Island," 655.

10. John K. Ford, West Coast Whale Research Foundation, Vancouver, B.C., stated in a personal communication dated 21 July 1986: "Recently, we have begun to question the validity of the pod as a social entity. The most important social group is the maternal group, several of which may travel together for some time to form a pod. Pods actually may fragment quite frequently, with maternal groups spending considerable time on their own."

It has long been assumed that orca pods are led by adult males, but recent findings in British Columbia suggest that some pods may be matriarchies, as is the case with elephant herds. Unlike bull elephants, however, mature orca males seem to stay with the extended families into which they are born.

CHAPTER TWO *(pages 20–32)*

1. Ford and Ford, "Killer Whales of B.C.," 15. The Fords saw an orca repeatedly release a six-pound salmon, then suck it back into its mouth. The interaction with the little calf is fictional embellishment on my part.

2. I have no data to confirm that orcas skin birds before eating them. However, other species that prey on birds avoid eating the feathers, so I presume that orcas do the same. I borrowed the skinning technique from the leopard seal, which skins a penguin with a violent sideways whipping motion of the head that wrenches the bird right out of its pelt. Orcas do

not have the neck mobility of seals, but in Patagonia, big bull orcas have been filmed tossing sea lion pups around in much the same way and with considerable force. (When doing this, a given orca seems always to flip its prey in the same direction, say to the right. Perhaps, like us, they tend to be right-handed or left-handed.)

In *Icebound Summer,* p. 35, Sally Carrighar depicts an orca snapping a seal out of its skin to get rid of the indigestible fur. The rest of her book was carefully researched, so I presume that this behavior is documented.

3. Marden, "The Continental Shelf," 496–98, 510–11. This article includes beautiful, informative paintings of the shelf's undersea topography.

4. Apollonio, *Gulf of Maine,* 18, 19.

5. Burton and Burton, *International Wildlife Encyclopedia,* 1395.

6. Bigelow and Schroeder, *Fishes of Gulf of Maine,* 26.

7. Ellis, *Book of Sharks,* 90.

8. Ibid., 81.

9. Ibid., 67.

10. Bigelow and Schroeder, 27.

11. Ellis, 91.

12. Burton and Burton, ibid.

13. Ellis, 97.

CHAPTER THREE *(pages 33–42)*

1. By traveling eighty miles in about thirteen hours, our orcas would have averaged five knots. Based on my readings, this speed is well within reason, even if the animals stopped to rest or feed. *Alaska Geographic*'s 1978 special issue on whales states that "killer whales have been clocked at a steady 25 knots" (p. 101) and that "some tracked groups averaged 75 miles a day" (p. 103). "The Orca (Killer) Whale" states: "Orcas are rapid swimmers, reaching speeds in excess of 30 miles per hour [26 knots]. One B.C. transient pod covered 550 km (350 miles) in 6 days" (p. 7).

2. Bigelow and Schroeder, *Fishes of Gulf of Maine,* 346.

CHAPTER FOUR *(pages 43–59)*

1. This scene is based on an incident reported to me by harpoon fisherman Frank Budges of East Sandwich, Mass., in a letter dated 10 October 1986. See appendix sighting #174.

2. Mayo et al., *Humpback Whales,* 53; Mattila, Guinee, and Mayo, "Humpback Whale Songs." Until recently, it was assumed that humpbacks sang only on their tropical breeding grounds, but scientists are now finding that

they do a fair amount of singing in the Gulf of Maine. The cited references indicate that humpbacks apparently start singing before migration to their low-latitude wintering grounds, and that singing on the high-latitude feeding grounds is common in autumn.

Singing on the northern feeding grounds may be associated with courtship behavior, for most female humpbacks with new calves seem to be accompanied by male escorts. This could be a sign that females come into a second heat while nursing, which may be nature's way of compensating for inevitable mortalities among the calves. Then again, singing activity on the northern feeding grounds could simply be a warm-up exercise. During this period, males may exchange songs and settle on the major musical theme that all will use after they reach their tropical breeding grounds.

3. Other species have been observed seeking safety alongside vessels. A photo caption (p. 103) in *Alaska Geographic*'s special 1978 issue on whales reads: "When chased by killer whales, sea lions will take shelter against whatever they can, in this case a boat. In top photo, a killer whale (spy-hopping) watches sea lion herd, which is huddled off bow of a Japanese stern trawler. In photo above, sea lions swim frantically off bow of ship, with killer whales (about 6) in foreground. The sea lions are porpoising and scared." (Photo credit: Mil Zahn, National Marine Fisheries Service.)

While preparing this manuscript for typesetting, my copyeditor, Mary Anne Stewart, attached a note relating that a California salmon fisherman working outside Half Moon Bay, just south of San Francisco, saw a sea lion escape a great white shark by jumping into a small boat.

4. Captain Charles Mayo (father of Dr. Charles "Stormy" Mayo) related this and other orca incidents to me over dinner in Provincetown on 8 May 1986. The incident described here occurred sometime during the 1960s. I modified it somewhat to fit my narrative. Now retired, Captain Mayo had taken sport fishing parties out of Provincetown since 1920. He originated rod-and-reel bluefin fishing in 1937. From 1950 on, he contributed many valuable observations to Frank Mather and Frank Carey, tuna experts at Woods Hole Oceanographic Institute in Woods Hole, Mass.

5. This scene is fictionalized around fragmentary reports given me by two harpoon fishermen, Sonny McIntyre of Ogunquit, Maine, and Dana Kangas of Gloucester, Mass. (See appendix sighting #186). Neither man could recall just when the incident occurred, but they believe it was in the late 1960s. Dana Kangas recalls it as taking place in September, because he had to go back to school while it was happening. The publisher of the Provincetown *Advocate* vaguely recalls the event. Charles Mayo (see note 4) was at sea when it happened. My ads seeking reports of orca sightings drew no additional witnesses to this event. The scientists in the small boat are pure fiction.

CHAPTER FIVE *(pages 60–68)*

1. This hunting scene is based on field observations shared with me by William W. Rossiter, vice-president of Cetacean Society International, in a personal communication dated 20 November 1987. Using an inflatable boat, he followed this large herd of whitesides for five hours on 26 April 1985 and recorded his observations in a seven-page report complete with detailed chart. There were no orcas in the area at the time; that part of the scene is fictional.

The Atlantic white-sided dolphin (*Lagenorhynchus acutus*) is Bill Rossiter's favorite species for study, and he has spent many hours on and in the water with them. Knowing how many years it takes before you can observe marine life and really grasp what you are seeing, I find Bill Rossiter's powers of observation enviable.

2. Orcas in British Columbia have been studied closely since 1971 (Bigg, "Killer Whale Stocks off Vancouver Island"; Ford and Fisher, "Killer Whale Dialects"). It appears that these animals spend their entire lives in extended family pods with a high degree of genetic isolation.

3. These scenes are based on events related to me by Dr. "Stormy" Mayo during an inteview at Provincetown's Center for Coastal Studies on 9 May 1986. (See appendix sighting #136.) Despite his many years of working with marine mammals, he said it was "a daunting experience" to be in the water so close to a wild orca.

4. The orca/finback encounter, also related to me by Dr. Mayo (see note 3), actually occurred closer to Provincetown than I indicate in my narrative. (See appendix sighting #189.) Expecting a bloodbath, Dr. Mayo recorded the scene with his video camera, but the orcas and finbacks passed through each other's ranks "like cards being shuffled" and went their separate ways with no sign of hostility. Dr. Mayo noticed no evasive maneuvers on the part of the finbacks.

It seems to me that there must be clues in the body language (or more likely, the sounds) of orcas that let other species know whether they are hunting. Prey animals in Africa seem to known when lions or wild dogs are hunting or simply passing through an area. The same appears true of caribou vis-à-vis wolves.

CHAPTER SIX *(pages 69–91)*

1. Scientists have been able to hear and identify orca calls over distances of nine to ten miles in British Columbia, even with noisy vessel traffic in the area (Ford and Ford, "Killer Whales of B.C.," 29). I speculate that the funneling effects of Great South Channel and Northeast Channel, together

with the orcas' sensitivity to their own sounds, would enable them to hear each other over much greater distances.

2. International Whaling Commission, "Report of the Workshop on Killer Whale Populations," 13. See also chap. 1, note 10; chap. 5, note 2.

3. Ford and Ford, "Killer Whales of B.C."

4. John Ford, personal correspondence, 21 July 1986.

5. Lilly, *Dolphins,* 302–23.

6. Bigg, "Killer Whale Stocks off Vancouver Island"; Ford and Ford, ibid.; Ford and Fisher, "Killer Whale Dialects."

7. Ford, per. corr., ibid.

8. Ford and Fisher, ibid.

9. Ford, per. corr., ibid.

10. Hoyt, *Orca,* 54.

11. Ibid., 81.

12. Ibid., 106.

13. Lilly, ibid., 70, 102, 186–94, 338–64. Vocal exchanges between human and dolphin were recorded by Dr. Lilly on *Sounds and Ultrasounds of the Bottle-nose Dolphin.* Side 2 of the record describes Lilly's attempts to get dolphins to speak English.

14. Ford, "Acoustic Traditions of Killer Whales," 6.

CHAPTER SEVEN *(pages 92–105)*

1. Matthews, *The Whale,* 259. Kenneth S. Norris introduced here the concept of "ringing," suggesting that some objects sonared by cetaceans may resonate as well as returning echoes. Dr. Norris speculated that the "ringing" might tell cetaceans something about the objects they sonar.

2. Norris and Mohl, "Can Odontocete Cetaceans Immobilize Prey by Sound?"

3. Tangley, "A Whale of a Bang."

4. "Hearing Could Be Herring's Red Herring," 238.

5. Ibid.

6. Beardsley, "Sonic Punch," 36.

7. Hertz (Hz) has replaced cycles per second (cps) as the international standard of frequency. KHz stands for 1,000 Hz or 1,000 cycles per second.

Decibel (dB) is a measurement of sound intensity relative to the softest sound the average person can hear. Each dB represents about a twenty-five percent increase in loudness above the threshold of human hearing. Ordinary conversation has about a 70 dB intensity. A pneumatic drill of the type used to excavate streets reaches sound levels of about 100 dB. Sound intensities of 120 dB are one trillion times louder than the softest sounds we can hear and are at our threshold of pain. That is, above 120 dB, we do not perceive the stimulus as sound per se, but feel it as pain.

The higher pulse repetition rates achievable by dolphins are about 1,200 pulses per second. The highest frequencies emitted by dolphins are about 208 kHz (208,000 cycles per second). A pulse is made up of many different frequencies ranging from very low to high, all bunched together in a sudden, sharp burst of sound. The sharper the pulse (i.e., the more steeply it rises and falls), the higher the frequencies it contains. Pulses may contain frequencies as high as 208,000 cycles per second, but the repetition rates at which the dolphins emit the pulses are much lower, probably 1,200 pulses per second or less.

8. Mayo et al., *Humpback Whales*, 52–53.

9. My use of a bubble-blowing finback in the narrative is based on some interesting observations made by Scott Mercer of New England Whale Watch. One day in May of 1986 while I was at sea with him, he said he had noticed finbacks blowing bubble clouds over the last several years. I asked whether he thought they might be adopting this behavior as a result of observing humpbacks. If so, he said, they showed no signs of following through and swallowing fish trapped in their bubble clouds.

This could be the first stage in a fascinating case of interspecies learned behavior. If so, we may someday see finbacks using bubble-feeding techniques.

On p. 62 of Faith McNulty's *The Great Whales*, Roger Payne is quoted as suspecting that humpbacks might exhale underwater to avoid showing vapor, then surface for quick, quiet inhalations. At the time Dr. Payne expressed these thoughts (pre-1974), I believe the use of bubble clouds was not yet understood to be a feeding mechanism, so he may have mistaken bubble-feeding for furtive breathing. Still, his hypothesis is valid. Some survivors of whaling may have had the good sense to adopt furtive breathing habits. Finbacks in our area are notorious among whale watchers for giving them the "finback slip." Perhaps furtive breathing is another aspect of the wariness many finbacks show toward vessels that try to follow them.

In "At Home with Right Whales," p. 332, Dr. Payne describes right whales exhaling underwater to reduce their time at the surface, thereby exposing themselves as briefly as possible and maintaining greater speed (surface drag slows them). He neglects to point out that this exhaling technique also avoids sending talltale vapor columns into the air.

On p. 333 of the same article, Dr. Payne also mentions that he has had many whales breathe on him at close range, but only once has he smelled fetid breath. This is in marked contrast to my experience with humpbacks in the Gulf of Maine, some of which I have actually smelled before I saw them.

I never noticed humpback halitosis until 1986, though some local whale watchers say humpbacks have always smelled bad. This may be a matter of degree or subjective response. A number of times prior to 1986 (the year most humpbacks stayed far offshore), individuals exhaled into my face close enough to blow off my hat, and I noticed only a fishy odor, much like the breath of a dolphin. While I do not find that odor objectionable, it may repel other people. But the fetid breath I noticed in 1986 was not merely fishy; it smelled like *rotten* fish.

While observing North Atlantic humpbacks on their mating/calving grounds over Silver Bank in the Dominican Republic, I detected no signs of bad breath, nor have scientists who observe the whales there each year. Humpbacks do not feed while on their mating/calving grounds, so the odor may relate to feeding. To my knowledge, fetid breath has not been reported among any other whale species that visit the Gulf of Maine. Finbacks and minkes in the Gulf of Maine are often seen feeding together with humpbacks on the same prey species, so if the odor relates to feeding, it may be peculiar to humpbacks.

Or, bad breath may be peculiar to certain individuals. Having had a number of close encounters with odorless humpbacks, I am inclined to think that those with foul breath are ill. During a three-week period in December of 1986, ten humpbacks (two percent of the regional summer population) washed up dead along the Massachusetts coast. Red-tide poisoning (via ingested mackerel) is thought to be the cause of death, but I wonder whether some sort of respiratory infection may have been at work, as well. Humpbacks are known to carry a strain of diphtheria similar to that found in humans.

10. Ford and Ford, "Killer Whales of B.C.," 18–19.

11. Hoyt, *Orca,* 72–73.

12. Larson, "Minke/Orca Encounter," 2.

13. Personal interview conducted by telephone with Tudor Leland, Massachusetts sport fisherman, 11 May 1986.

14. Ford and Ford, ibid.

15. Altruistic behavior has many times been observed between cetacean species in captivity. Similar behavior has been seen in the wild (e.g., dolphins appearing to lead stranded whales into the safety of deeper water), though we have no way of knowing for certain the intentions behind such actions.

CHAPTER EIGHT *(pages 106–116)*

1. This type of foraging behavior may explain many reports of orca singletons and pairs, which are often seen making beelines toward points unknown.

2. While I was on a research expedition in Canada's Gulf of St. Lawrence in 1986, Richard Sears, founder and director of the Mingan Island Research

Center, gave an interesting lecture about blue whales. Aware of my interest in orcas, he included among his slides a photograph of a right whale being attacked by several orcas off the coast of South Africa, at the confluence of the Indian and Antarctic currents. The orcas reportedly managed to bite chunks out of the whale, but by rolling belly-up (presumably to protect its vitals) and defending itself with flippers and flukes, the right whale managed to fight off its attackers. The scene was photographed from a clifftop.

The scene in which the cow protects her calf by lifting it on her belly has no basis in fact as far as I know, but while at play, right whale calves often swim atop their mothers.

3. This attack was mentioned on page 130 of my book *A Dolphin Summer,* but that description was based on an erroneous report. I subsequently learned that the attack was reported not by Jay Neeland but by William Neelon of Newburyport, Mass. I interviewed Mr. Neelon and his brother Michael on 19 May 1986 aboard the New England Whale Watch vessel *Cetacea* in Newburyport. (See appendix sighting #99.)

4. The original report published by the Gulf of Maine Whale Sighting Network (GMWSN) cited forty to fifty orcas. When I interviewed William Neelon on 19 May 1986, he said it may have been more like twenty-five to thirty. He said the orcas divided into three groups before attacking, and that he seemed to recall no more than ten in each group. Other reports for that month and area (see appendix sightings #98, #100, #101) confirm that forty to forty-five orcas were in the vicinity, so Mr. Neelon's original estimate of forty to fifty may have been correct.

5. There is some evidence that finbacks are monogamous. They are most often seen in pairs, though identification of sex is difficult, and these dyads could be mother–calf pairs. Farley Mowat's *A Whale for the Killing* provides well-documented evidence for monogamy. In Mowat's factual account, a pregnant finback is trapped in a small Newfoundland bay for weeks, and during all that time a male remains just outside the bay, calling to her.

6. My scenario is speculative, but the concept of two mates protecting their calf would explain why three of the finbacks in the area that day did not flee when the orcas approached. Were the calf ill or injured, the trio would make a likely target for orcas. Whalers historically harpooned calves first, knowing that the mothers (and perhaps mates, as well) would try to save them. This way, the whalers were assured of more kills.

7. I see no need for orcas to impose passive restraint on finbacks from the rear, for finbacks cannot swim backward. They may be able to scull backward with their flippers, but certainly not with much speed or power. As for the orcas in front, if a sixty- to seventy-foot finback in fear of its life wanted to swim away, I doubt that the mere presence of two orcas at its snout would prevent it from moving. Given the reported lack of move-

ment on the part of the finbacks, my guess is that the orcas were gripping their flukes and snouts to prevent them from thrashing or turning belly-up, a maneuver large whales have been seen using to protect their vital organs from orcas. Also, the finbacks would have sunk once they lost consciousness or died, so the orcas would have had to hold them up.

8. I doubt that the finbacks were already dead at this point in the attack. It can take hours for an entire pride of African lions to kill one large buffalo, so I doubt that some forty orcas could kill three big finbacks in a matter of minutes. Perhaps, held head and tail by pairs of big orcas, the whales could scarcely move.

Another possibility is that orca attacks render some whales senseless with shock. On p. 9 of his article "Dolphin Sacred, Porpoise Profane," George Reiger includes the following description of killer whales in action, as set down in 1911 by naturalist Roy Chapman Andrews while he was aboard a Japanese whaler off the Korean coast:

> We were chasing a big gray whale about fifty feet long close inshore where he was trying to escape by sliding behind rocks. Suddenly, the high dorsal fins of a pack of killers appeared, cutting the water like giant black knives as the beasts dashed in. Utterly disregarding our ship, the killers made straight for the gray whale. The beast, twice the size of the killers, seemed paralyzed with fright. Instead of trying to get away, it turned belly up, flippers outspread, awaiting its fate. A killer came up at full speed, forced its head into the whale's mouth and ripped out great hunks of soft, spongy tongue. Other killers were tearing at the throat and belly while the poor creature rolled in agony. I was glad when a harpoon ended its torture.

Contrary to this account, gray whales have a reputation for being courageous fighters (whalers called them devilfish), but there are exceptions to every rule.

9. The actions of the harpoon fishermen are fictional, but two harpoon boats actually were on the scene that day. William Neelon (see note 3) recalled that the harpoon boats were from Maine, but he did not remember their hailing ports. I checked with harpoon fishermen in a number of Maine ports but could locate no one who had witnessed the attack.

The Neelon brothers suspect that most of the people out there that day were unaware of the attack. Even those who noticed the orcas and finbacks, if they were any distance away, probably did not realize what was happening.

10. On p. 76 of *A Dolphin Summer,* I wrote that orcas need ten percent of their body weight in food each day, but my files show no record of how I arrived at that figure. Estimates in the literature, based on the food consumption of captive orcas, range from three to eight percent of body weight per day. Active animals in the wild probably need more food than captives, but ten percent sounds high to me now.

Even using high-side figures, say ten percent of body weight and an average weight of six tons per orca, the daily food requirement for the three pods in this scene would figure out to only twenty-seven tons. Many tons of finback meat would have been left over for scavengers.

CHAPTER NINE *(pages 117–129)*

1. Such problems can result from respiratory infection and congestion or severe infestation of the nasopharyngeal passages by parasitic worms.

2. "Shad Tagging in the Bay of Fundy," 20.

3. *American Shad,* 8.

4. Grosslein and Azarovitz, *Fish Distribution,* 59–61.

5. "Shad Tagging in the Bay of Fundy," ibid.

6. Ibid.

7. *American Shad,* 4.

8. Appolonio, *Gulf of Maine,* map, 42.

9. Greenberg, "Modeling Tidal Power," 106.

10. The driving power and acceleration of orcas must be seen to be believed. From a standing start, I once saw a large bull (twenty-two to twenty-five feet long) immediately achieve several fluke beats per second. With only a few thrusts of his flukes, that bull covered a distance of some ninety feet within a matter of seconds. Imagine the strength required to move flukes six to nine feet broad that rapidly in a dense fluid.

Orcas dramatically demonstrate their strength off the coast of Patagonia, where they are often seen lobbing sea lions weighing several hundred pounds twenty to thirty feet into the air. I find it difficult to believe that orcas can move their big flukes broadside through the water fast enough to deliver such blows. Might they instead move their flukes edgewise? In "Patagonia's Wild Shore," pp. 314–15, Des and Jen Bartlett show an orca in the act of lobbing a sea lion aloft, and the flukes appear twisted to the whale's right. An edgewise chop would be far faster underwater than a broadside blow, and much more punishing to the prey. Then again, it might also damage the orca's flukes, which are largely soft tissue. I expect an orca could start with an edgewise chop, then just before striking the prey, twist its flukes to deliver a broadside blow.

11. Sperm whales often breach. So do gray and right whales. Humpbacks breach most frequently of all. While watching large whales breach, I have often wondered what speeds they must reach in order to hurl bodies weighing thirty to sixty tons out of the water. In *A Whale Called Killer,* p. 111, Erich Hoyt notes that orcas must reach exit speeds of at least twenty-two miles per hour (nineteen knots) in order to breach. It would seem that heavier animals, such as humpbacks, grays, sperm whales, and right whales,

would have to reach even higher exit speeds when breaching. Is this possible? These four species are generally considered slowpokes. (Sperm whales can maintain speeds of fifteen to twenty knots for ten minutes or more, but this usually constitutes escape behavior.)

In Chapter One I have humpbacks maneuvering with considerable speed and agility when attacked by orcas, but at the time I wrote that, I did not realize just *how* quickly they can move. Then I read "Why Whales Leap," in which (p. 85) Hal Whitehead calculates an exit speed of fifteen knots for breaching humpbacks. I take it that similar speeds would apply to right whales.

Apparently these seemingly slow whales can move very quickly when the need arises. This suggests to me that ramming might be another defense against orcas. The combination of flukes and long flippers certainly enables humpbacks to accelerate quickly over short distances. Imagine how an orca would fare, were it rammed at thirteen to seventeen knots by a forty-ton whale. Having come across no evidence of ramming, I did not use it in my narrative, but it is a possibility.

12. Watkins, Moore, and Tyack, "Sperm Whale Acoustic Behaviors," 1. Among other things, this paper reported that five sperm whales apparently remained submerged for at least *two hours and eighteen minutes!* Also, intense military submarine sonar activity during the Granada invasion made sperm whales silent and shy.

13. Arnbom et al., "Sperm Whales React to Attack." This article describes fifteen to twenty-five orcas attacking twenty to thirty sperm whales near the Galapagos Islands on 18 April 1985. Surrounding a calf, the sperm whales bunched together and tried to keep facing the orcas, which for their part tried to attack from the rear. Bloody parallel gashes up to two feet long were seen near the blowholes of at least three sperm whales. Apparently no sperm whales were seriously injured. When the orcas broke off the attack, the sperm whales left the area.

My readings suggest that orcas seldom attack sperm whales. When they do, it is probably because the odds are heavily in their favor.

CHAPTER TEN *(pages 130–137)*

1. Baumgartner, "Whales Anger Alaska Fishermen"; Freeman, "Orcas and Longliners Battle." Earlier in my narrative, the orcas could conceivably have raided herring weirs, which are in heavy use along the coast of Maine and around its offshore islands during the autumn spawning season. I did not include this in my narrative because I have no evidence that orcas enter these fish traps. Other cetaceans, including minkes and young humpbacks, are frequently trapped in Maine weirs. Fishermen usually report such en-

trapments to authorities so that the animals can be freed, or if already drowned, recovered for study purposes. None of the weir-related reports I have on file involve orcas.

2. This devotion to the old cow, before and after death, is fairly typical behavior among cetaceans. In *A Dolphin Summer,* p. 186, note 2, I cite several cases of cetaceans carrying dead babies, even after they are badly decomposed. In *Orca,* p. 92, Hoyt cites a case in which a young orca was struck and slashed by the propeller of a British Columbia ferry. A male and a female immediately supported the bleeding calf between them. Fifteen days later, two orcas supporting a third—presumably the same group—were observed at the same place.

Reluctance to abandon the dead and dying has been observed in terrestrial species, as well. Jane Goodall described (and her husband filmed) a wild female chimpanzee who, having lost her infant to polio, carried the little corpse on her back for days. Elephants are also very devoted to their ill and injured and will attempt with dogged persistence to get kin back on their feet, even after they are dead.

3. Although albatrosses and tropicbirds are rare in the western North Atlantic, some wanderers (usually solitary) do visit our area from time to time. I open and close this book from the viewpoints of these exotic birds merely to dramatize the fascinating mixture of tropical and boreal life found along the Georges Bank shelf break.

BIBLIOGRAPHY

American Shad. Biological Report 82 (11.37). TR EL-82-4. Slidell, La.: U.S. Department of the Interior, Fish and Wildlife Service, National Coastal Ecosystems Team, April 1985.

Apollonio, Spencer. *The Gulf of Maine.* Rockland, Maine: Courier of Maine Books, 1979. A guide to the Gulf of Maine's history, geology, geography, currents, and inhabitants.

Arnbom, Tom, Vassili Papastavrou, Linda S. Weilgart, and Hal Whitehead. "Sperm Whales React to an Attack by Killer Whales." *Journal of Mammalogy* 68, no. 2 (May 1987).

Au, D., and D. Weihs. "At High Speeds, Dolphins Save Energy by Leaping." *Nature* 284, no. 5756: 548-50.

Au, W. W. L., R. W. Floyd, R. H. Penner, and A. E. Murchison. "Measurement of Echolocation Signals of the Atlantic Bottlenose Dolphin, *Tursiops truncatus* Montagu, in Open Waters." *Journal of the Acoustical Society of America* 56, no. 4 (1974): 1280-90.

Balcomb, Kenneth C. III. "The Occurrence and Status of Three Resident Pods of Killer Whales in Greater Puget Sound, State of Washington." An Ocean Research and Education Society Reprint, December 1982.

Balcomb, Kenneth C. III, J. R. Boran, and S. L. Heimlich. "Killer Whales in Greater Puget Sound." *Report of the International Whaling Commission* 32 (1982): 681-85.

Bartlett, Des, and Jen Bartlett. "Patagonia's Wild Shore: Where Two Worlds Meet." *National Geographic* 149, no. 3 (March 1976): 298-321. On pages 314-17, orcas are shown slapping sea lions high into the air and stranding themselves in pursuit of sea lions on shore.

Batteau, D. W., and P. R. Markey. Final Report to U.S. Naval Ordnance

Test Station, China Lake, Calif., Contract N00123-67-C-1103, 1967.

Baumgartner, Mark. "Whales Anger Alaska Fishermen: Tolerance Dissipates As Man and Mammal Compete for Same Valuable Black Cod Catch." *Christian Science Monitor,* 7 May 1986.

Beardsley, Timothy M., ed. "Sonic Punch" (column). *Scientific American* 257, no. 4 (October 1987): 36.

Bel'kovich, V. M., and A. V. Yablokov. "The Whale: An Ultrasonic Projector." *Yunyi Tekhnik* (Young Technologist Magazine) (USSR), March 1963, 76–77. (In *Dolphins and Porpoises,* Richard Ellis shows the spelling of this periodical as *Yuchnyi Teknik.*)

Benjamin, Molly. "Where Are the Dogfish? P'town Boats Wishing Dogs Would Come Home." *Commercial Fisheries News,* September 1986, 14. This article discusses some of the many changes in the Gulf of Maine during 1986, especially the sudden "disappearance" of the once-ubiquitous dogfish, which Massachusetts fishermen had just begun exploiting for England's fish-and-chips market.

Berzin, A. A. *The Sperm Whale.* Jerusalem: Israel Program for Scientific Translations.

Berzin, A. A., and V. L. Vladimirov. "A New Species of Killer Whale (Cetacea, Delphinidae) from the Antarctic Waters." *Zoologicheskii Zhurnal* 62, no. 2 (1983): 287–95. Soviet scientists report a possible new species *(Orcinus orca glacialis),* based on morphological differences found in animals from the Indian Ocean sector of the Antarctic. Mitchell (1985) questions whether the "comparative description" qualifies as a formal diagnosis distinguishing the taxon from *Orcinus orca.*

Bigelow, Henry B., and William C. Schroeder. *Fishes of the Gulf of Maine.* Fishery Bulletin 74. Washington, D.C.: Fish and Wildlife Service, 1953.

Bigg, Michael. "An Assessment of Killer Whale *(Orcinus orca)* Stocks off Vancouver Island, British Columbia." *Report of the International Whaling Commission* 32 (1982): 655–66.

Bigg, Michael, Ian MacAskie, and Graeme Ellis. "Photo-identification of Individual Killer Whales." *Whalewatcher (Journal of the American Cetacean Society)* 17, no. 1 (Spring 1983): 3–5.

Bloch, Dorete, and Christina Lockyer. "Killer Whales *(Orcinus orca)* in Faroese Waters." In *North Atlantic Killer Whales,* a special issue of *Rit Fiskideildar* (Journal of the Marine Research Institute, Reykjavik, Iceland) 11 (1988): 55–64.

Bonner, N. *Whales.* Blandford Press, 1980.

Bowles, Ann E., W. Glenn Young, and Edward D. Asper. "Ontogeny of Stereotyped Calling of a Killer Whale Calf, *Orcinus orca,* During Her First Year." In *North Atlantic Killer Whales,* a special issue of *Rit Fiskideildar* (Journal of the Marine Research Institute, Reykjavik, Iceland) 11 (1988): 251–75.

Braham, H. W., and M. Dahlheim. "Killer Whales in Alaska Documented in the Platforms of Opportunity Program." *Report of the International Whaling Commission* 32 (1982): 643–46. Cites 2,500 orcas seen in Alaskan waters.

Brown, David H., David K. Caldwell, and Melba C. Caldwell. "Observations on the Behavior of Wild and Captive False Killer Whales, with Notes on Associated Behavior of Other Genera of Captive Delphinids." *Contributions in Science,* nos. 70 and 95. Natural History Museum of Los Angeles County.

Brunenmeister, Susan. "A Summary and Discussion of Technical Information Pertaining to the Geographical Discreteness of Atlantic Bluefin Tuna Resources." ICCAT Working Document SCRS/79/95.

Bullock, T. H., and S. H. Ridgway. "Neurophysiological Findings Relevant to Echolocation in Marine Mammals." *Animal Orientation and Navigation.* Edited by S. R. Galler et al. National Aeronautics and Space Administration Publication SP-262 (1972): 373–95.

Bunnell, Sterling. "The Evolution of Cetacean Intelligence." In *Mind in the Waters,* ed. Joan McIntyre. New York: Scribner's/Sierra Club, 1974, 58. Also see marginal note by Peter Warshall.

Burton, Maurice, and Robert Burton, eds. *The International Wildlife Encyclopedia.* New York: Marshall Cavendish Corporation, 1969.

Busnel, R.-G., and A. Classe. *Whistled Languages.* New York: Springer-Verlag, 1976. English edition, p. 98.

Butler, Michael J. A. "Plight of the Bluefin Tuna." *National Geographic* 162, no. 2 (August 1982): 220–39. On p. 232, orcas are shown crippling giant bluefin tuna by biting off their tails.

Caldwell, D. K., and M. C. Caldwell. *The World of the Bottlenose Dolphin.* New York: J. B. Lippincott, 1972.

Carrighar, Sally. *Icebound Summer.* New York: Knopf, 1953.

CETAP (Cetacean and Turtle Assessment Program). *A Characterization of Marine Mammals and Turtles in the Mid- and North Atlantic Areas of the U.S. Outer Continental Shelf.* Contract AA551-CT8-48, Final Report. University of Rhode Island, Graduate School of Oceanography, for U.S. Department of the Interior, Washington, 1982.

This study was part of an effort to determine the potential environmental impact of oil drilling on the continental shelf. During the survey period, covering thirty-nine months from 11-1-78 through 1-28-82, CETAP reported only 85 orcas in twelve sightings (less than one percent of the large whale sightings and less than one percent of the odontocete sightings). The number of individual orcas per sighting ranges from 1 to 40, the average being 7.1, the largest for all large whale species. About half of the sightings were made in slope waters, the rest close to the coast.

Christensen, Ivar. "Distribution, Movements and Abundance of Killer Whales

(Orcinus orca) in Norwegian Coastal Waters, 1982–1987, Based on Questionnaire Surveys." In *North Atlantic Killer Whales,* a special issue of *Rit Fiskideildar* (Journal of the Marine Research Institute, Reykjavik, Iceland) 11 (1988): 79–88.

Coffee, D. J. *Dolphins, Whales and Porpoises.* New York: Macmillan, 1977.

Conly, Robert Leslie. "Porpoises: Our Friends in the Sea." *National Geographic* 130, no. 3 (September 1966): 396–425.

Cousteau, Jacques-Yves and Philippe Diole. *Dolphins.* New York: Doubleday, 1975.

——. *The Whale: Mighty Monarch of the Sea.* New York: Doubleday, 1972.

Crail, Ted. *Apetalk & Whalespeak: The Quest for Interspecies Communication.* Chicago: Contemporary Books, Inc., 1983.

Dahlheim, Marilyn E. "A Review of the Biology and Exploitation of the Killer Whale, *Orcinus orca,* with Comments on Recent Sightings From Antarctica." *Report of the International Whaling Commission* 31 (1981): 541–46.

Dearden, J. C. "A Stranding of Killer Whales in Newfoundland." *Canadian Field Naturalist* 72, no. 4 (1958): 166–67.

Dobbs, Horace. *Follow the Wild Dolphins.* New York: St. Martin's Press, 1982.

Duffield, D., and L. Cornell. "Observations on Population Structure and Dynamics in *Orcinus orca.*" Abstracts from presentations at the Third Biennial Conference on the Biology of Marine Mammals, 7–11 October 1979, Seattle, Wash. Includes chromosomal and biochemical evidence that orcas live in genetically isolated groups having only limited exchanges with other pods.

Duffield, Deborah A., and Karen W. Miller. "Demographic Features of Killer Whales in Oceanaria in the United States and Canada." In *North Atlantic Killer Whales,* a special issue of *Rit Fiskideildar* (Journal of the Marine Research Institute, Reykjavik, Iceland) 11 (1988): 297–306.

Earle, Sylvia A. "Humpbacks: the Gentle Whales." *National Geographic* 155, no. 1 (January 1979): 2–17.

Ellis, Graeme, ed. *Killer Whales of Prince William Sound and Southeast Alaska.* A Catalog of Individuals Photoidentified, 1976–1986. San Diego: Sea World Research Institute, 1987.

Ellis, Richard. *The Book of Sharks.* New York: Grosset & Dunlap, 1976.

——. *The Book of Whales.* New York: Knopf, 1985.

——. *Dolphins and Porpoises.* New York: Knopf, 1982. Orca material on pp. 167–89, 246–51.

Evans, Peter G. H. "Killer Whales *(Orcinus orca)* in British and Irish Waters." In *North Atlantic Killer Whales,* a special issue of *Rit Fiskideildar* (Journal of the Marine Research Institute, Reykjavik, Iceland) 11 (1988): 42–54.

Evans, W. E. "Echolocation by Marine Delphinids and One Species of Freshwater Dolphin." *Journal of the Acoustical Society of America* no. 54 (1973): 191–99.

Evans, W. E., W. W. Sutherland, and R. G. Berl. "The Directional Characteristics of Delphinid Sounds." In *Marine Bio-Acoustics,* ed. W. N. Tavolga, vol. 1, 353–72. New York: Pergamon Press, 1964.

Evans, W. E., A. V. Yablokov, and A. E. Bowles. "Geographical Variation in the Colour Pattern of Killer Whales *(Orcinus orca)." Report of the International Whaling Commission* 32 (1982): 687–94.

Ferreira, Ernesto. "La pesca dell' 'Albacora' nelle Azzorre." *Note dell' Instituto Italo-Germanico di Biologia Marina di Rovigno d'Istria,* N. 1, 1932. On 10-14-86 Frank J. Mather III, Scientist Emeritus at the Woods Hole Oceanographic Institution, kindly supplied me with an English abstract of this paper, which describes the hook-and-line tuna fishery in the Azores between 1924 and 1931. Bluefin tuna and three other species were taken regularly from October to March, the bulk of the catch being taken between November and January. Sometimes large schools of *Phocoena communis* (a species of porpoise referred to locally as *boto*) and *Globicephalus melas* (blackfish or pilot whales) appeared on the banks and chased away the tuna, at times for the season.

Ford, John K. B. "Acoustic Traditions of Killer Whales." *Whalewatcher* (Journal of the American Cetacean Society) 19, no. 3 (Fall 1985): 3–6.

———. "Group-Specific Dialects of Killer Whales *(Orcinus orca)* in British Columbia." Abstracts from Presentations at the Fifth Biennial Conference on the Biology of Marine Mammals. Boston, Mass., November 1983.

Ford, John K. B., and Dean H. Fisher. "Killer Whale *(Orcinus orca)* Dialects as an Indicator of Stocks in British Columbia." *Report of the International Whaling Commission* 32 (1982): 671–79.

Ford, John, and Deborah Ford. "The Killer Whales of B.C." *Waters* (Journal of the Vancouver Aquarium) 5, no. 1 (Summer 1981): 2–33.

Freeman, Kris. "Orcas and Longliners Battle for Black Cod." *National Fisherman,* May 1986, 2–4, 79.

Fritts, Thomas, A. Blair Irvine, Randy Jennings, Laura Collum, Wayne Hoffman, and M. Angela McGehee. *Turtles, Birds, and Mammals in the Northern Gulf of Mexico and Nearby Atlantic Waters.* An overview based on aerial surveys of OCS areas, with emphasis on oil and gas effects. Prepared for Fish and Wildlife Service, U.S. Department of the Interior. Albuquerque, New Mex.: Denver Wildlife Research Center, Museum of Southwestern Biology, University of New Mexico. (This survey team sighted no orcas in the Gulf of Mexico. Thus, it appears doubtful that orcas prey on bluefin tuna to any major degree on their spawning grounds.)

Gaskin, D. E. *Ecology of Whales and Dolphins.* Heinemann, 1982.

Gentry, Roger L. "Seals and Their Kin." *National Geographic* 171, no. 4 (April 1987): 492–93. Incredible Jeff Foott photographs of orcas stranding themselves to snatch sea lions and southern elephant seals off sharply sloping beaches in Patagonia.

Geraci, J. R., S. Testaverde, D. J. St. Aubin, and T. Loop. "A Mass Stranding of the Atlantic White-sided Dolphins *(Lagenorhynchus acutus)*: A Study into Pathobiology and Life History." National Technical Information Service Publication No. PB289361. Washington, D.C., 1978.

Giddings, Al. "An Incredible Feasting of Whales." *National Geographic* 165, no. 1 (January 1984): 88–93. Some great Giddings photographs of humpbacks bubble-net feeding in groups of up to six whales. Also a nice Ocean Images photograph on pp. 50–51.

Gormley, Gerard. *A Dolphin Summer.* New York: Taplinger, 1985.

Gosline, John M., and M. Edwin DeMont. "Jet-propelled Swimming in Squids." *Scientific American* 252, no. 1 (January 1985): 96–103.

Graves, William. "The Imperiled Giants." *National Geographic* 150, no. 6 (December 1976): 722–51.

Greenberg, David A. "Modeling Tidal Power." *Scientific American* 257, no. 5 (November 1987): 106–13.

Griffin, Donald R. *Animal Thinking.* Cambridge: Harvard University Press, 1984.

———. *The Question of Animal Awareness.* Los Altos, Calif.: William Kaufman, 1981.

Griffin, Edward I. "Making Friends with a Killer Whale." *National Geographic* 129, no. 3 (March 1966): 418–46.

———. *Namu: Quest for the Killer Whale.* Gryphon West Publishers, 1982.

Grosslein, Marvin D., and Thomas R. Azarovitz. *Fish Distribution* MESA New York Bight Atlas Monograph 15. Albany: New York Sea Grant Institute, 1982.

Hall, John D., and Lanny H. Cornell. *Killer Whales of Prince William Sound, Alaska.* Results of 1985 Field Research. San Diego: Sea World Research Institute, 1986.

Hammond, Philip S. "Abundance of Killer Whales in Antarctic Areas II, III, IV, and V. *Report of the International Whaling Commission* 34 (1984): 543–48.

Hammond, Philip S., and Christina Lockyer. "Distribution of Killer Whales in the Eastern North Atlantic." In *North Atlantic Killer Whales,* a special issue of *Rit Fiskideildar* (Journal of the Marine Research Institute, Reykjavik, Iceland) 11 (1988): 24–41.

Hamner, William M. "Blue-Water Plankton." *National Geographic* 146, no. 4 (October 1974): 530–45.

Hancock, David. "Killer Whales Kill and Eat a Minke Whale." *Journal of Mammalogy* 46, no. 2 (1965): 341–42.

"Hearing Could Be Herring's Red Herring." *Science News* 130 (11 October 1986): 238. A report from the Third International Animal Sonar Systems Symposium, Helsingor, Denmark.

Heezen, B. C., and G. L. Johnson. "Alaskan Submarine Cables: A Struggle with a Harsh Environment." *Arctic* 22, no. 4 (1969): 413–24.

Heide-Jorgensen, Mads-Peter. "Occurrence and Hunting of Killer Whales in Greenland." In *North Atlantic Killer Whales,* a special issue of *Rit Fisk-ideildar* (Journal of the Marine Research Institute, Reykjavik, Iceland) 11 (1988): 115–35.

Heldt, H. "Reperage des Bancs de Thons par avion: applications à la pêche — étude des migrations." Notes No. 26, Station Oceanographique de Salammbo, Regence de Tunis, Protectorat Français, June 1932. On 10-14-86 Frank J. Mather III, Scientist Emeritus at the Woods Hole Oceanographic Institution, kindly supplied me with an English abstract. Part of Dr. Mather's translation describes large cetaceans preying on giant bluefin tuna outside tuna traps along the coast of Tunisia near Gibraltar. The cetaceans that terrify tuna the most are called *roass* (grampus) or *arroas* by the fishermen of Spain and Morocco. The fishermen's descriptions do not mention color, but the information given suggests that the cetaceans are false killer whales *(Pseudorca crassidens).*

Herman, Louis, ed. *Cetacean Behavior: Mechanisms and Functions.* New York: Wiley, 1980.

Hill, David. "Vanishing Giants." *Audubon,* January 1975.

Hoyt, Erich. *Orca: The Whale Called Killer.* Camden East, Ontario: Camden House, 1984. This book contains one of the most comprehensive orca-related bibliographies available.

——. *"Orcinus orca:* Separating Facts from Fantasies." *Oceans,* July–August 1977, 22–26.

——. *A Whale Called Killer.* New York: Dutton, 1981.

Hult, R. W. "Another Function of Echolocation for Bottlenose Dolphins *(Turpsiops truncatus)."* *Cetology,* no. 47 (27 November 1982). Hult describes captive bottlenose dolphins using high-intensity click trains to herd sea bass from one area of their tank to another, and to separate individual fish from their school. The dolphins appeared to be playing with the fish.

International Whaling Commission. Committee-authored reports.

SC/33/Rep4 (draft). "Report of the Workshop on Identity, Structure and Vital Rates of Killer Whale Populations — Cambridge, England — June 23–25, 1981."

——. "Report of the Scientific Committee, Annex H (Small Cetaceans)." *Rep. Int. Whal. Commn.* 33 (1983): 161–162.

——. "Report of the Scientific Committee, Annex H (Small Cetaceans)." *Rep. Int. Whal. Commn.* 34 (1984): 148–49.

_____. "Report of the Scientific Committee, Annex I (Small Cetaceans)." *Rep. Int. Whal. Commn.* 35 (1985): 136.

_____. "Report of the Scientific Committee, Annex I (Small Cetaceans)." *Rep. Int. Whal. Commn.* 36 (1986): 114.

Jonsgard, A., and P. B. Lyshoel. "A Contribution to the Knowledge of the Biology of the Killer Whale *Orcinus orca* (L.). *Nytt magasin for Zoologi* (a Norwegian journal of zoology) 18, no. 1 (1970): 41–48.

Kanwisher, John W., and Sam H. Ridgway. "The Physiological Ecology of Whales and Porpoises." *Scientific American* 248, no. 6 (June 1983): 110–20.

Kasamatsu, F., D. Hembree, G. Joyce, L. Tsunoda, R. Rowlett, and T. Nakano. "Distribution of Cetacean Sightings in the Antarctic: Results Obtained from the IWC/IDCR Minke Whale Assessment Cruises, 1978/79 to 1983/84." *Report of the International Whaling Commission* 38 (1988): 449–87.

Katona, Steven K., Judith A. Beard, Philip E. Girton, and Frederick Wenzel. "Killer Whales *(Orcinus orca)* from the Bay of Fundy to the Equator, Including the Gulf of Mexico." In *North Atlantic Killer Whales,* a special issue of *Rit Fiskideildar* (Journal of the Marine Research Institute, Reykjavik, Iceland) 11 (1988): 205–24.

Katona, Steven K., Valerie Rough, and David T. Richardson. *A Field Guide to the Whales, Porpoises and Seals of the Gulf of Maine and Eastern Canada (Cape Cod to Newfoundland).* New York: Scribner's, 1984. Orca material, 109–17.

Kellogg, Remington. "Whales, Giants of the Sea." *National Geographic* 77, no. 1 (January 1940): 35–90.

Kellogg, W. N. *Porpoises and Sonar.* Chicago: University of Chicago Press, 1961.

Kelly, H. R. "A Two-Body Problem in Echelon-Formation Swimming of Porpoise." U.S. Naval Ordnance Test Station, China Lake, Calif. Technical Note 40606-1, 1959, 1–7.

Kenney, Nathaniel T. "Sharks: Wolves of the Sea." *National Geographic* 133, no. 2 (February 1968): 222–57.

"Killer Whales Destroyed. VP-7 Accomplishes Special Task." *Naval Aviation News,* December 1956, 19. Apparently due to complaints about damage to nets in Icelandic waters, the U.S. Navy was asked to rid the coastal areas of orcas. Last year VP-18 [U.S. Navy planes] destroyed "hundreds of Icelandic killer whales with machine guns, rockets, and depth charges."

Kirkevold, Barbara C., and Joan S. Lockard, eds. *Behavioral Biology of Killer Whales.* Alan R. Liss, 1986.

Larson, Dotte. "Minke/Orca Encounter." *Journal of CETA-RESEARCH* 3 (Fall 1982): 2.

Leatherwood, S., D. K. Caldwell, and H. E. Winn. *Whales, Dolphins and Porpoises of the Western North Atlantic: A Guide to Their Identification.* NOAA Technical Report, NMFS CIRC-396. Seattle: NOAA, NMFS, 1976.

Leatherwood, S., R. R. Reeves, and L. Foster. *The Sierra Club Handbook of Whales and Dolphins.* San Francisco: Sierra Club Books, 1983.

Leatherwood, S., R. R. Reeves, W. F. Perrin, and W. E. Evans. *Whales, Dolphins and Porpoises of the Eastern North Pacific and Adjacent Arctic Waters: A Guide to Their Identification.* NOAA Technical Report, NMFS CIRC-396. Seattle: NOAA, NMFS, 1982.

Lewis, David. "Icebound in Antarctica." *National Geographic* 166, no. 5 (November 1984): 634–63. On p. 655, a leopard seal is shown snapping an Adelie penquin out of its skin.

Lien, Jon, Ivar Christensen, Maren Lien, and Peter W. Jones. "A Note on Killer Whales *(Orcinus orca)* Near Solvaer, Norway, in November–December, 1984." In *North Atlantic Killer Whales,* a special issue of *Rit Fiskideildar* (Journal of the Marine Research Institute, Reykjavik, Iceland) 11 (1988): 95–98.

Lien, Jon, Garry B. Stenson, and Peter W. Jones. "Killer Whales *(Orcinus orca)* in Waters off Newfoundland and Labrador, 1978–1986." In *North Atlantic Killer Whales,* a special issue of *Rit Fiskideildar* (Journal of the Marine Research Institute, Reykjavik, Iceland) 11 (1988): 194–201.

Lilly, John C. *Lilly on Dolphins: Humans of the Sea.* New York: Anchor/Doubleday, 1975.

Lilly, John C. *Sounds and Ultrasounds of the Bottlenose Dolphin.* Vocal exchanges between human and dolphin. Experiments by Dr. John C. Lilly. New York: Folkways Records, 1975.

Linehan, Edward J. "The Trouble with Dolphins." *National Geographic* 155, no. 4 (April 1979): 506–41.

Little, E. A., and J. C. Andrews. "Drift Whales at Nantucket: The Kindness of Moshup." *Man in the Northeast* 23 (1982): 17.

Lopez, Juan Carlos, and Diana Lopez. "Killer Whales *(Orcinus orca)* of Patagonia, and Their Behavior of Intentional Stranding While Hunting Nearshore." *Journal of Mammalogy* 66, no. 1 (February 1985): 181–83.

Lowenstein, Jerold. "Cetacean Evolution." *Oceans* 19, no. 1 (January-February 1986): 70–71. Using radioimmunoassay techniques, Lowenstein claims to have traced cetaceans back to the hippopotamus. For a conflicting view, see Miller (1983).

Lyrholm, Thomas. "Photoidentification of Individual Killer Whales, *Orcinus orca,* off the Coast of Norway, 1983–1986." In *North Atlantic Killer Whales,* a special issue of *Rit Fiskideildar* (Journal of the Marine Research Institute, Reykjavik, Iceland) 11 (1988): 89–94.

McIntyre, Joan, ed. *Mind in the Waters.* New York: Scribner's/Sierra Club, 1974.

Mackay, R. Stuart, and H. M. Liau. "Dolphin Vocalization Mechanisms." *Science* 212, no. 4495 (9 May 1981): 676–77.

McNally, Robert. "Echolocation." *Oceans* 10, no. 4 (July–August 1977): 27–33.
_____. *So Remorseless a Havoc.* Boston: Little, Brown, 1981.
_____. "To Kill a Whale." *Oceans* 10, no. 1 (January–February 1977): 62–65.

McNulty, Faith. *The Great Whales.* New York: Doubleday, 1974.

Marden, Luis. "The American Lobster, Delectable Cannibal." *National Geographic* 143, no. 4 (October 1973): 462–87.

_____. "The Continental Shelf: Man's New Frontier." *National Geographic* 153, no. 4 (April 1978): 494–531. Article includes beautiful, informative paintings of the shelf's undersea topography.

Mart, Jeff. "Cosmic Plot: The Last Catch of Killer Whales in Puget Sound." *Oceans* 9, no. 3 (May–June 1976): 56–59.

Mather, Frank J. III. "A Preliminary Note on Migratory Tendencies and Distributional Patterns of Atlantic Bluefin Tuna Based on Recently Acquired and Cumulative Tagging Results." A manuscript (SCRS/79/76), later included in the ICCAT's 1980 Collected Volume of Scientific Papers. Dr. Mather reports preliminary conclusions regarding migratory movements of giant bluefin tuna. Present indications are that, although some transatlantic movements occur, the two major populations of Atlantic bluefin remain largely isolated from each other on their respective sides of the Atlantic.

Matthews, L. Harrison. *The Whale.* New York: Crescent Books, 1975.

Mattila, David K.; Linda N. Guinee, and Charles A. Mayo. "Humpback Whale Songs on a North Atlantic Feeding Ground." *Journal of Mammalogy,* Vol. 68, No. 4, November 1987, pp. 880–883.

Mayo, C. A. *Observations of Cetaceans: Cape Cod Bay and Southern Stellwagen Bank, Massachusetts, 1974–1979.* Final Report to U.S. Marine Mammal Commission, No. MMC-80/07, 1982, 68 pp.

Mayo, Charles, Carole Carlson, Phil Clapham, and Dave Mattila. *Humpback Whales of the Southern Gulf of Maine.* Provincetown, Mass.: Center for Coastal Studies, 1985.

Mercer, Scott N. *Observations of Cetaceans on Jeffrey's Ledge and in Ipswich Bay in Spring, Summer and Autumn 1985, Including References to Previous Seasons.* Newburyport, Mass.: New England Whale Watch, Inc., 1985.

_____. *Seasonal Distribution of Humpback Whales in the Southern Gulf of Maine, 1978 to 1983.* Report No. 2, 1984. Newburyport, Mass.: New England Whale Watch, Inc., 1984.

_____. *Sighting Records and Notes on the Occurrence of Large Whales, Dolphins, and Porpoises off the New Hampshire and Massachusetts Coastlines, 1980 and 1981.* Report No. 1, 1984. Newburyport, Mass.: New England Whale Watch, Inc., 1984.

Mikhalev, Y. A., M. V. Ivashin, V. P. Savusin, and F. E. Zelenya. "The Distribution and Biology of Killer Whales in the Southern Hemisphere." *Report of the International Whaling Commission* 31 (1981): 551–65. Soviet scientists report a possible new species, *Orcinus nanus*. Mitchell (1985) refers to the taxon as a *nomen nudem*.

Miller, Julie Ann. "When Whales Abandoned the Land." *Science News,* 23 April 1983, 271. Cites findings of Gingerich and Wells at University of Michigan, Ann Arbor, that *Pakicetus* is the "perfect missing link" between whales and their terrestrial forebears. *Pakicetus,* a fossil about fifty million years old, was found in freshwater deposits with land animal fossils, and is therefore thought to have spent much of its time on land. For a conflicting view, see Lowenstein (1986).

Minasian, S., K. Balcomb, and L. Foster. *The World's Whales.* Washington, D.C.: Smithsonian Books, 1984.

Mitchell, Edward. "Canada Progress Report on Cetacean Research June 1977–May 1978." *Report of the International Whaling Commission* 29 (1979): 111. "A pod of 14 killer whales were trapped in Usualuk, a small fjord on Kikertelung Island about 40 miles from Pangnirtung, Cumberland Sound, Baffin Island, in the last week of September 1977. The killers became trapped in the fjord, actually a salt water lake, when the tide went out. Inuit hunters killed all of the killer whales; seven on 1 October (2 beached, 5 sank); seven on 3 October (2 beached, 5 sank). One male calf was 11 ft. 8½ in. (3.55 m) long, and a tooth was collected from it. RCMP Constable Harris took photographs, and subsequently J. Parsons (Mac-Laren Atlantic Ltd.) sampled teeth and stomach contents from the carcasses."

_____. *Porpoise, Dolphin and Small Whale Fisheries of the World: Status and Problems.* Morges, Switzerland: International Union for Conservation of Nature and Natural Resources, Monograph No. 3, 1975. Information on commercial whaling and capture of orcas.

_____. "Relationships of Killer Whale *Orcinus orca* within Delphinidae." A paper presented at the Sixth Biennial Conference on the Biology of Marine Mammals, Vancouver, British Columbia, 22–26 November 1985. Dr. Mitchell cites chromosomal, pigmentary, pathological, and behavioral evidence that orca pods and local communities the world over are sympatric — i.e., they tend to overlap geographically without interbreeding. This genetic isolation gives rise to distinct races, including smaller or differently pigmented orcas that some scientists have classified as new species *(Orcinus orca glacialis, O. nanus, O. glacialis,* and *O. morzerbruynsis).* Dr. Mitchell sees only *O. orca glacialis* (dwarf killer whale) as a possibly useful subspecies, and questions whether even that taxon should be distinguished from *O. orca.*

Mitchell, Edward, and Alan N. Baker. "Age of Reputedly Old Killer Whale, *Orcinus orca*, 'Old Tom' from Eden, Twofold Bay, Australia." *Report of the International Whaling Commission,* Special Issue 3 (1980): 143–54.

Mitchell, Edward, and Randall R. Reeves. "Records of Killer Whales in the Western North Atlantic, with Emphasis on Eastern Canadian Waters." In *North Atlantic Killer Whales,* a special issue of *Rit Fiskideildar* (Journal of the Marine Research Institute, Reykjavik, Iceland) 11 (1988): 161–93.

Moore, Sue E., Jon K. Francine, Ann E. Bowles, and John K. B. Ford. "Analysis of Calls of Killer Whales, *Orcinus orca,* from Iceland and Norway." In *North Atlantic Killer Whales,* a special issue of *Rit Fiskideildar* (Journal of the Marine Research Institute, Reykjavik, Iceland) 11 (1988): 225–50.

Mowat, Farley. *A Whale for the Killing.* New York: Little, Brown, 1972.

Murchison, A. E. "Detection Range and Range Resolution of Echolocating Bottlenose Porpoise *(Tursiops truncatus)*." In *Animal Sonar Systems,* ed. R.-G. Busnel and J. F. Fish. New York: Plenum Press, 1980, 43–70.

Myrick, Albert C., Pamela K. Yochem, and Lanny H. Cornell. "Toward Calibrating Dentinal Layers in Captive Killer Whales by Use of Tetracycline Labels." In *North Atlantic Killer Whales,* a special issue of *Rit Fiskideildar* (Journal of the Marine Research Institute, Reykjavik, Iceland) 11 (1988): 285–96. The authors conclude that because of the difficulty in reading cemental growth layer groups (GLGs) and linking them in some consistent manner to dentinal GLGs, the method of using cemental layers alone for age determination is unreliable. They suggest that new methods for estimating age in orcas older than twenty years should be explored.

Nayman, Jacqueline. *Whales, Dolphins and Man.* London: Hamlyn, 1978.

Nishiwaka, M., and C. Handa. "Killer Whales Caught in Coastal Waters off Japan." *Scientific Report of the Whales Research Institute, Tokyo* 13 (1958): 85–96.

Norris, Kenneth S. *The Porpoise Watcher.* New York: Norton, 1974.

Norris, Kenneth S., and W. E. Evans. "Directionality of Echolocation Clicks in the Rough-Toothed Porpoise *(Steno bredanensis* [Lesson])." In *Marine Bio-Acoustics,* ed. W. N. Tavolga, vol. 2, 305–16. Elmsford, N.Y.: Pergamon Press, 1967.

Norris, Kenneth S., and Bertel Mohl. "Can Odontocete Cetaceans Immobilize Their Prey by Sound?" A paper presented at the Fourth Biennial Conference on the Biology of Marine Mammals, San Francisco, 1981.

Norton, A. H. "The Mammals of Portland, Maine, and Vicinity." *Proceedings Portland Society of Natural History* 4, no. 1 (1930): 1–150.

"The Orca (Killer) Whale *(Orcinus orca)*." *Whale Report,* Autumn 1980, 7. Washington D.C.: Center for Environmental Education.

Oien, Nils. "The Distribution of killer whales *(Orcinus orca)* in the North

Atlantic Based on Norwegian Catches, 1938–1981, and incidental sightings, 1967–1987." In *North Atlantic Killer Whales,* a special issue of *Rit Fiskideildar* (Journal of the Marine Research Institute, Reykjavik, Iceland) 11 (1988): 65–79.

Payne, Roger. "At Home with Right Whales." *National Geographic* 149, no. 3 (March 1976): 322–39.

———. "Humpbacks: Their Mysterious Songs." *National Geographic* 155, no. 1 (January 1979): 18–25.

———. "New Light on the Singing Whales." *National Geographic* 161, no. 4 (April 1982): 463–77. New findings regarding Pacific humpback migrations, together with some excellent Flip Nicklin photographs of humpbacks.

———, ed. *Communication and Behavior of Whales.* Westview Press, 1983.

Perez, J. M., W. W. Dawson, and D. Landau. "Retinal Anatomy of the Bottlenose Dolphin (*Tursiops truncatus*)." *Cetology,* no. 11, 31 December 1972. The authors found that *Tursiops* has a duplex retina (i.e., containing two types of photoceptors — rods and cones) in which cones are by no means rare. This suggests functional color discrimination. The paper cites other research by Mann (1946) showing that cones are also present in the retinas of sperm whales (*Physeter catadon*) and fin whales (*Balaenoptera physalus*). These findings dispute the belief that cetaceans are colorblind.

Plutte, Will. "The Whaling Imperative: Why Norway Whales." *Oceans* 17, no. 2 (March–April 1984): 24–26.

Pryor, Karen. *Lads Before the Wind: Adventures in Porpoise Training.* New York: Harper & Row, 1975.

Purves, P. *Echolocation in Whales and Dolphins.* Academic Press, 1983.

Quinn, Virginia. "Killer Whales Deserve a Better Name." *National Wildlife,* February–March 1984, 48–50.

Reeves, Randall R., and Edward Mitchell. "Distribution and Seasonality of Killer Whales in the Eastern Canadian Arctic." In *North Atlantic Killer Whales,* a special issue of *Rit Fiskideildar* (Journal of the Marine Research Institute, Reykjavik, Iceland) 11 (1988): 136–60.

———. "Killer Whale Sightings and Takes by American Pelagic Whalers in the North Atlantic." In *North Atlantic Killer Whales,* a special issue of *Rit Fiskideildar* (Journal of the Marine Research Institute, Reykjavik, Iceland) 11 (1988): 7–23.

Reiger, George. "Dolphin Sacred, Porpoise Profane." *Audubon,* January 1975, 7–11.

———. "Marine Mammal Muddles." *Audubon,* March 1976.

Ridgway, S. H., D. A. Carder, R. F. Green, A. S. Gaunt, and W. E. Evans. "Electromyographic and Pressure Events in the Nasolaryngeal System of Dolphins During Sound Production." In *Animal Sonar Systems,* ed.

R.-G. Busnel and J. F. Fish. New York: Plenum Press, 1980, 239–49.

Scheffer, Victor B. "Alaska's Whales." *Alaska Geographic* 5, no. 4 (1978): 5–14.

_____. "The Case for a World Moratorium on Whaling." In *Mind in the Waters,* ed. Joan McIntyre. New York: Scribner's/Sierra Club, 1974, 229–31.

_____. "Exploring the Lives of Whales." *National Geographic* 150, no. 6 (December 1976): 752–66.

_____. *A Natural History of Marine Mammals.* New York: Scribner's, 1976.

_____. *The Year of the Whale.* New York: Scribner's, 1969.

Schevill, W. E., and W. A. Watkins. "Sound Structure and Directionality in *Orcinus* (Killer Whale)." *Zoologica* 51, no. 2 (1966): 70–76.

Scordia, Concettina. "Intorno alle incursioni del *Globicephalus melas* (Trail) nello Stretto di Messina, e ai danni che ne vengono apportati alla pesca del Tonno." *Memorie di Biologia Marina a di Oceanografia* 6, no. 2 (1939): XVII, Universita di Messina. On 10-14-86 Frank J. Mather III, scientist emeritus at the Woods Hole Oceanographic Institution, kindly supplied me with an English abstract. Part of Dr. Mather's translation describes a school of about thirty *G. melas* (regional variant on *Globicephala melaena,* pilot whale?) attacking and devouring bluefin tuna in the Strait of Messina in February 1933, when the hook-and-line fishery was active. Two of the cetaceans were harpooned, and the skull of one is shown in a photograph. In a telephone conversation with me, Dr. Mather quoted William Schevill of the Woods Hole Oceanographic Institute as saying that the skull was that of *Pseudorca crassidens* (false killer whale), not *Globicephalus melas.*

Sergeant, D. E. "Age Determination in Odontocete Whales from Dentinal Growth Layers." *Norsk Hvalfangst-tidende* 48, 6 (1959): 273–88.

_____. "Ecological Aspects of Cetacean Strandings." In *Biology of Marine Mammals: Insights Through Strandings,* ed. J. R. Geraci and D. J. St. Aubin. U.S. Marine Mammal Commission Report MMC-77/13, 1979, 94–113.

Sergeant, D. E., and H. D. Fisher. "The Smaller Cetacea of Eastern Canadian Waters." *Journal Fisheries Research Board of Canada* 14, no. 1 (1957): 83–115.

Sergeant, D. E., A. W. Mansfield, and B. Beck. "Inshore Records of Cetacea for Eastern Canada, 1949–68." *Journal Fisheries Research Board of Canada* 27, no. 11 (1970): 1903–1915. Orca material on pp. 1910–11. A twenty-four-foot male orca found dead, seal in stomach, stranded at Green Island Cove, Strait of Belle Isle, late February 1960. A twenty-foot orca, probably female, found dead at Cape Wolfe, P.E.I., 25 June 1968. Article also cites 1957 mass stranding at Trinity Bay, Nfld (see Dearden 1958), and a single stranding in the Bay of Fundy in 1957. All these strandings are included in the appendix.

Sergeant, D. E.; D. J. St. Aubin, and J. R. Geraci. "Life History and North-west Atlantic Distribution of the Atlantic White-Sided Dolphin, *Lagenorhynchus acutus.*" *Cetology* 37, 27 September 1980.

"Shad Tagging in the Bay of Fundy." *The Sou'wester* (a commercial fishing newspaper), Yarmouth, Nova Scotia, 15 February 1984, 20.

Sigurjonsson, Johann, and Stephen Leatherwood. "The Icelandic Live-Capture Fishery for Killer Whales, 1976–1988." In *North Atlantic Killer Whales,* a special issue of *Rit Fiskideildar* (Journal of the Marine Research Institute, Reykjavik, Iceland) 11 (1988): 307–16.

Sigurjonsson, Johann, Thomas Lyrholm, Stephen Leatherwood, Erlendur Jonsson, and Gisli Vikingsson. "Photoidentification of Killer Whales, *Orcinus orca,* off Iceland, 1981 through 1986." In *North Atlantic Killer Whales,* a special issue of *Rit Fiskideildar* (Journal of the Marine Research Institute, Reykjavik, Iceland) 11 (1988): 99–114.

A Socio-Economic and Environmental Inventory of the North Atlantic Region. Submitted to the Bureau of Land Management, Marine Minerals Division, as partial fulfillment of Contract 08550-CT3-8. South Portland, Maine: Research Institute of the Gulf of Maine, 1974.

Steiner, William W., James H. Hain, Howard E. Winn, and Paul J. Perkins. "Vocalizations and Feeding Behavior of the Killer Whale (*Orcinus orca*)." *Journal of Mammalogy* 60, no. 4 (1979): 823–27.

Stone, G., S. Katona, and J. Beard. *Whales in the Gulf of Maine, 1978–1981.* Report of the Gulf of Maine Whale Sighting Network. College of the Atlantic, Bar Harbor, Maine.

Talbot, Lee. "The Great Whales and the International Whaling Commission." In *Mind in the Waters,* ed. Joan McIntyre. New York: Scribner's/Sierra Club, 1974, 232–36.

Tangley, Laura. "A Whale of a Bang." *Science 84* (May 1984): 73–74. Overview of the Norris/Mohl/Marten hypothesis that odontocetes use loud bursts of sound to stun prey, together with some peer skepticism.

Tarpy, Cliff. "Killer Whale Attack!" *National Geographic* 155, no. 4 (April 1979): 542–45. Incredible photographs of orcas feeding on a live blue whale. The attack was observed from the research vessel *Sea World* off the tip of Baja California. About thirty orcas were attacking a young sixty-foot blue whale, biting away great slabs of flesh as the whale swam slowly along, unable to escape because its flukes had been shredded by the orcas. The researchers followed the whales for five hours, recording the event with movie and still cameras. About 6:00 P.M., the orcas suddenly broke off the attack and left the area. The severely wounded blue whale continued swimming slowly on, probably to its death.

Sea World scientists later studied and edited the hours of film. According to a staff member's remarks to me, at least some of the scientists suspect that the adult orcas were using the unfortunate blue whale to teach the pod's juveniles how to kill. The edited version of the film is available for viewing at Sea World, on a restricted basis, I believe. Brief segments have been aired on television.

Taylor, C. K., and Saayman, G. S. "The Social Organization and Behavior of Dolphins (*Turpsiops aduncus*) and Baboons (*Papio ursinus*): Some Comparisons and Assessments." *Annals Cape Provincial Museum (Natural History)* 9, no. 2, 11–49.

Thomas, Gary L., and Fred L. Felleman. "Acoustic Measurement of the Fish Assemblage Beneath Killer Whale Pods in the Pacific Northwest." In *North Atlantic Killer Whales,* a special issue of *Rit Fiskideildar* (Journal of the Marine Research Institute, Reykjavik, Iceland) 11 (1988): 276–84.

Tomilin, A. G. *Mammals of the USSR and Adjacent Countries.* Moskva: Dzdatel'stvo Akademi Nauk SSSR 9 (1957): 605–26.

Voss, Gilbert L. "Squids: Jet-powered Torpedoes of the Deep." *National Geographic* 131, no. 3 (March 1967): 386–411.

Walker, Theodore J. *Whale Primer.* Rev. ed. San Diego: Cabrillo Historical Association, 1975.

Watkins, William A. Comments on "Spectral Analysis of the Calls of the Male Killer Whale." *IEEE Transactions on Audio and Electroacoustics,* AU-16, 4, 1968, 523.

Watkins, W. A., K. E. Moore, and P. Tyack. "Sperm Whale Acoustic Behaviors in Southeast Caribbean." *Cetology,* no. 49, 8 November 1985.

Watson, Lyall. *The Romeo Error: A Matter of Life and Death.* New York: Anchor Press/Doubleday, 1974.

Wenzel, Frederick, and Richard Sears. "A Note on Killer Whales in the Gulf of St. Lawrence, Including an Account of an Attack on a Minke Whale." In *North Atlantic Killer Whales,* a special issue of *Rit Fiskideildar* (Journal of the Marine Research Institute, Reykjavik, Iceland) 11 (1988): 202–4.

White, D., P. Spong, N. Cameron, and J. Bradfor. "Visual Acuity in the Killer Whale (*Orcinus orca*). *Experimental Neurology* 32 (1971): 230–36. Studies conducted at Vancouver Aquarium showed that an orca can see about as well underwater as a cat can in air.

Whitehead, Hal. "The Unknown Giants: Rare Look at Sperm and Blue Whales." *National Geographic* 166, no. 6 (December 1984): 776–89. Some great Flip Nicklin photographs of sperm and blue whales.

———. "Why Whales Leap." *Scientific American* 252, no. 3 (March 1985): 84–93.

Whitehead, Hal, and Carolyn Glass. "Orcas (Killer Whales) Attack Humpback Whales." *Journal of Mammology* 66, no. 1 (1985): 183–85.

"Wolves of the Sea: Men Watch as Orcas Kill Minke Whale." *Alaska* 52, (September 1986): 46.

Wursig, Bernd. "Dolphins." *Scientific American* 240, no. 3 (March 1979): 136–48.

Wursig, Bernd, and Melany Wursig. "Day and Night of the Dolphin." *Natural History* 88, no. 3 (March 1979): 60–67. In distinct patterns, the dusky dolphin hunts the elusive anchovy, jumps for "joy," and tries to avoid killer whales.

INDEX

A

A Dolphin Summer (book), 76, 140
Albatross, 1–2, 182
Anadromous fish, 49, 120–21

B

Balling (containing prey in dense
        masses), 50, 61–62
Bigg, Michael, 18, 77, 174
Blackcod (Alaska), 47
Blubber,
    consistency, 14;
    function of, 47–48;
    sensitivity to pain, 16, 169;
Bluefish, 40, 49, 52–53
Bubbles, use of by cetaceans, 51,
        61–62

C

Cachalot — *See* Sperm whale
Cass, Virginia L., 97
Cod, 44, 46, 94, 107
Cold water tolerance vis-a-vis
        body size, 30, 40
Cunner, 107

D

Dadswell, Mike, 120
Dolphins,
    general, near shore, 118;
    general, evasive tactics, 83;
    Atlantic white-sided,
        evasive tactics, 89, 109;
        interaction with humpbacks,
            99;
        hunting/feeding techniques,
            60–62, 83;
        juvenile herds, 99–100;
        interaction with orcas, 62–63,
            88–91;
    bottlenose, 97;
    saddleback (common), 4

E

Earthwatch, 140
Ellis, Graeme, 77, 81

F

False killer whale (*Pseudorca
        crassidens*), 170
Fish traps, 34, 42, 57

Fishing,
  harpoon, 51–52, 56, 87, 115, 172;
  longline, 131–32;
  seining/purse-seining, 37–40, 110, 111;
  rod and reel, 86–87, 110–11;
  trawling/pair-trawling, 27, 83;
  trolling, 53–54;
Flounder, 46
Ford, John K.B., 73–82, 99, 103–04, 174
Ford, Deborah, 103–04

G
Gannet, 23, 27–28, 109
Gulls,
  general, 36, 57, 58, 85, 113, 115;
  herring, 50, 61, 99;
  black-back, 99;
Gurry, 92–93

H
Haddock, 44, 46, 94, 107
Hake,
  general, 49, 92;
  silver hake, 22, 107
Halibut, 8
Heiser, John B., 30
Herring, 46, 50, 83, 92, 95, 97, 99, 106, 111, 117, 119
Hoyt, Erich, 81, 99, 102
Hunter, James, 102

I
Ice Age and glaciation in Gulf of Maine, 25

K
Kittiwake, 10
Krill, 100, 114

L
Lilly, John, 76, 81, 175

M
MacAskie, Ian, 77
Mackerel, 28, 46, 55, 57, 67, 83, 94, 111
Marten, Kenneth, 97
Mayo, Charles (Capt.), 53–55, 173
Mayo, "Stormy" (Ph.D.), 66, 174
Menhaden, 83
Mercer, Scott, 176
Meteor shower, 136
Mohl, Bertel, 97

N
National Marine Fisheries Service, 37, 40, 94
Neelon, Michael, 111–15, 178, 179
Neelon, William, 111–15, 178, 179
New England Whale Watch, Inc. (Newburyport), 176, 178
Norris, Kenneth S., 96–98

O
Ocean mixing, 9
"Old Tom" (orca), 169, 171
Orcas,
  acoustic dialects, 62, 73–82;
  acoustic repertoires, 62, 73–82;
  activity vis-a-vis sounds made, 74;
  ailments, illnesses, injuries, 2–3, 10, 119, 125, 131, 169, 180;
  altruism, 124–137, 132, 182;
  breaching, 22, 72, 180–81;
  call-sign hypothesis, 76–79;
  calls, discrete, 74;

calls, pulsed vs. non-pulsed (tonal), 75;
daily food intake vis-a-vis body weight, 36, 85, 179–80;
distinctive body markings, 2, 71;
diving, 3, 85;
extended families, 18, 174;
exploitation of fishermen, 29, 34, 36–39, 44, 47, 49, 86–88, 131–32, 181–82;
exploitation by fishermen, 39, 56;
forced to resort to less desirable prey, 47;
hunting/feeding methods, 6–9, 11–16, 34–36, 44–46, 49–52, 52–59, 82–85, 87–88, 92, 106, 107–08;
in Antarctica, 102–03;
in British Columbia, 99, 103;
in Canadian Maritimes, 140;
leadership of experienced elders, 48–51, 53;
language hypothesis, 79–82;
life expectancy, 17–18, 169, 171;
loners, 62–66;
mating, 72, 110;
natural history in Pacific Northwest, 73–82;
nursing, 6, 20;
nursing calves, appearance, 2;
peaceful interaction with other cetaceans, 62–63, 99, 102–105, 174;
with finbacks, 103, 174;
with humpbacks, 99;
with minkes, 102–03;
with white-sided dolphins, 62–63;
physical differences, bulls and cows, 2;

play, 3, 8, 21–23, 171;
pod leadership, 171;
pod size in eastern North Pacific, 73;
pod size in western North Atlantic, 73;
pod permanence/variability, 78, 171, 174;
predation on bluefin tuna, 38–39, 44–45, 52–59, 83–87;
predation on finback whales, 110–16, 179;
predation on gray whales, 179;
predation on humpback whales, 11–16, 170;
predation on minke whales, 6–8, 16, 104, 169–70;
predation on sharks, 89
protection of young, 91
reactions to sonar beams from vessels, 133–34;
reputaton for wanton killing, 85;
retaliation against, by fishermen, 47, 88, 132;
sightings in western North Atlantic, 139–68;
skinning furred/feathered prey, 23, 171–72;
sleep, 17;
"snacking" on whale blubber, 15, 17;
strength, 180;
swimming speed, 14, 17, 33, 172, 180;
teaching of young, 90–91;
temporary amalgamations of pods, 19, 71–73, 82–91, 109–22;
"toying" with prey, 22–23;

use of sound,
  to identify prey, 175;
  to confuse prey, 95–99, 134;
  to stun prey, 95–99;
  whalers' tolls, 143

P
Phalarope, 20, 135
Pollock, 107
Pollution, 27
Porpoise, Dall's, 102
Portugese Man-of-War, 4
Prey/predator relationships,
    102–05
Prey seek safety alongside vessels,
  bluefin tuna, 55;
  sea lions, 173

R
Risks facing predators, and how
    weighed, 15
Rosefish, 107
Rossiter, William W., 174

S
Salmon,
  Atlantic, 49;
  Pacific, 99, 103
Sand lance, 10, 71, 83, 92, 94–95,
    99, 107, 111
Scattering layers, 131
Scoters, 118
Sea level, rising, 121
Sea temperature gradients, 45, 118
Seals,
  general, 124;
  gray, 48, 118;
  harbor, 30, 48
Shad, 35, 49, 119–21, 126
Sharks,
  attacks on people, 32;
  basking shark, 31;

cold water tolerance vis-a-vis
    body size, 30, 40;
  general, 85, 130, 131;
  great white, 28–32, 131;
  Greenland shark, 31;
  mako, 5, 31, 131;
  porbeagle, 31, 89, 131;
  sand shark, 35;
  "warmblooded" species, 30–31
Shearwaters,
  greater, 11, 23, 99
Shelf break (continental shelf),
    4–9, 24–25, 126, 131, 134
Shoals Marine Laboratory, 30
Skua, 11
Slope water (continental slope), 9
Smelt, 123
Squid,
  general, 83, 111;
  short-finned, 10, 71, 137;
  giant, 128–30
Storm petrels,
  Wilson, 106–07;
Striped bass, 46, 49
Suffering of prey, 16–17
Surface tension, 33
Swimming speed vis-a-vis body
    length, 35
Swordfish, broadbill, 5, 131

T
Tidal range, 121–22
Tornado (waterspout), 135
Tropicbird, 137, 182
Tuna,
  bluefin ("horse mackerel"),
    effects of Japanese market de-
      mand, 86, 111;
    evasive tactics, 86;
    general, 11, 31, 38–42,
      44–47, 49, 50–59, 83–87,
      92, 106, 110–11, 131;

migration routes, 142;
primary prey for orcas?,
142;
school formations, 83;
swimming/feeding with
whales, 99;
Yellowfin, 41

W

Waterspout (tornado at sea), 135
Whales,
blue, 5–6;
finback,
general, 41, 92, 94;
evasive tactics, 101, 176;
peaceful interaction with
orcas, 66–67, 103;
possible use of bubbles, 176;
predation on by orcas,
110–16, 179;
respiratory ailments, 112;
gray (Pacific), 179;
humpback,
change of feeding grounds,
93–95, 123;
defense mechanisms, 11–15;
evasive tactics, 176;
feeding techniques, 100–01;
general, 67, 92, 111;
importance of sand lance to,
93–95;
peaceful interaction with
orcas, 99;
predation on by orcas, 11–16,
170;
singing on northern feeding
grounds, 53, 172–73;
use of bubbles, 100–01;
minke,
general, 92, 94, 101, 118;
predation on by orcas, 6–8,
16, 169–70;
peaceful interaction with
orcas, 102–03;
pilot whale, 4;
right whale,
general, 94;
defensive tactics, 108, 178;
sperm whale (cachalot),
general, 4,14, 126–29;
dive time, 127, 181;
predation on giant squid,
128–30
Whale-watching, 93, 94